Making All Things New

Making All Things New

Dialogue, Pluralism, and Evangelization
in Asia

Michael Amaladoss, S.J.

ORBIS BOOKS

Maryknoll, New York 10545

BV
2183
.A52
1990

The Catholic Foreign Mission Society of America (Maryknoll) recruits and trains people for overseas missionary service. Through Orbis Books, Maryknoll aims to foster the international dialogue that is essential to mission. The books published, however, reflect the opinions of their authors and are not the official position of the society.

Library of Congress Cataloging-in-Publication Data

Amaladoss, M. (Michael), 1936-
    Making all things new: dialogue, pluralism, and evangelization in
Asia / Michael Amaladoss.
        p.   cm.
    Includes bibliographical references.
    ISBN 0-88344-677-4 (pbk.)
    1. Catholic Church—Missions.   2. Missions—East Asia.
3. Missions—Theory.   4. Christianity and culture.   5. Christianity
and other religions.   6. East Asia—Religion.   7. Asia—Religion.
I. Title.
BV2183.A52   1990
261'.9054—dc20
                                                        90-40483
                                                            CIP

To My Mother

Contents

Foreword

I must start with a confession. I am not a professional missiologist. So I have not written a formal treatise on evangelization. In this volume, I have brought together a number of my rather recent papers on themes connected with evangelization. All these papers have their origin in a question, usually raised in the context of a seminar or a consultation. Occasionally I have raised a question myself to clarify an idea.

Though the origin of the papers is occasional, there is a clear convergence of theme. All of them have to do with God's call to us to collaborate in building the Reign promised to all peoples. God is making all things new (Rev. 21:5). God invites us to participate in creating this newness.

Whatever may have been the origin of the questions, my attempts at an answer start from my experiential context, namely our situation in India. India shares with Asia many elements of its situation and experiences: religious pluralism, need for inculturation and liberation, similarity of world views and problems. Therefore my reflections will also have an Asian resonance. Theological reflection is no longer universal. It is always marked by the context in which it is done. I am happy to acknowledge it and accept its limitations. To accept one's limited perspective is to be open to other points of view and to be ready for conversation. This openness is necessary in the face of pluralism. It is also an experience of freedom.

Though I have revised all the papers, there has been no substantial modifications. Reading these papers again I am surprised to find an idea or a suggestion in an earlier paper which I have later developed more in detail. Thus there is a continuity and development, even if some repetition is unavoidable in a collection like this. In the Orient we speak of a concentric way of developing a theme. You may have examples of it here.

A search is always tentative and calls for dialogue. My aim is not so much to have the last word, but to provoke reflection and call for a dialogue.

I am grateful to the many friends who have dialogued with me and have helped me to clarify my own ideas. Special thanks are due to Fr. Juan Ochagavia who has read through the whole manuscript and made useful suggestions and to Miss Sulogini Francis who helped with some of the typing.

All these papers, except three, have appeared in a number of Asian reviews: *Vidyajyoti Journal of Theological Reflection* (Delhi): Chapters 2, 3, 7, 8, 9, and 11; *Jeevadhara* (Kottayam): Introduction, Chapters 1 and 12;

East Asian Pastoral Review (Manila): Chapters 3, 10 and 14; *Indian Eccle-siastical Studies* (Bangalore): Chapter 5; *Progressio* (Rome): Chapter 13. Chapter 6 appeared in a collection published by the Indian Theological Association on *Communalism in India*. The Conclusion appeared in the *International Review of Mission* (Geneva). My sincere thanks to the various editors for their encouragement.

I am particularly grateful to my friends at Orbis Books for their encouragement and for making this international edition possible.

MICHAEL AMALADOSS, S.J.

Introduction

The Future of the Church
in Asia

The aim of evangelization is to promote a dialogue between the Word of God and the human community to which that Word is addressed as a call to conversion—*metanoia*. This dialogue is conditioned by the historical situation, the socio-economic circumstances and the cultural background of the community. The Word that comes to this community is not an abstract Word, but comes as the "Good News" with the power of liberation and wholeness in this situation. The Christian community is but the messenger, but one that not only conveys the message, but does so by living it, embodying it, witnessing to it and showing how the "Good News" is operative in its own life. This dialogical process therefore situates the double focus of evangelization: the Reign of God and the Church. The primary focus is spelt out by the Lord's Prayer: "Thy Kingdom come." It is by living out this primary objective that the Church is built up as a sacrament of the Reign.

In this introduction and throughout the volume, the focus of my reflection will be India, because today theological reflection arises out of and refers to the particular experience of the theologian and his community. But I venture to suggest that the problems affecting evangelization in India are very similar to the problems elsewhere in Asia, particularly regarding religious pluralism, the millennial cultures, dialogue with the great and the popular religions, modernity, liberation, ecumenism and the context of a post-colonial situation. In the light of the growing awareness of global evangelization as the collaborative task of the entire Church, our Indian experience and reflection will certainly interest also other Churches in the world.

A TWO-FOLD INCULTURATION

It is in the context of this double objective of evangelization that we must understand today the complex and complete meaning of inculturation. Culture is the way a people live and express themselves in community relationships and celebration. When the Word of God comes to a particular

1

cultural situation, it can transform that culture. This transformation is not only for the benefit of the small or big Christian community that might emerge in that cultural situation, but through that Christian community, sometimes even in spite of it, it is possible to transform that whole culture, often in ways known only to God. If I take my own country as an example, while it is true that the "Unknown Christ" has been and continues to be operative, it is also true that the "Acknowledged Christ" has also had an impact, through various leaders and reformers, in the transformation of the country. That a person like Gandhi would not attribute the Christian influence on him to any Church community in India is secondary. What is important is that Christ did have some influence in shaping his vision and policies. It is of course more difficult to measure the influence of the many Christian institutions that we have in the country on the thousands of beneficiaries who pass through them. But we cannot deny that they have had some influence. Insofar as this influence has had an impact in transforming them in some way and, through them, the culture of the people as a whole it is already evangelization. The point I wish to make here is that when we speak of our mission in India, we should think not merely in terms of building up a local Church that is inculturated and relevant, but also consider what the Church could do to transform the culture and people of India and thus contribute towards the building up of the Reign of God.

In the following pages, my focus will be more on what the Church today could and should do for India in view of the Reign. I suggest that what the Church could do for itself should be determined in view of its wider mission to the whole people of India.

A CONTEXTUALIZED MISSION

Every one knows the famous words of Gandhi that to a hungry person, even God would dare to appear only in the form of bread. One cannot reflect on what the Church could do for India today without briefly evoking the situation of India today. So much is being said and written about the situation in the country that it will suffice to be brief and indicative.

It sounds almost platitudinous to say that India is a poor country. Perhaps it would be more relevant to say that nothing much is done to improve the lot of the poor. Successive Governments have spoken about Socialism. We have had many five-year plans. But on the whole it is only a small proportion of the middle class, upper middle class and the rich who have profited by them. They continue to become more and more wealthy while the poor continue to become more and more destitute.

The problem of caste cuts at the very roots of the equality that our democracy so proudly proclaims in the preamble of its Constitution. The "Untouchables" are nearly 25% of the population and there is no sign of any improvement in their lot, either economically or socially. The affirmative action through quotas in educational institutions and job opportunities reaches a small portion of the elite among them. While there is some mobility in the intermediate castes through sanskritization, economic betterment or access to political power, as far as the whole system is concerned there has been no structural change. The fact that the "untouchables" are becoming increasingly aware of and resentful of their situation is only making matters more painful for them and does it without bringing about any change. The change will have to come from the total community as such, because change involves a total social restructuring of the community.

At the moment, our country is a very divided country. It is true that India was really one country until 1947 and its birth was marked by the painful process of division along religious lines. Communalism has been a problem since its birth. It has now been aggravated by economic and political circumstances. Communal conflicts, based not only on religion, but also on language, ethnicity, caste, etc. are tearing the country apart in various ways. Some years ago, one used to talk seriously about national integration. Today we do not seem even to talk about it. We should not however think of communalism purely in terms of the political unity of the country. Even if tomorrow we divided India into various units, pluralism of castes, ethnic groups, languages and religions would still be a problem in every unit. Hence community building is as important and difficult in a village, a city, a state, or a region. as in the whole country. Communalism also has economic aspects. For example, Indira Gandhi had no difficulty in granting the purely religious requests of the Sikh agitators. The real bone of contention was matters like territory and share of the river waters. More deeply, communalism has cultural and even spiritual roots. One has a strong sense of group identity. While one wishes for power and wealth, one does not wish it for everybody. It is a sort of collective selfishness, the collectivity extending not even to the whole community, but only to an elite that has the political and economic power. This is the opposite of a broad humanism.

COMMUNITY BUILDING

What can be done to tackle these problems? Reflecting, perhaps at an abstract level to begin with, I think that we have to build up communities of people. These communities would be characterized by the following basic attitudes: respect for the dignity and individuality of every human person, irrespective of his caste, creed or ethnicity; a sense of concern for each other that is ready to share without being selfish; a sense of togetherness and participation shown in dialogue and collaboration. These are the marks of a genuinely democratic society. These values and attitudes will have to be worked out in terms of appropriate economic, social and political structures. But these structures would not emerge, nor will they be effective, if these basic attitudes are not there as the source from which the structures originate. Without these attitudes, legal frameworks, political rhetoric and even economic planning are useless. These attitudes can only be cultivated in local communities of a reasonable size.

THE FAILURE OF THE CHURCH

How can the Church help in this process? Ideally speaking, every Christain community should be a fellowship, such as the one described above. But one would be hard put to find today many communities who live up to this ideal. These are not new ideals. In a sense the Church has been promoting these in ways it considered adequate. But an honest evaluation would show that its efforts have not been really effective. The visibility of the Church in India today stems from its institutions: educational, health and developmental. Our educational institutions have perhaps helped our own Christians to emerge into the middle class and become as selfish as any other middle- and upper-class population any where. We have rendered a similar service to the better off people of other religions. We have not been able to fulfill even the limited objective of communicating the faith to our Christian students. Our developmental programs have shared the same fate as those of the Government. They have helped the better off or those who have an easy access to our resources. They have not really reached the marginalized or the really poor.

Church communities are as notorious proportionately for their disputes along ritual, linguistic or communal lines as any other communities. As regards caste, the Church has also made little headway. By simply accepting caste and not doing anything about it, the Church has placed itself in an unenviable position. The Hindus and the Government consider that Christians (and Muslims) do not have discrimination of castes. However, an untouchable community that becomes Christian does not on that account improve its status in relation to the other caste communities around it. Neither does it improve its status with regard to the other caste communities within the Church. So, untouchables become doubly disadvantaged. The recent movements among Christians to demand the same concessions and quotas for caste Christians as for others of a similar status could only strengthen their caste identity and consequent discrimination both in the Church and in the world. In this manner, the Church is effectively abandoning any pretensions about trying for a casteless society. Maybe it is a more honest attitude; but neither more evangelical — nor prophetic.

This is the record of the Church so far. What then should the Church do? What India needs today is an ideology for a pluralistic society at the theoretical level and a people's movement for liberation and wholeness at the practical level. The Church can contribute to the development of such an ideology and also be one of the moving forces behind the people's movement. Through the process the Church itself can become more authentically Church in the very act of being the servant of the people. Let me try to explain this.

A NEW GREAT TRADITION

Every country has an image of the kind of society it wishes to become in the light of which it strives to create the approriate socio-economic and political structures and the necessary means in terms of action plans. Gandhi had the ideal of the *Ramrajya*. J. P. Narayan spoke of *Total Revolution*. Some speak of Socialism, while others of a classless society. India's Constitution envisages a secular democracy, that commits itself "to secure to all its citizens: justice, social, economic and political; liberty of thought, expression, belief, faith and worship; equality of status and of opportunity; and to promote among them all fraternity assuring the dignity of the individual and the unity of the Nation." These elements constitute a socio-political ideal and the structures appropriate to work towards it. In the context of the religious pluralism in the country, the Constitution has chosen secularism, not as anti-religious, but as open to all religions, shown particularly by its recognition of minority rights. But this ideal cannot be said to have been interiorized by the country as whole. Besides other obstacles of an economic and political character, it seems to be encountering two difficulties which have their roots in religion and culture. Though the Constitution has given the country a secular ideal, it will not become real until the various religious groups make this ideal their own and decide to build a new human community in India where each person would have the freedom and the respect of the others with regard to faith convictions, but at the same time seek to bring to the community the richness of these convictions, inspiration and values. In this manner, in a community of people mutually respecting and enriching each other, religion would not be a force for division, but a matter of "roots," of identity and of openness, in an atmosphere of tolerance and collaboration.

Such a collaboration and participation is possible only where every citizen feels equally involved and accepted. I think that at the moment there is a cultural block to this. If we today ask some one: "What is Indian culture?" we would probably hear of the Vedas and the Upanishads, the Bhakti traditions and the Epics, the Architecture and the Arts, etc. That is, by and large, the Indian cultural tradition will largely be seen as a Hindu tradition. Yet, Islam and Christianity and many other smaller religions and various ethnic groups in the middle of India and in the Northeast have had their own creations and contributions. They are present in our history and cultural tradition. But somehow they are not integrated into the mainstream of the cultural tradition. For whatever reason, these groups feel marginal and even foreign in the Great Tradition of the country. Talk about a Hindu India, or of an India where the Hindus will dominate because they form the majority of the population makes matters only worse. These fears and this experience of marginalization on the part of the minorities can disappear only if we can create a new Great Tradition that succeeds in integrating the contributions of all the various cultural traditions of India. There must be a totality in which, the Christian, the Muslim and the Sikh, the tribal and even the most oppressed groups can identify their contributions in an integrated whole—a totality which every Indian can collectively acknowledge as one's own because each one has contributed to it. Such a totality can evolve only through dialogue, through give and take, through the respecting of each one's individuality and identity. This mutual respect must reach out beyond the cultural to the religious. This can only be the collective work of all.

In the perspective of an unity in pluralism, this new Great Tradition will create a "we" feeling which will not discriminate among people on the basis of caste, creed, language, ethnic origins, and religion. This would provide the foundations for a broad humanism that is secular and democratic. Obviously it would not resolve problems of a moral nature like selfishness, corruption and violence. It would not either provide ready-made economic and political solutions to the problems the country is facing. But it can provide a cultural basis conducive to a successful handling of problems at other levels. The different religions would be called on to provide to their own believers the ultimate meaning and motivation to this common project in the first place and jointly through dialogue to the community as a whole. It will be the task of interreligious dialogue to respect the identity of each religion, and, even while all believers bear witness to their own religious convictions, these convictions do not become obstacles to an active collaboration at all levels, economic, social, political and cultural and even religious—such as was shown in Assisi when leaders of all religions came together to pray for peace.

A FACILITATING ROLE FOR THE CHURCH

What could be the role of the Church in this project? First of all, I really think that the Church can play a mediating and facilitating role in bringing everyone together. In a way Hindu-Muslim conflict has become endemic in the country. The Church can be an instrument of peace. It has already been playing such a role though in a very limited way in the various kinds of dialogues and live-in sessions which it has been organizing in India for many years. But this has so far been only an activity of the experts. Such meetings continue to be necessary. Yet at the same time we should widen participation to include people at all levels. We should also broaden the focus to include not only interreligious exchange but also a common effort to make a religious impact on common human problems.

If this dialogue is done seriously, one would probably find that there is a large amount of consensus on most of the basic values among the various religious groups, even if each religious group seeks to justify it according to its beliefs and world view. We speak often about a secular humanism. (Do we think of it only as a purely rational affair that keeps clear of religious belief, with the real risk of becoming atheistic on the claim of being purely rational or also as something that searches for the least common denominator on which all would agree or finally as something that emerges out of the contribution of every one rooted in one's own faith, without forcing it on anybody else, but through dialogue seeking to enrich and challenge each other and in this manner growing by assimilating the positive values from the other and renouncing the negative values in oneself). This is a difficult process. Yet in a multireligious society, it is through such a process that the Church would be able to establish its identity in comparison with others, become a strong and relevant witness to its message and its values, yet at the same time make its contribution to the totality of values in the service of the human community.

The question, therefore, in the kind of situation we have in India today, is whether the Church, instead of simply being exclusive and self-defensive, can take the initiative in bringing people together around common tasks, in promoting mutual understanding and in sharing through dialogue, thus facilitating the emergence of a new Great Tradition that would not simply be Hindu, but Indian and therefore multireligious. This would be a model, not only for India, but for the whole world. This will have to be at once an intellectual and a practical process. With its educational institutions and its action groups, the Church has already a basis for this task. Among the various religions, the Church is perhaps the best organized so that it can really take a planned and systematic approach to the project. This would also be a much better and a more effective way of witnessing to its own identity as being for the Other as a relevant and involved group of people with clear convictions, who are also open to the convictions of others, with a goal not centered on itself but on fulfillment for every one.

A PEOPLE'S MOVEMENT

It is in this context that I would like to propose that the Church must really become the center of a people's movement. First of all the Church must be in itself a people's movement. The whole Church is on mission: to build a new heaven and a new earth—a new humanity, which is the Reign of God. This cannot be done by simply concentrating on personal conversion and on personal salvation. Faith today manifests itself in working for justice. Given the present oppressive structures this would involve a struggle. This struggle must be engaged in by the people themselves. The Church cannot really bring about any transformation in the world without in some way getting involved, struggling with the people. In short, it must become a people's movement. But in a multireligious community like that of India, one cannot think of a people's movement that is exclusively Christian. Just as the Christians are oppressed with all the others they will also struggle with the others. Here also the Church can play a role of animation—not being exclusive, but by facilitating and coordinating. The new Great Tradition itself would emerge dialectically from a multireligious struggle for liberation and wholeness.

In this whole process the Church as a religion would also have a religious role. That is the role of animation, inspiration, clarification and motivation, relating the action to ultimate values and world views. This religious role — of the Church as of the other religions — would be integral to any process for a holistic liberation. This is what we mean by rejecting a merely rational humanism, however noble. But the Church is not simply a religion. It is people. That is why even this religious contribution would not be made in the classrooms of theologates, but in the fields of struggle where people live and experience their faith and have an opportunity for an ongoing reflection on what they are doing in the light of their faith.

A RENEWED MISSION

So I suggest that in the years to come the Church should dedicate itself to this as a priority and focus all its energies, its communities, its institutions and its resources on this goal. This people's movement has already started in the form of various action groups. Will the Church in India make this its own priority and in this way combine in a creative manner the various dimensions of its mission, namely dialogue, liberation, inculturation and proclamation? As an authentic and living witness to the Good News of the Reign, it will be proclamation. As a process to transform Indian culture in view of building up a new Great Tradition, it will be creative inculturation. As a people's movement, it will promote liberation. All this will be done in collaboration with other believers through dialogue.

This mission should eventually condition the life and activity of the Church, the formation of its leadership, the role of the laity and the necessary and inevitable involvement of the people in public life.

PART I

DIALOGUE

1

The Encounter of Religions

Pluralism is always a problem. This is true whether one speaks of religions or economic systems or political ideologies or social structures. Where there is no open conflict, one seeking to dominate or suppress the others, there is a search to reduce pluralism to a unity. This search for unity can take various forms. If we take the field of religion as an example, one way is to affirm one's own legitimacy and deny any legitimacy to the others, even if those who claim legitimacy may be a minority and may face persecution. Another way is to order everything in a hierarchy, often placing oneself at the top. For instance, Christianity thinks of itself as the latest and most perfect covenant coming after the cosmic and Judaic covenants. A minor variation in the hierarchical system is compartmentalization, where each unit is assigned a special place and does not interfere with the others. The caste system is an example in the social sphere. Many sects in Hinduism tend to become castes. Still another solution is to acknowledge pluralism at a phenomenal level, but to affirm a basic unity that is either transcendental (that is, in the scheme of things) or eschatological (that is, a project for the future). Certain inclusivistic approaches in the Christian theology of religions and modern Advaitic approaches to other religions tend to be transcendental. In this spectrum, where can we place the contemporary encounter between religions? Is there an ideal situation towards which we should move? What are the prospects in the concrete, historical situation?

In the following pages, I would like to focus my attention on the Indian situation. The world situation is so mobile and complex that one might tend to lose oneself in generalities. On the other hand, what is true of India may be true in other societies, so that we can really rise from the particular to the general in our reflection. One could even say that India offers an ideal model to reflect on such a problem, not only because of the presence of all the great and other smaller religions, but also because of its efforts to build a secular society according to a democratic constitution that has a positive attitude to all religions. Our starting point then is that pluralism of religions in India is a fact. How can we come to terms with it in a creative

11

way so that it helps rather than hinders India's effort to build a better future for all its peoples?

THE SOUTH ASIAN CONTEXT TODAY

A New Situation: Emergence of Democratic States

I think that we are facing a new historical situation. In India people of different religious beliefs have always been living together, though in a rigidly structured and compartmentalized society. What is new is the effort made to integrate these groups into one democratic state. In order to understand this situation well, it will be helpful to explore a wider background.

Religion and culture are linked closely together. Religion is the deepest element in culture, giving it its meaning system in the context of ultimate perspectives. In its turn culture gives a socio-historical presence to religious belief and commitment. In simpler human communities with cosmic religions, there is no separation between religion and culture. Only some of the great religions claim to free themselves of cultural limits and through missionary movements make themselves present in various cultural contexts. But the tendency has always been for any given human group to find a basis for its identity in fundamental convictions that are derived from a particular religion. In monarchic societies, this condition is indicated by the principle: *cujus regio, eius religio* (that is, the people follow the religious beliefs of the king). Missionaries often make use of this principle by directing their proclamation to the political leaders of a community. This is also why many new religions were persecuted as threats to the State. The Islamic countries, Hindu Nepal and Buddhist Tibet are obvious contemporary examples. But the principle is more widespread than we might imagine. England has an established Church and Italy has special links to the Catholic Church. Hindu and Muslim minorities can bear witness to the Christian or "post-Christian" character of Europe. Even in the United States of America, a Hindu has little chance of being elected president. In all these countries, of course, believers in other religions are tolerated. But the basic inspiration of the culture remains Christian.

The situation, however, is changing because of developments both in experience and in ideology. In the past people belonging to a different religion may have been mostly temporary migrants for commercial or other purposes and did not pose a problem to social cohesion. But owing to missionary movements and migrations, followers of other religions form sizeable minorites among the residents of many countries today. For example, there is a greater percentage of Muslims in France, Belgium and Germany than there are Christians in many countries in Asia. In most countries in Africa, Christians and Muslims form large percentages of the population. Therefore religious pluralism has become a fact of life which cannot be ignored. It has always been so in India and has remained so even after the partition of the subcontinent along religious lines. Our pluralism is even more pronounced than elsewhere because of the number of religious groups—besides Hinduism and Islam, there is also Christianity, Sikhism, Jainism and Buddhism, not to speak of the various tribal religious groups.

This fact of pluralism becomes a problem everywhere today because of the democratic ideology. Democracy supports freedom, equality and fraternity of the citizens. But it does so not in terms of their race or religion. It is an individual person as an individual who possesses democratic rights. A person is equal to another simply because of basic humanity.[1] Religious, racial or caste identity becomes very secondary in relation to fundamental rights and freedoms. This does not mean that discrimination based on race or religion or caste disappear automatically. But it does mean that such discrimination, however actual, is illegal and against the ideology on which the national community is founded. This implies that the meaning system that provides a unifying basis for the national community is no longer that of a particular religion, whatever may have been the process of a nation's historical origins. The ideology on which the national community is based claims to be independent of any religious affiliation. This ideology would be true of most modern democratic constitutions. This means that religion in such societies is neither a cohesive nor a divisive factor by itself. It can help and support the unity. It should not undermine it. This is the theory, but the reality may not correspond to it. Just as caste is as strong as ever in India and just as race is as important a divisive factor in the United States of America today, religion also continues to be a divisive factor in multireligious societies. That is why pluralism of religion is not only a fact but a problem. Ideologically it should not be a problem, but as a matter of fact it is. This tension between fact and ideology provides an incentive to reform or to transform the facts in order to conform to the ideology. This is probably the most important element of the new situation—that is, the emergence of human communities whose ideology of unity does not depend upon a particular religion for its basic meaning. Thus there is a differentiation between religion and the political structure.

Secularization and Social Institutions

This differentiation is further strengthened by the phenomenon of secularization. One of the results of the secularization of society is precisely the emergence into at least a relative autonomy of the various institutions which constitute society.[2] Culture, economics, politics and science acquire autonomy as meaning systems with a certain legitimacy at their own level. Religion is still the provider of meaning from an ultimate perspective. Yet it no longer provides an over-arching, global meaning system as it did before the process of secularization. There is always the danger that the nonreligious meaning systems seek to absolutize their autonomy. Apart from this danger, the differentiation between, for example, culture and religion makes it possible that different cultural systems draw inspiration from the same religious system, just as a given cultural system may take inspiration from various religions. Thus differentiation makes possible a pluralism. The fact is that religiously pluralistic societies acquire a legitimacy in terms of a democratic ideology, with secularization and the consequent differentiation between social institutions providing the condition of possibility for such pluralism. Democratic ideology and secularization do not necessarily offer a positive role to religious pluralism in the building up of the national community. But neither do they prevent it.

The Need for Religion

I remarked above that the nonreligious socio-cultural institutions may tend to make their autonomy absolute. Though secularization may not make people less religious, it does tend to make religion a private affair. If religion becomes a private affair of individuals or groups, the pluralism of religions is not a problem. But it was Gandhi who remarked that those who say that religion has nothing to do with politics do not know what religion means.[3] Religion, it is true, has to do with ultimate perspectives, not only in themselves, but also insofar as they have an impact on life here and now. Religion is not merely a creed, it gives rise to a body of moral principles of behavior. This morality is not merely for the individual, but for the community. Correspondingly, other social systems may have a certain autonomy in themselves. But their autonomy is not absolute. They are not adequately meaningful in themselves. Left to themselves, economy will be governed by the profit motive, politics will be guided by the realities of power, science will pursue knowledge for its own sake without worrying about its social consequences, and technology will only worry about efficiency. They will forget that they are at the service of the human community. It is the task of religion to keep this perspective alive in terms of ultimacy and transcendence and keep challenging the limited autonomies of the other social institutions, just as the other institutions will keep challenging religion so that it does not become alienating and other-worldly.

Conditions of Pluralism

Religions tend to be absolute in their affirmations and do not easily tolerate other absolutes. Co-existence of religions, not merely as private belief systems, but as having a public role in society, becomes possible only on the following conditions: (i) when every religion, that is a community of believers, is able to make space for other believers, that is, other religions, not merely in the sense of their being tolerated as second class citizens, but accepted as full and equal participants; (ii) when every religion is able to distinguish between its faith convictions and their moral consequences;

(iii) when a certain consensus regarding moral imperatives for personal and social behavior can be arrived at by people who believe differently. When these conditions are present, one could go one step further and evoke the possibility that each religion is open to be challenged on what it sees as the inevitability of the process through which the moral consequences flow from faith convictions. Such openness would make the consensus not merely a minimum common denominator but something dynamic, ongoing, creative and mutually enriching. In a multireligious community, therefore, every religious group is rooted in its own faith; it accepts other religious groups as legitimate; it is open to dialogue with their members in view of a common commitment to build up the community.

To clarify further the ideal that I am proposing here, I would like to underline three points that are implicit in the foregoing vision. First, my focus has been not on religions, but on believers. Religions do not encounter each other in the abstract. Believers in different faiths live together and encounter each other. I am not comparing one religion to another as belief systems or moral codes or world views. The legitimacy that I ask to be accorded is not primarily to another *religion*, but to another *believer*. The root of religious freedom is the dignity and conscience of the human person. Therefore what is fundamental is the respect that we should have for the other as a person and to his religious and other basic convictions. I can dialogue with another and seek to persuade, but not dominate, much less suppress the other person. This personal and human perspective is that of the modern democratic constitutions. It is also the perspective of the Second Vatican Council, in its Decree on Religious Freedom, and later documents of the Church in the social field.[4]

Second, the Indian people have given to themselves a constitution, based on the fundamental rights and liberties of the human person, and committed to a national community guranteeing freedom, equality, fraternity and justice to all its citizens.[5] Therefore the religions in India do not have an option in the matter, but are faced with the challenge of collaborating in the building up of the national community, so that they can be positive and constructive and not divisive forces.

Third, I am not interested in interreligious encounter for its own sake. It is true that at a certain level such encounters can dispel prejudices, promote mutual understanding, discover common ground and provide mutual enrichment. Such interreligious dialogue is necessary and useful. But the real challenge of interreligious encounter today is not simply at the religious level, but what it can do together to promote a community of fellowship, justice and peace. Often one speaks of the pursuit of Truth or of the experience of God as if God can be experienced independently of the world and of the other. Such a perspective is alienating. Religions do not exist for their own sake. Their purpose is to facilitate a fuller human — and therefore divine — life for the people. Their purpose is to make life meaningful, and even revelations are oriented to that. Therefore, when religions meet each other and do not talk about life in the world, they are being untrue to their own identity. Only when religions stop being narcissistic and become fully involved with people, will they see religious pluralism as a challenge. It is in their common commitment to a fuller life for the whole of humanity that religions can discover their own community and complementarity.

In the Christian religious tradition, the theology of religions seeks to make space in the context of our own faith for other religions.[6] The Second Vatican Council spoke of God being the common origin and end of all peoples.[7] The Asian Bishops spoke of God manifesting God's self also in other religions.[8] Coming together with leaders of other religions to pray for peace in Assisi in 1986, Pope John Paul recognized the legitimacy of other religions and pointed out that what unites us is more profound and primary than what divides us.[9] The need and the possibility of collaboration of all believers in the promotion and defense of common human and spiritual values have been repeatedly affirmed in recent Church documents.[10] Theologians may continue to discuss the implications of this openness to other religions for our traditional views regarding revelation, sharing worship and the mediation of Jesus Christ. In a sense these are in-house discussions and we may or may not agree on the solutions suggested by scholars. But this discussion need not and should not keep us from interreligious encounter as a means of building up a new world.

OBSTACLES TO DIALOGUE

It is in the context of this vision of a multireligious community, that there is not only a hope for the future, but also a concrete challenge thrown to us by our Constitution, that we have to look at the obstacles that are preventing such a fruitful encounter today.

I would like to evoke here four obstacles: prejudice, secularism, fundamentalism and communalism. Prejudice has its roots often in ignorance. Especially in India, because of the caste system, we are accustomed to live in a society which is highly compartmentalized. This means that as a religious community we are living in a world of our own. We are ignorant of the beliefs and practices of other peoples. The gap left by ignorance is filled by prejudice. This may be transmitted from generation to generation. The other is simply an outsider. He does not exist as someone to whom we can relate. One is ready to believe every rumor. Even hatred is a relationship. But ignorance is simply the absence of relationship. Sometimes what is called tolerance may take this form. The other is not respected, much less accepted. There is no sense of community. Religious diversity is recognized, but it does not become a problem. I am afraid that the tolerance on which the Indians pride themselves is not positive, but is of this negative kind.

Secularism is not widespread in India. But one may see it among the more educated. Religion is privatized. Religious beliefs and practices are one's private affair. They have no place in public life. Provided one is faithful to the law of the land, one is to be left alone to hold whatever beliefs one wishes. The danger here is that bereft of their religious base moral principles in public life fall a prey to self-interest, efficiency, success and the profit motive.

Fundamentalism is a narrow affirmation of the truth of one's own beliefs. The others may not be considered insincere, but deluded. While we should tolerate people who are in error, because of their basic humanity, we need not take their errors seriously. Since polity and public life are to be built on the truth, people who believe differently are reduced to second-class status. No distinction is made not only between religion and morality, but also between what is moral and what is legal. A mild form of fundamentalism sees in religion the cementing force between people and tries to promote a state religion. This tendency is quite widespread in the world even today.[11] We have Buddhist, Islamic, Hindu and Christian States: sometimes in principle, often in practice. Even in India, in spite of its constitution, Hinduism does dominate public life, though the religious minorities are protected by the Constitution and the courts. Most religions have smaller groups of active fundamentalists: the RSS in India, the Muslim Brotherhood in some Islamic countries, the Moral Majority in the U.S.A., Communion and Liberation in Italy. They confuse too quickly religion and society, faith and politics. The fundamentalists have no use for interreligious encounter. The other believers are reduced, in practice, if not in principle, to second-class status.

Another aspect of fundamentalism is proselytism. Witnessing to one's own faith, even with the intention of calling the other to conversion, if it is respectful of the other and his convictions, is always done in dialogue. But proselytism is aggressive and dominating. Even if only a small group in a religious community, for instance some evangelical groups among Christians, is engaged in proselytism, it throws suspicion on the whole community and creative and positive encounter between religions becomes difficult.

A milder form of fundamentalism may show itself in a self-sufficient attitude that has eyes only for what is lacking in others. However perfect may be the object of our faith, our own understanding, expression and practice of it is culturally and historically conditioned and limited. An awareness of these limitations would keep us more open to receive as much as to give in the process of encounter. For instance, the Eastern religions have a more cosmic, holistic and harmonious approach to reality compared to the anthropocentric, abstract and dichotomous approach characteristic of the Christian tradition influenced by Greco-Roman culture.[12] From this point of view, cultures and religions may be seen as complementary and dialogue as an element of growth. A similar difficulty arises when religions do not realize that their language is evidently symbolic and that ongoing interpretation, the goal of which is to make the original memory relevant to contemporary reality, is necessary to make religion historically pertinent. A religion that cannot do this is not only incapable of dialogue, but is also unable to provide a prophetic challenge to society.

While fundamentalism is a religious attitude, communalism is a political one. Communalism believes that the people who share the same religious beliefs also share the same economic and political interests. Hence it seeks to turn the religious community into a political power bloc. While communalism may be based also on other factors like caste, race and language religious communalism seems the most dangerous, because it uses all the emotional power of faith, which has an absolute character, to support its crusade for political control. The other believers are not merely second-class citizens: they are enemies. There is not only no respect and no acceptance; there is a nursing of hatred and mistrust. One cannot any longer speak of a national community. Communalism reduces religion to its lowest level, by making it a political tool. Religion then loses its prophetic role and legitimates the pursuit of political power as a means of controlling people.

MEANS OF PROMOTING INTERRELIGIOUS ENCOUNTER

What are the ways of promoting a profitable interreligious encounter? My intention here is not to give a list of activities that one could engage in, but rather to indicate areas to which one must pay attention.

First of all, we must strive to promote an experiential awareness of one's own religious identity. Often identity is not affirmed in positive terms of what one is and has, but in terms of what some one else does not have — that is, identity is determined by difference. It would be better if we can be positive about ourselves, be aware of our strengths as well as our limitations, be proud of what we have and be articulate of what we can contribute to the enrichment of others, leaving others to witness to their own identity, without presuming to tell them what they have or do not have.

Second, we must be really committed to a national human community, based on the freedom and dignity of the human person and promoting equality, fellowship and justice for all. We must see the role of religions as prophetic, not divisive, contributing, in dialogue with each other, a common human, moral and spiritual foundation to public life. In doing so religions are not playing politics, but doing precisely what they should do as religions in human society. All citizens must be formed to such a democratic world view through precept and practice. Religions must be able to distinguish between what can be demanded of all, even legally, even in terms of a moral consensus, and what each one of them has a right to demand from its own adherents in terms of its beliefs. Each religion has certainly the democratic right to seek to enlarge the area of consensus through dialogue and persuasion, but not to impose it through legislation.[13] In India we are still moving towards a common civil code based on fundamental rights and freedoms. Though the courts have consistently supported such a move, religions and interested politicians have not always been enlightened and constructive in their policies and behavior.

Third, an interreligious community is built up by living and acting as one, not just by talking. Theological discussions and sharing of spiritual experiences do have a role, but only as elements of common projects to promote freedom, fellowship, equality and justice. One could think of basic human communities that engage themselves in such a process.

CONCLUSION

One can see that such an interreligious encounter is not primarily of the religious leaders and experts, but of the people who live, work and struggle in the world. It must primarily be a dialogue of and about living. Sometimes one speaks of various levels of dialogue starting with the dialogue of life and ending with dialogue of spiritual experiences. The order should be reversed. Or rather one could say that it must be circular: from dialogue of life, to dialogue of spiritual experiences, back to dialogue of life, to be tested in the crucible of praxis. The criterion of authentic religion and spirituality lies in their commitment to the promotion of a more authentic and fuller human life, because "the glory of God is the living human person."

2

Approaches to Popular Religion

In a developing country like India, popular religion is an interesting theme for study. "Popular" may point to something that is liked by a big majority of the population. We speak of a popular film, a popular TV program, a popular sport. Popular may also mean "of the people" as different from an elite. The obvious implication is that the elite is a minority. In the second sense popular is not a value-neutral term since it is the elite who use it to refer to phenomena that they look down upon in some way. Religion refers to a complex of beliefs, rituals and community structures which are expressive of the deeper meanings of life and reality. One should distinguish religion from a religiosity that indicates an attitude which might find expression even in nonreligious ways.

The scientific elite look at popular religion as obscurantist, superstitious and an obstacle to progress. The religious elite may see it as primitive. The intellectual elite may look at it as ignorant, fundamentalist and fanatical. The political elite often misuse it as a power-base. For the people themselves, it is the way they live their religion. It is open to use or abuse like any human and social institution.

My intention here is not to offer you a phenomenological analysis of popular religion. I only wish to raise a few questions with regard to our approach to it. I do not wish to offer any answers, though the way in which a question is posed and clarified may already indicate a possible answer. I am taking for granted that religion, as a dimension of life, is to be considered seriously and positively. I am not going to make an apology for it. I shall focus my attention on three questions: What is popular religion? How seriously do we take it? Is it a help or a hindrance for human and social development?

WHAT IS POPULAR RELIGION?

Even if we try to avoid a value-laden use of this term and use it only descriptively, popular does correlate to a term like the "elite," whether intellectual or spiritual. The approach to things religious of a theologian or a *sanyasi* will be different from that of a lay person. Symbols and rituals that seem to be spontaneous expressions of the experience of the people can be differentiated from what is official, determined as such by the group, guarded by its hierarchical officials and handed down in a tradition. In a stratified society, popular could refer to the experience or expression of the poor and the powerless as compared to what is controlled by those in power, whether this power is political or religious. These contrasts describe popular in a negative way by comparing it with what it is not. But this reference to the other pole seems almost constitutive of the description of the popular. This is clear if we compare it with a term like tribal.

Tribal and Popular Religion

Tribal religions are religions of the people. But they are not popular in the sense described above because there is no elite group within tribal society that would stand apart from the people and consider their beliefs and rituals as different and popular. It is a unified, closed system that does not have the two poles. This does not mean that an outsider may not find analogies between popular and tribal religions with regard to their beliefs, symbols and rituals and their psychological and social rootedness. But popular religion seems to me to be an open system with fluid frontiers which it shares with "great" or "higher" religion.

Popular and Popularized

One use of the word popular refers to something that is preferred by a great number of the people. In contemporary society one speaks of the mass: mass culture or mass media. The characteristic of the popular in the age of the media is that it does not really emerge from the people but from a group, often of the elite, who produce it for and in the name of the people and diffuse it. They create popular taste. Such products are not so much popular as "popularized."[1] Whereas in earlier ages the people had some say in what was happening, today they have no influence at all except the negative ability of rejecting what does not please them. The production of films is the best example of this in India. But the process can also be found in the sphere of religion. The media can make or unmake gurus, promote temples and pilgrim centers. Such popularization is alienating for the people and manipulative on the part of the popularizers, because it is really not "of the people."

Polarities

Keeping in mind the popular-elite polarity we can try to explore the meaning of the popular further by evoking other similar polarities in the field of religion. These polarities are in no way synonymous. They bring out complementary aspects and enrich our understanding of the popular. Mandelbaum speaks of the *pragmatic* and *transcendental* aspects of religion. The pragmatic deals with the needs of life in the world, with suffering and sickness. The transcendental concerns the mysteries of life and death and the after-life. The former brings the gods down to earth through shamans and ecstatic rituals. The latter perceives the ultimate meanings of life in the world; it establishes and renews a timeless order through ritual. While the one caters to the life-needs of individuals and society, the other leads to salvation.[2]

Pieris evokes a distinction between the *cosmic* and *metacosmic* dimensions of religion. The cosmic deals with this world and its cosmic forces as well as the powers of the human psyche, with the cycles of the seasons and the adventures of agriculture and hunting, with rites of passage and kinship relations that structure the group. The metacosmic, while rooted in the cosmic, rises beyond it to point to salvation, with special myths of origins and ends, and speaks about union with the Absolute which calls for gnosis or renunciation and transformation. Pieris borrows this distinction from the Buddhist tradition which speaks of *lokiya* and *lokottara*.[3]

From a cultural point of view, Redfield[4] proposes the dialectic between the *Little* and the *Great Traditions*. The Little Tradition is localized geographically and historically. The Great Tradition embraces many Little Traditions and, in the process, it becomes more abstract, universal, reflective and refined. The Little Tradition is not simply an incipient or degenerate form of the Great One. The two strands interact mutually and dialectically through a process of universalization and parochialization which keeps the tradition dynamic, as Marriott has described this process.[5]

From the point of view of expression and communication, one could speak of the *oral* and the *written*. Oral is linked to spontaneity, variation, emotional expression and immediacy. But writing makes possible standardization and a wider spread both in time and space. Oral cultures can be very developed. On the other hand, one must distinguish between writing and printing. Where writing may remain an elite activity, printing may help to democratize and popularize elite as well as popular culture.

From the point of view of praxis, one could evoke the distinction between religion *as lived* and religion as *reflected on*. Religion as lived takes life for granted in the sense that it goes on with its appropriate rituals and symbols. Reflection is a second-order activity that seeks for meaning and articulation and gives rise to speculation and discussion.

Stirrat speaks of two models of the sacred, those of Eliade and Durkheim respectively.[6] The sacred of Eliade may seem socially irrelevant. It transcends space and time. It is an absolute which is the object of individual striving and offers salvation. It is not a model of social life; it is concerned with universals. The sacred of Durkheim is concerned with social life, with space and time, whether it is thought of as cyclical or progressive. It is the "sacralized social" of the here and now.

"Popular" and "Elite"

Considering these various polarities, one may be tempted to equate the popular-elite polarity either with all or one of them. That would be a mistake. I take them all as heuristic classifications which refer to two aspects and levels of the same continuum, but looked at from different points of view. They are not mutually exclusive. The "higher" or more developed forms are rooted in the "lower" or less developed, and the lower ones are open to the higher. One can very well see how they are two dimensions of the great religions. The elite, too, as long as they are human and practice ritual, participate in popular religion, even if they are able to talk about its meaning. Those who are practicing popular religion, unlike those who are engaged in tribal religious practices, know that the symbols and rituals that they live in a matter-of-fact way can be explained by people who are more informed than they are. They may even have some vague awareness of such explanations. Obeyesekere points out that in southern Asia

> intellectuals not only continue to believe in their higher religions, like Buddhism and Hinduism, with increased conviction, but, more surprisingly, continue to adhere to those spirit cults which are decried and sometimes condemned by these higher doctrinal traditions.[7]

This behavior can very well be substantiated from India. Similarly Ursula Sharma shows how a person who is sick, besides going to a doctor, may take steps to remedy other possible causes like sorcery and unintentional or known offense against the deity and finally have recourse to the explanation of the *karma* theory.[8] Similarly Gabriele Dietrich, speaking of peasants, says: "They may worship God in a certain form, but their understanding of God also transcends this form."[9]

Thus we see that already at the level that we would call popular there is a reflection, even if it is unsystematic and unarticulated. On the other hand, access to systematic reflection is not a hindrance to participation in popular religious forms. This could be understood if we distinguish between symbol and reflection. With symbols, one is at the level of the human, of life, of community, of time and space. No one can escape this level, though the symbols may be more or less refined. With reflection, symbols are not denied but are relative with reference to the reality symbolized. Symbols (and gods) are susceptible to reinterpretation.[10] Correspondingly, the meaning system of a great religion cannot have an impact on life and society unless it finds new expression in the living, popular symbols of a new culture.

Francis Jeyapathy, after an interesting analysis of the meaning of popular religion, concludes:

> The unique configuration of the so-called popular religion can then be seen to lie in the strong local colouring of the symbols and rituals, in the close correspondence these religions have with the social life of the people, in the way local histories and socio-political conditions are gathered up, expressed, enacted and sought to be changed in the symbolic realm, in the ambivalent relation they enjoy with the official religions.[11]

I think that popular and elite religions should be seen as two symbolic forms of one religion, two moments on one continuum of expression. They cannot be understood one without the other, even if they have specific characteristics and can be looked at separately. But the separate focus should not assume a dichotomy. They are different expressions at different levels of the same meaning. We need not attach value connotations to them. Living the faith in a human, social way in symbol and ritual, is to live it popularly and this is a part of every religion. There is a popular component in each one of us. Some of us may be capable of reflecting on what we live, rising to higher levels of abstraction and expression, relativizing, not doing away with, the symbol, and adapting it to different circumstances. While life can continue without reflection, reflection cannot cut itself off from life without losing its significance.

THE SIGNIFICANCE OF POPULAR RELIGION

How seriously do we take popular religion? With a view to answering this question, I would like to start with a sort of case study. Rituals connected with sickness and healing is a common focus of popular religious practice. How do we look at them? Investigators take various attitudes.[12] Some will deny everything as superstitious and advise the sick person to go and see a doctor.[13] Others would take the spirits seriously, but substitute healing rituals of a new religion seen by them as true and superior.[14] Some would see the rituals as symbolic ways of handling realities that are basically psychological and/or sociological. Among these latter, I see three different approaches: one group would prefer to do away with the mystery and substitute modern scientific methods, which, in any case, resemble in their own ways;[15] another group, without believing in the spirits, will act "as if" and keep the ritual since it is effective;[16] a third group will respect the symbolic world of the ritual in its own cultural context and appreciate its efficiency without pronouncing on its truth value.[17] A final approach tries to substitute a new elite reflection from a new faith perspective.[18]

The Rituals of Healing: An Analysis

The people who practice these rituals do not indulge in all these reflections. But on the other hand, we should not think that they are naive and
do not know how to articulate the various causes of sickness and remedies
for them. Sickness may have physical, psychological, social, personal and
supra-human dimensions. In a tribal ritual, the witch doctor treats the sick
person holistically in relation to all these dimensions, though he does it
symbolically: he gives herbal medicine, involves family and friends in the
ritual to promote reconciliation, builds up self-confidence through suggestive ritual, dispels the guilt feeling, and propitiates the spirits. At the level
of popular and elite religion, this unity is broken. At the elite level, there
is a differentiation of functions: in a hospital, the doctor handles the physical aspects, the counsellor looks after the psychological and social
problems, the chaplain calms the guilt feelings and assures spiritual support. At the popular religious level, we see the same differentiation, but
the functions are managed in a different way. Recourse to medicine will
be a first step. Where there is no known medicine, a goddess will be
invoked. Where medicine does not bring healing, one will try to make
propitiation for one's unknown faults or amends for known ones. Sometimes one may suspect sorcery and approach a shaman, because there seems
to be no other convincing explanation. If nothing succeeds, one would
blame one's karma or fate. Sometimes two or more of these means of
healing may be tried at the same time.[19]

One notices, however, a certain mobility of consciousness without detriment to the final goal which is healing. With the progress of medicine,
for example, some of the goddesses who were considered as the causes for
the disease disappear from the scene or their function is reinterpreted.[20]

Three Types of Rituals

Popular religion has many more rituals than the ones of healing. We can
broadly distinguish three types of these: need-based, social and transcendent. Let us briefly look into each of these. The *need-based rituals* cater to
all human and social needs. As long as one does not feel fully master of
oneself and is aware that one is dependent on the divine, these rituals will
continue, though symbols and Gods may keep changing according to history
and culture. Of course some one who no longer feels such dependence does
not need religion. Use of need-based ritual does not mean that the persons
ignore other means of satisfying their needs. As the proverb goes: "God
helps those who help themselves." God is not a substitute for other human
and natural means. But God continues as the hidden presence in all that
befalls the humans. Speaking of peasants who were organizing themselves
for a liberative struggle with the help of Marxist ideology, Dietrich says:
"There was a strong feeling of reliance on the gods in the people despite

their consciousness of their own power to organize."[21]

The *social rituals* contribute to the construction and maintenance of the community. These are principally the rites of passage. These rituals are normally symbolic representations of community structures. They seem to act on the community through a "structure—anti-structure—communitas" dynamic.[22] While there is a liminal moment of confusion and catharsis, the community structure is strongly and clearly reaffirmed.[23] The ritual is socially determined and controlled by the representatives (the clergy) of the group.

The *rituals of transcendence* refer to the world of God. It is oriented to salvation. They are rituals of thanksgiving and praise. They mediate symbolically, not only a world that is seen as future, but also a world that is present, but transcendent. These symbols of what will be and what ought to be challenge what is.

In the spectrum going from popular to elite religion, the social rituals are shared by all, at least in a minimal form: birth, marriage, death. Even if the religious element is secularized, the social structure would remain and would be mediated symbolically. The need-based rituals will be found more on the popular side of the spectrum. The rituals of transcendence will characterize the elite pole. But all three types will be present, though in varying proportions, throughout the spectrum.

An Advaitic Perspective on Symbol

What is the significance of these different dimensions of symbol and ritual? If we take the phenomenon of symbol seriously, then I would suggest that the relation between the symbol and the reality it symbolizes is an *advaitic* one. The symbol is not the reality; it has no meaning independently of the reality. But the reality cannot be reached except through the symbol. But the symbols of reality arise out of the dialectic between the reality on the one hand and the human person and society on the other. This process is the emergence of culture. The psychological structures of the human person, the relationships of social structures and the cosmic manifestation of the reality in space and time—all of these in their own ways determine the kinds of symbols that emerge. Among many others, Eliade (for cosmos and history)[24] Jung (for psychology),[25] and Mary Douglas (for society structures)[26] have tried to show the intimate link between their respective fields of study and the kinds of symbols which emerge. But the symbols should always lead beyond these conditioning structures to the reality they symbolize. The reality of the symbolic world is then a relative one: it is relative to the reality it symbolizes; it is also relative to the human, socio-historic and cultural conditions of its own emergence. This double relativity is the principle of variety, change, transformation.

What, then, is the significance of popular religion? Its significance is that of the symbolic world. The symbolic world is not the simple reflection of the real one. But it is not an empty, imaginative creation either. In the light of ongoing experience, change of circumstances and fresh discoveries, the symbols will change or will be reinterpreted. But the inadequacy and mobility of the symbol does not belie the reality even if the persons who respond to and use the symbol may not be reflectively aware of it.

POPULAR RELIGION AND DEVELOPMENT

Is religion an obstacle to development? In a well-known quotation, Marx speaks about religion being the opium of the people.

The abolition of religion as the illusory happiness of the people is required for their real happiness. The demand to give up the illusions about its conditions is the demand to give up a condition which needs illusions.[27]

Weber, who was more positive about the role at least of a particular type of religion, namely Calvinist Protestantism, was critical of Asian religions.

For the various popular religions of Asia, in contrast to ascetic Protestantism, the world remained a great enchanted garden, in which the practical way to orient oneself, or to find security in this world or the next, was to revere or coerce the spirits and seek salvation through ritualistic, idolatrous, or sacramental procedures. No path led from the magical religiosity of the non-intellectual classes of Asia to a rational, methodical control of life.[28]

Gunnar Myrdal thinks that religion usually acts as "a tremendous force for social inertia" and says that he "knows of no instance in present-day South Asia where religion has induced social change."[29] These criticisms will apply more particularly to popular religion because it seems superstitious and magical and nonrational.

Re-Interpretation of Religion

One can suggest that precisely because popular religion is concerned with their present needs, the people will not be averse to use appropriate means, even if that leads to a reinterpretation of their religious symbols. Dietrich says:

People's organization does not necessarily have a very secularizing effect on people even though the ideology under which they are organized may have an atheistic bias. Most people tended to feel that their trust in the gods was either strengthened by or not affected in the struggle; certainly, it was not weakened. . . The presence of God is very much experienced as the presence of energy in nature, in things and in people. . . Since the presence of God is energy, it is only natural if most people feel their trust in God is not weakened through political organization.[30]

Studying rural Hinduism and its evolution in the context of modernity, Ayrookuzhiel says:

While in some cases new meanings are put into old symbols, there is also the process of dropping some old religious symbols and integrating new ones like humanity, scientific truth, reason, etc. into their symbol complex.[31]

Both the symbol systems may sometime coexist because they are perceived to meet different needs and to point to different meanings. Vieda Skultans, studying a healing temple, points out how a mentally ill person is brought there often because they cannot go to a psychiatrist. But when they are in the temple the ritual centers around the accompanying female caretaker, who feels responsible for the health of the family.[32] Some who are staying in the temple keep seeing the local psychiatrist too. Obeyesekere shows how the popularity of the gods and their identity and role in the life of the people change according to the developing circumstances and needs of the people.[33] Similarly some of the new religious movements that are developing in India can be seen as attempts to modernize Hinduism supported by the people of the middle class.[34] The experience of Latin America shows that when people acquire a new awareness, they either create new popular religious symbols or reinterpret traditional ones so that popular religion becomes a force for liberation.[35]

How do we understand these phenomena? If, as I have argued above, the symbol system emerges from the dialectic of life-experience and faith, when experience changes and faith remains the same, the symbol system readjusts itself to suit the new situation. Because faith and symbols are at different levels, though related to each other, transformation at one level need not imply transformation at another. This means also that in an ongoing process of change, the symbolic world is dependent on the world of experience. Hence the symbolic world need not be seen as an obstacle to social change. Or to put it in another way, social change is no threat to the symbolic world, though it might involve adjustment and even transformation.[36] The symbolic world may not bring about social change on its own. But it cannot continue unchanged in the face of experience. If there is stagnation, the cause may be more human and political rather than religious.

Rituals of Social Structure and the Reality of Power

In the previous section, I spoke of three kinds of symbol and ritual. They do not react to social change in the same way. The rituals of transcendence are normally not affected. The need-based symbols and rituals easily adapt themselves or are reinterpreted or even disappear in the context of changing experience. The symbols and rituals that do not easily change are the socio-structural ones. Social roles continue even if they are played by different groups of people.[37] The legitimation of the caste system through ritual is a good example. It is true that the Bhakti schools tried to rise beyond the caste structure. But beyond affirming the availability of salvation to all irrespective of caste, they did not affirm social equality. Similarly some of the need-based cults may serve as a counter-point to the official ritual structure of the priests.[38] But they have no effect on social structure.[39] Similarly the ritual process described by Victor Turner speaks about communitas as resulting from the process.[40] But while the communitas may be a happy resolution of the threatening liminal state, it does not radically change the structure, but reaffirms it. In rites of passage, the individual may move to another level in relation to the group. In social rituals like pilgrimages, the liminal state may recall to all the participants nonstructural values. But these values are institutionalized in the social group as a consequence of the rite. It is more prophetic than transformative.

This means that a socio-structural ritual can only be changed with difficulty. Besides the creation of a new awareness among every one in the social hierarchy, a two-fold strategy seems indicated. At the social level, development and mobility characteristic of industrialization and urbanization, can break up existing social structures and bring about new ones, even though slowly. At the ritual level a process of what has been called "Sanskritization" which leads the Harijans to "abandon" their proper gods in the celestial hierarchy and to worship higher gods destroys the ritual legitimation of the social hierarchy. That is why the movement to open the doors of all the temples to the Harijans may be significant not only socially, but also ritually.

CONCLUSION

The structuralist tradition in anthropology has shown us that our ancestors did not have less intelligence and wisdom though they may have had different worldviews and symbol systems. Such a point of view helps us to avoid value judgments. This does not mean that there are no differences or change or development. I have tried to show that popular religion cannot be simply dismissed as magical or superstitious. It can be understood only in the context of a higher form of the same religion. It presents a complex structure with the symbol systems mediating between experience and reality. One can distinguish the symbolic ritual into three kinds: need-based, socio-structural and "transcendent." It is this complexity which makes change possible. Like everything human, religion can be abused. One can show that evils like fundamentalism and communalism have their roots, not in religion, but in psychological need or social rivalry for power. While it is necessary to reflect on religion, it is lived religion which ultimately makes life meaningful and leads it to fulfillment.

3

Other Scriptures and the Christian

Are the scriptures of other religions inspired? Do we hear God speaking to us through them? Can they nourish our prayer, reflection and action? Can we proclaim them in our liturgy? A Christian cannot avoid these questions when one realizes that all peoples share a single origin and goal, that God's loving plan extends to all peoples and that the people look to the various religions for answers to the mysteries of life.[1] The questions become even more urgent when one believes that the religions are not merely human efforts searching for God or the ultimate, but represent also, at least partially, God's effort to reach out to people. Whatever be one's view regarding the precise place to be given to other religions in the plan of God for the world in the context of his self-revelation in Jesus, most theologians would agree today that people find salvation in and through their religions, not merely in spite of them.[2] Some of these religions have scriptures, acknowledged as such: for example, Hinduism and Islam. If our appreciation of other religions is not to be merely negative, what value do we give to their scriptures?

THE BANGALORE SEMINAR

Some years ago, these questions were addressed by a group of exegetes, theologians, liturgists, philosophers and students of Hinduism and Islam, at a seminar in Bangalore, India.[3] The answers of that seminar may be a good starting point for the present inquiry.[4]

Professing a functional approach, the seminar places the other religions and their scriptures in the context of the "Universal economy of the Spirit, who is bringing peoples in diverse ways to the eschatological realization of fellowship in God" (49).[5] Though it is aware of possessing "the guaranteed sacramental sign of Christ's word," and it has in the gospel a sure criterion of true revelation, the church is called to show respect and openness to the Spirit speaking through other scriptures (56). In the liturgy, the other scriptures open the Christian community to a living contact with the authentic religious experiences of the non-Christian community and relates these experiences to the Christian faith expressed in the liturgical celebration. The seminar foresees that such use of the Indian scriptures "would ultimately result in a radical re-orientation of the Indian Church. . . Never can the Church be truly Indian without imbibing her religious and humanistic traditions, without being familiar with and feeding on her Scriptures." (71). A strong christocentric understanding of the history of salvation, progressing through the Cosmic, Judaic and Christian covenants, constitutes the background of the final statement. The focus is on the use of non-Christian texts in prayer and liturgy. One realizes that such texts need not be Scriptures. Therefore other religious scriptures are not considered as such in the statement and the word "inspiration" is studiously avoided. There is, for instance, this disarming statement: "Considering the nature of the Scriptures of other religions and their place in the liturgy, it would seem less appropriate to finish their reading with the relatively recent formula 'this is the word of the Lord' "(61).[6]

The statement obviously represents the consensus of the whole group. While it favored the use of other religious scriptures in prayer, reflection and liturgy, it did not wish to pronounce itself clearly on their inspired character. But in the preparatory research papers and in the reports of workshop discussions, there are a few ideas which I would like to evoke here. Some see the other scriptures as "Seeds of the Word," which are to be discerned in the light of the Word in the Bible.[7] Others point to the positive use and appreciation of ancient Near Eastern religious and wisdom material by the Old Testament and suggest that we can do the same.[8] The exegetes see the term inspiration as analogical and speak of three types: eschatological (New Testament), prophetic (Old Testament) and illuminative (other scriptures).[9] One places christocentrism in the context of the cosmic economy of the Spirit.[10] Another tries to move away from a christocentric to a theocentric perspective.[11] There is a clear and definite shift from the "natural/supernatural" to the "cosmic/historical" perspective which sees a unity in difference among Christianity and other religions.

The situation has not changed much in the last ten years. However, further reflection can help us to pose the questions more sharply, offer a more nuanced answer, point to directions along which our search should continue and suggest possible avenues of action. This is what I shall try to do in the following pages. While the problem should not be narrowed down to the inspiration of other scriptures, that remains the central question. Any inspiring text can nourish our prayer and reflection. The question is precisely about some texts that claim to be in some way God's word in a given religious tradition. We cannot talk about them without talking about "inspiration." Hence the question: Can the scriptures of other religions be considered inspired? What does that mean? What is the living context in which such an assertion could be made? What would be the practical consequences with regard to the way in which they are used? What difference would it make to our attitude to and our use of our own scriptures?

A PHENOMENOLOGICAL ANALYSIS

To call any text "scripture" is to imply that it is sacred, inspired. A religious community has a memory of its beginnings. This memory refers back to a time when, through a founder or founders, the community as such came to be. The ultimate founder, operating through human intermediaries, is recognized to be God himself. This foundational event consists of three elements: community structures, rituals and narrative. The community structures regulate order and internal relationships in the group in view of the style of life or goal that the community has set itself. The group is animated by leaders and priests. The same person(s) may fulfill both roles. They derive their authority from God himself through means recognized as such by the group. The community comes together occasionally to celebrate events in the ongoing life of a member or of the community, finding in these events a meaning related to the foundational experience and to the goal towards which the community is moving. This meaning is spelt out in stories and other texts which are proclaimed during the ritual, making it meaningful. These texts, when written down, become the scriptures. To call a text scripture therefore is to refer to the foundational experience which it proclaims in the context of a ritual which actualizes that experience here and now.

Though it is customary to call scripture only the written texts, the term could legitimately be extended to all foundational texts. All the written texts of today have had their oral stages and what is oral tradition today could be written down later. The foundational experience need not refer to a single event or to a limited stretch of time. The foundational experience of the Bible covers a few thousand years and a series of events or periods. Though the Vedas are considered eternal and basic to Hindu tradition, the Bhagavad Gita, the Bhagavatam and the corpus of devotional literature may be more important to different subgroups within the Hindu tradition.[12]

Scriptures are normally spoken of within the theistic tradition. Do the Buddhists have scriptures? They do have their foundational texts. One speaks of the "Pali Canon." It is not necessary for us here to discuss whether Buddhism is a religion and whether it has scriptures, though one can justifiably answer both the questions in the affirmative.

Inspiration-talk is therefore meaningful only in the context in which a religious community attributes divine or superhuman influence and authority to its foundational experience and all its elements. The general process is called revelation—God's self-communication to people. People then respond in faith. Such a dialogue takes place in the context of a community, its symbol-system and particularly its language. The foundational experience becomes institutionalized and normative. The text, oral or written, not only shares in this normative, authoritative character. It has a double individuality. It is the text that spells out and specifies the meaning of the symbolic structures that are closer to life. In that very process, it becomes a fixed, autonomous element that needs constant re-interpretation. It is in this broader context that we must understand the words of the Second Vatican Council which says that the Old and New Testaments, "having been written under the inspiration of the Holy Spirit, have God for their author and have been handed on as such to the Church herself."[13]

Though inspired by God, the text is in human language, expressing the experience of a prophet or a community conditioned by space, time and culture, but meaningful to the ongoing life of the community and hence needs to be continually reinterpreted to make it relevant to the moment. The context of this reinterpretation is the current experience of the community which is made meaningful in relation to the foundational experience.[14]

What I have been trying to do in the preceding pages is to outline a phenomenology of the reality of scripture as such, to whatever religious tradition it may belong. I am not here interested in the way the theologians explain this phenomenon in each religious tradition. The Hindus may think of their Vedas as eternal sound, heard by seers and recorded in their present form. The Muslims may consider the Suras of the Koran as dictated by an angel.[15] The scholastic theologians of the Christian tradition may spin intricate theories of instrumental causality. These theories do not interest me at the moment. What interests me is the scriptural function in the on-going life of a religious community.

INSPIRED SCRIPTURES?

After these necessary preliminary observations, I come back to the question: Are the scriptures of other religions inspired?[16] It would be clear from what I have been saying so far that inspiration is not an independent, self-evident characteristic that can be discerned in itself in a given text. It is not like asking: Has this text literary merit? I do not either ask this question in a relative sense: Scriptures are considered inspired by the people whose scriptures they are. Neither do I ask a question in the manner of a student of the phenomenology of religions, who finds that every religion has a text (myth), oral or written, considered foundational and authoritative. I am asking two direct questions: Can I, a Christian, accept that God speaks to my brothers and sisters of other religions through their scriptures? Can I discover God speaking to me in and through the scriptures of other religions?

My answer to these questions will depend on the value I give to the other religions. If I believe that other religions mediate a salvific dialogue between God and a community, this dialogue will certainly take place through their scriptures as an element of their foundational experience.

Such religions then belong to the salvific plan of God for the world, and God, in some way, also speaks to me through them. In what way will depend on how I picture the plan of God. Let me now elaborate these two answers.

EXTREME POSITIONS

Let me state from the very beginning that I am distancing myself from two extreme positions that some may be holding as not being worth our consideration at the moment.[17] One extreme would be a negative view of all other religions or of religion as such. Either one holds to the axiom: there is no salvation outside the Church or one opposes religion as such, including Christianity, to salvific faith. This extreme simply denies the universal salvific will of God and the human, social and tangible ways in which this will operates. Another extreme view would be a relativistic view of all religions as equally salvific: all rivers lead to the sea. So it does not matter which religion one follows. Each is self-sufficient. But, if God has one plan of salvation for the world, then the various religions must be somehow related to one another as elements in the one divine plan. Concrete visions of the plan might vary, but the plan is there. With these two extremes out of the way, let us look at the other options.

ALL SCRIPTURES ARE INSPIRED?

It is the common opinion of theologians today that God's universal salvific will, which extends to all, reaches out to the members of other religions not only in the secrets of their hearts but in and through their religions so that these can be called ways of salvation. Some may call it the cosmic activity of the Spirit. Others may see in it the active presence of the unknown Christ. In whatever way, God's saving love has been present to people through their prophets, their scriptures and their rituals. Not that these are free from human limitations. But these limitations do not radically vitiate God's self-manifestation in them. In the words of J. Dupuis:

> By speaking personally to the prophets of the nations in the secret of their hearts, God intended to manifest and to reveal himself in his Spirit to the nations themselves. This was the way in which, secretly and unobtrusively, he entered into the history of the nations and directed that history towards the realization of his own designs. Hence the social character of the "sacred scriptures" of the nations may be said to be willed by God himself. . . . They contain words of God to men in the words of the rishis.[18]

These words of the rishis, then, may be called in a certain sense inspired words of God. The inspired nature of their scriptures does not simply depend on their belief. It is an objective revealing act of God. This leads me to my second question. If God has really spoken through these scriptures, are not his words relevant to any one who is open to God's self-manifestation, even if one does not belong to the community to which God's words are addressed? A complete answer will depend on how I perceive the interrelationships of the various religions in the one plan of God for humankind and the particular place given to Christianity in this plan. I can see three broad perspectives emerging in the discussion among theologians on this question. All the three would agree that we can hear God's word in the scriptures of other religions. But they would differ in the value they give to it and in the way they relate it to the Christian scriptures.

AN ESCHATOLOGICAL PERSPECTIVE

The first view holds that God's self-manifestation in Jesus Christ is final, definitive, eschatological and historical. The other manifestations of God do not share these characteristics. They do not lack authenticity, but they are not historically related to the only normative one. Inspiration can be attributed in the strict sense only to the scriptures that are part of this eschatological, normative manifestation. G. Gispert-Sauch writes:

> Christian theology acknowledges a divine causality in the order of grace which is not however of the same type as the absolute will with which God "decrees" the Incarnation of the Son or brings the Church to existence, inspiring the Bible as one of its constituent elements. Such a causality is the outcome of the salvific presence of the Spirit of God in the world, both before the Resurrection of Jesus Christ as an "entelechy" leading to the risen Lord, and after the Resurrection as the manifestation of his victory in the lives of those who share in it.[19]

The scriptures of other religions therefore are as meaningful to us as St. Augustine's Confessions or the Poems of St. John of the Cross. We discern in them the work of grace or the Spirit. But we cannot place them alongside the Christian scriptures.

THE THREE COVENANTS

The second point of view sees a continuity in the self-manifestation of God in human history. Jesus Christ is the final, definitive Word. Every other word leads to it. One speaks, for instance, of three progressive covenants of God with humanity: the Cosmic, the Judaic and the Christian. J. Dupuis writes:

> The sacred scriptures of the nations can only contain initial and hidden words of God which do not have the official character that must

be attributed to the Old Testament, much less the definitive value of the New Testament. These hidden words may nevertheless be called divine words, in so far as they are spoken by God through his Spirit; and the sacred books in which they are contained deserve, in a certain sense, to be called from a Christian theological view-point, sacred scriptures.[20]

Jesus Christ is the final word, the fulfillment. All that precedes must be read and interpreted in the light of the final word. In the words of J. Neuner:

> Not only all individuals, but all values contained in religious traditions are at once to be judged, purified, fulfilled in Jesus Christ. The aspirations of these religious communities are expressed in their sacred writings. If, therefore, the religions are related to Christ and through him to the Church, and are to be perfected in him, also their sacred books belong in a broad sense to the Church and have to find their final interpretation in Jesus Christ. They wait to be read by Christians who would be able to place them into the wide context of God's Universal plan of salvation in Jesus Christ ... The Christian is able to read texts of other religions in a fuller sense.[21]

G. Soares-Prabhu speaks of the possibility of considering the scriptures of other religions inspired, but only when they are related to the New Testament. He cites the analogy of the Old Testament. He says:

> The Old Testament is authoritative, inspired, God's word, not in itself but in as much as it is illumined by the New. In itself the Old Testament is a Jewish book: it becomes an inspired Christian text (and so the normative word of God for the Christians) only when read and interpreted in the light of Christ. Inspiration is not a static property somehow in the material text of the Old Testament, but a quality which comes to it from its interaction with the New.[22]

It is interesting to stop here for a moment and visualize the images that picture the relationship between the scriptures of other religions and the New Testament. Partial–full, implicit–explicit, anonymous–acknowledged, first–final, tentative–definitive, promise–fulfillment. The view of God's plan for the world is strongly Christ-centered. One who has Christ has everything. That person may be interested in discovering traces of his passage in the scriptures of other religions. But they do not bring anything which the Christian does not already have.

PLURALISM AND COMPLEMENTARITY

The third view evokes a perspective of complementarity of the scriptures of various religions. This perspective is based on two related approaches.

First of all, there is a hesitation to identify the Church (and its various foundational elements, including the scriptures) with the Reign of God. A difference is seen between the mystery of God and its historical manifestation in Jesus Christ. The action of Christ and the activity of the Spirit are not simply identified without distinction. Secondly revelation is effected through symbols. A symbol is never an adequate manifestation of the mystery it symbolizes. Besides, different symbols of the same mystery reveal its different aspects; they are complementary. Let me further explain these approaches. It is not my intention here to develop a treatise on the theology of religions. I shall limit myself to a few indications that will throw the required light on the question that we are busy with at the moment.

We make usually too many and too easy identifications. The Bible is the book of the Church, but the Church is not simply identified with God's Reign. The Bible is not a full and adequate report of God's action and self-manifestation in the world. Even the New Testament is an official, but not an adequate expression of God's word in Jesus Christ. J. Dupuis writes:

> The fullness of revelation is not, properly speaking, the written word of the New Testament, but the person of Jesus Christ himself, his deeds and his words, his life, death and resurrection, in one word, the event of Jesus Christ, of which the New Testament itself claims to contain an incomplete record.[23]

The Christ-event, which is reported to us in the New Testament, however inadequately, and which took place in Palestine 2000 years ago, cannot be simply equated with the Mystery, the plan of God for the world of which Paul speaks. Whatever be the key place we give to the Christ-event in this plan, the Mystery itself is cosmic and would be complete only on the "last day." It is not simply a question of distinguishing Christ from the Spirit or from God and christocentrism from theocentrism. It is to point out that even the Christ-event has both a historical and a transhistorical or cosmic aspect that correspond to his reality as God-Man. *Communicatio idiomatum* should not lead one to a simple identification of the two aspects. If one understands this, it is easier to accept what Avery Dulles has to say:

> Could a Christian affirm that the same divine Lord whom Christians worship in Jesus is worshipped, under other symbols, by the devotees of the Lord Krishna and of the Lord Buddha? Fidelity to the Christian Confession, it would seem, excludes the idea that there is any Lord except Jesus (cf. 1 Cor. 8:6). In company with Lucien Richard, I would reject an extreme "archetype Christology" that would see the Jesus story as "the historicization of an archetype which is already found at work everywhere". On the other hand, it need not be denied that the eternal Logos could manifest itself to other peoples through other religious symbols. Raimundo Panikkar, who proposes a "universal

Christology," stands in a long Christian tradition of Logos-theology that goes back as far as Justin Martyr. On Christian grounds, it may be held that the divine person who appears in Jesus is not exhausted by that historical appearance. The symbols and myths of other religions may point to the one whom Christians recognize as the Christ.[24]

Therefore the different symbols of different religions and their scriptures, refer to the same Mystery, but reveal different aspects of the mystery. Even for me, as a Christian, the scriptures of other religions have something to say that I have not heard from my own scriptures.

If this is the case, I can hardly use my scriptures as a criterion to judge the scriptures of other religions. The principle of Judgement is God, the Spirit, the Mystery of Christ which I have experienced in my own scriptures as well as in the scriptures of other religions. It is a criterion of compatibility and consistency, not of conformity. This is the same criterion we use to interpret the Bible itself with its variety of perspectives and theologies. If I may permit myself another long quotation, J. Wijngaards has written:

> The Word of God is a living reality that cannot be pinned down to any external expression. In fact, Christ himself is the Spirit (2 Cor. 3:17). He is the Word of God whom we encounter in the celebration of the Eucharist and in the fellowship we have with our brethren. The New Testament itself is a sign of this living Word, which is Christ. It is not the Word itself *secundum se et simpliciter*. The scriptural traditions of other religions also are "signs" of God's presence in them, records of the work of the Spirit, tokens of the same "Word" proclaimed in the New Testament. When we compare the Bible and non-Christian Scriptures, we are opposing sacred realities that exclude one another. We are asking the question how the "sign" which is the Bible relates to the "sign" contained in other Scriptures. It is not the Bible that should pronounce a "judgement" on other Scriptures, but the Spirit of Christ in us who should make us discern all that is "true, noble, right, pure, lovely and honourable" (Phil. 4:8). "Only God's Spirit knows all about God" (1 Cor. 2:11).[25]

In order to understand and accept a complementarity between the Scriptures of various religions therefore, it is not necessary to move away from a christocentric to a theocentric perspective.

I think we have enough theological grounds to say that, speaking as a Christian, I can affirm that the scriptures of other religions are inspired and that they have a message for me, which is not just a repetition, much less an inchoate version, of Biblical revelation.

This does not mean that we need to say that all the scriptures are the same or that they say the same thing. This perspective would be as wrong as saying that all religions are the same or are only different names for the same reality. We have rejected this position. Qualities like inspiration and prophecy are neither univocal nor absolute attributes. If these terms are meaningful only in the concrete context of God manifesting himself to a particular group of people, then they are primarily and fully valid only in that particular context. Thus a prophet sent to a particular people for a particular occasion need not necessarily be a prophet for everybody at all times. So I can acknowledge that person as a prophet to these people, without accepting that he/she has the same prophetic character for me in my situation.

But if God has indeed spoken to a particular people through scriptures and prophets, then this factor is not a matter of indifference to me. Of course, first of all, these manifestations have to be interpreted in their proper religious and social context. This can obviously be done only by those who believe in them. My respect for these manifestations and their significance are proportional to my respect for the other believers and what God has done for them. Therefore, a proper approach to the other scriptures can be made only in the context of interreligious dialogue. In and through the witness of the other believers, I admire, understand, and praise God's self-manifestation. What I so understand is certainly meaningful to me and challenges me. That is the purpose of interreligious dialogue. The overall context, of course, is the plan of God for the world and it is through such interreligious encounter that we try to catch glimpses of the Mystery.

Once we have come into contact with other scriptures in this way, it is certainly legitimate for us to read and interpret them in our own faith and living context so that they become meaningful to us here and now. But as we have clarified above, the criteria for such interpretation cannot simply be my own scriptures but my sense of the Mystery, guided by my experience of Christ and the Spirit. It is in this sense that they could complement my scriptures and deepen my experience and understanding of the Mystery.

CONSEQUENCES

What are the consequences of this attitude to other religious scriptures? I can see three. First of all, I am called to listen to God speaking to me through the scriptures of other religions, in the two ways specified above. Such listening will enlarge my understanding of the horizons of the mystery of God. Secondly, such a broadening of horizons will lead me to interpret my own scriptures in a new light, the light coming not so much from the other scriptures, but from my deepened experience of the mystery of God. Thirdly, it will challenge me to enter into dialogue with others and to commit myself to a joint project of building up a new humanity, because we understand together slowly the plan God has for all of us, because he is our common origin and goal. I shall say a few words on each of these consequences.

Prayer

If, according to the seminar referred to above, the scriptures of other religions can have a place in our prayer, spiritual reflection and worship, the new realization regarding their inspiration will almost demand such a place. Moreover, some of these other scriptures, the Indian scriptures, for example, are my own patrimony and will help me to discover my own deeper and fuller identity. The use of these scriptures in the Liturgy will be further facilitated, if the Liturgy is not understood in an overly christocentric manner, as the Seminar did,[26] but it makes room for broader mysteric and pneumatic dimensions in the manner of the Oriental Churches.

Interpretation

It is already a fact of experience that Indians reading St. John's Gospel in the light of their scriptures discover in it themes, perspectives and depths that an European Christian would not find.[27] Talking about a Biblical hermeneutic for India today, G. Soares-Prabhu suggests

> Such an "Indian" method will not be a matter of elaborating specifically Indian techniques for interpreting the Bible, but of adopting a specifically Indian perspective from which the Bible will be interpreted. An Indian reading of the Bible is a reading from an Indian point of view: a reading guided by a sensibility shaped by Indian culture, and provoked by questions emerging from the Indian situation.[28]

Religions are an important part of the Indian cultural situation and their scriptures would certainly help us acquire that Indian sensibility. The seminar recognized this: "Never can the Church be truly Indian without imbibing her religious and humanistic traditions, without being familiar with, and feeding on her scriptures."[29]

Common Commitment

But the function of scriptures in a community is not primarily to be vehicles of its culture. Its role is to make the life of the community meaningful in the context of its foundational experience and in reference to its goal, namely self-realization and fulfillment, *Moksha*. It supports moral values and promotes the quality of life. In a country like India where people of all religions are working together to build up a new humanity, religion should be a cause neither of alienation nor of division. Rather it should be a force for collaboration. The kind of complementarity that I have suggested would enable the followers of different religions to help each other through earnest dialogue to develop an integral vision of people and the world that would provoke and support a common commitment to creative action. Each religious group, without losing its identity, would be taken up in a converging movement which would be a historic, dynamic expression of God's plan for humanity. I have traced elsewhere the possible path that such a dialogue between Hinduism and Christianity could take in India. A mutual understanding and interpretation of the scriptures would certainly be an essential element of such a dialogue. One recalls the prayer meetings of Mahatma Gandhi in which scriptures of the various religions were read and people prayed together. It is certainly an easier form of dialogue than common liturgical celebration or community organization.

In the history of the world, religious pluralism has always been a source of strife, more or less serious. But religions can also become sources of unity and collaboration and not of division. Common reading of the scriptures can be a means of promoting such unity. The analysis of the problem of inspiration of the scriptures of other religions that I have attempted here seems to indicate that a common reading of the scriptures is not only tolerated or allowed, but even demanded. Perhaps, today, that is the best way of proclaiming and making effective the Good News of the Reign of God.

4

Dialogue and Mission: Conflict or Convergence?

There is a widespread feeling today in the Church that its traditional missionary dynamism is growing weaker. This phenomenon is being blamed on an emerging theology of religions on the one hand and on the other, on a broadening of the focus of mission effort. Proclamation leading to conversion is seen only as one aspect of evangelization, the other aspects being dialogue, liberation and inculturation.[1] Increasing secularization and dechristianization has made the whole world the field of mission so that one speaks of the mission in and to six continents. The other religions are seen in a more positive light as "ways of salvation" calling for interreligious dialogue.[2] Some theologians have not only moved from christocentrism to theocentrism, but even propose the possibility of many incarnations.[3] Are we finding facile solutions to the problem of religious pluralism, sacrificing in the process the identity of the Church? In this atmosphere, the dialectical relationship between mission and dialogue becomes radicalized into an opposition, with the result that a variety of middle positions that try to hold on to both poles of the dialectic tend to get overlooked. I think that mission and dialogue are in a convergent rather than conflictual relationship. I shall try to explain why in the following pages. It is not my intention here to explore elaborately the implications of mission and dialogue taken separately. I shall rather focus on their interrelationships.

A PARADIGM SHIFT?

Karl Rahner has suggested that with the Second Vatican Council, the Church has entered a new stage of awareness and development: from being a European dominated reality into a World Church.[4] He considers this transition as important as the transition of the Church from being a Jewish sect into a Christian community open to the gentile Greco-Latin world. However, this awareness of becoming a World Church is not a triumphalistic one of a giant multinational corporation with power and influence everywhere. It is the awareness of a community-in-diaspora, which is everywhere—even in the so-called Christian countries—a little flock, vigorously witnessing to and proclaiming the Good News.[5] Corresponding to this self-awareness of itself as a world Church, there is an experiential realization of the universal salvific will of God which makes God present to all people of every time through the Word and the Spirit. Combined with these new perspectives is a new method of theological reflection which does not descend from above deductively from the truths of faith, but rather starts from below with the experience of the world and, reading the signs of the times, moves on to interpret the perennial tradition in order to make it relevant to the present. Such an exploration of human and social experience needs the help of the social sciences.

I think we are actually living a process that could be called a paradigm shift. In science, a paradigm is a framework of meaning that makes sense of a body of data perceived as a system. New data brought in by new discoveries tend to be interpreted and integrated into the existing framework. Then comes a stage when some incoming data cannot be so integrated. Under this challenge, the framework itself undergoes a transformation. This process is a paradigm shift. The Copernican revolution is a well-known example. The theology of evangelization is undergoing a Copernican revolution. Under the impact of a positive experience of other religions the center of the framework is shifting from the Church to the Reign of God. This change is making us look in a new way at Christ, at the Church, at salvation and at mission. In the following pages, let us first look at the various elements of the paradigm. We would then be able to look at the whole. We shall then draw appropriate conclusions for reflection and action.

A POSITIVE VIEW OF OTHER RELIGIONS

The Second Vatican Council declared in its *Constitution on the Church:*

> Those also can attain to everlasting salvation who, through no fault of their own do not know the Gospel of Christ or His Church, yet sincerely seek God and, moved by grace, strive by their deeds to do His will as it is known to them through the dictates of conscience.[6]

This text reaffirms traditional doctrine. It might however seem to limit itself to the interior, personal relationship between God and an individual in the secrecy of his conscience. This perspective is further deepened in a Trinitarian context, by the *Constitution on the Church in the Modern World* which stresses the common vocation of all to salvation.

> Since Christ died for all men, and since the ultimate vocation of man is in fact one, and divine, we ought to believe that the Holy Spirit in

a manner known only to God offers to every man the possibility of being associated with his paschal mystery.[7]

The Declaration on Other Religions seems to go further by talking of "ways," consisting of "teachings, rules of life and sacred ceremonies." It develops further the theme of a common vocation. All peoples make up a single community, which has God as its origin and goal. "His providence, His manifestations of goodness, and His saving designs extend to all men (cf. Wis. 8:1; Acts 14:17; Rom. 2:6-7; 1 Tim. 2:4)." The Christians, therefore, are exhorted, through dialogue and collaboration and in witness of Christian faith and life, to "acknowledge, preserve, and promote the spiritual and moral goods found among these men, as well as the values in their society and culture."[8]

Continuing this tradition and talking from an experience of the great religious traditions of Asia, the Asian Bishops affirm:

> We accept them as significant and positive elements in the economy of God's design of salvation. In them we recognize and respect profound spiritual and ethical meanings and values. Over many centuries they have been the treasury of the religious experience of our ancestors, from which our contemporaries do not cease to draw light and strength. They have been and continue to be the authentic expression of the noblest longings of their hearts, and the home of their contemplation and prayer. They have helped to give shape to the histories and cultures of our nations. How then can we not give them reverence and honour? And how can we not acknowledge that God has drawn our peoples to himself through them?[9]

In systematizing these insights, theologians have explained that given God's universal salvific will on the one hand and the socio-historical nature of the human person on the other, the salvific dialogue between them takes place not merely in the interiority of conscience but through the teachings, rules of life and sacred ceremonies that constitute religion.[10] We can therefore say that the followers of other religions attain to salvation not in spite of them, but in and through them, though it is always God who saves. Religions are therefore ways of salvation. Of course they are not free of human error and sin. Some have called the Church an extraordinary way as opposed to other ordinary ways. We shall discuss this difference later. For the moment let us stay with the idea—or rather the experience—of many ways to salvation: not many salvations, but many ways of participating in the one salvation from the Father through Christ in the Spirit.

THE PLURALISM OF RELIGIONS

As soon as one speaks of many ways to salvation, one will be accused of relativism. Is it not like saying: "all religions lead to God as all rivers lead to the sea?" The *Document on Religious Freedom* states it very clearly:

The highest norm of human life is the divine law—eternal, objective, and universal—whereby God orders, directs and governs the entire universe and all the ways of the human community, by a plan conceived in wisdom and love. Man has been made by God to participate in this law ... Hence every man has the duty, and therefore the right, to seek the truth in matters religious ... Truth, however, is to be sought after in a manner proper to the dignity of the human person and his social nature. The inquiry is to be free, carried on with the aid of teaching or instruction, communication, and dialogue ... In all his activity a man is bound to follow his conscience faithfully ... Of its very nature, the exercise of religion consists before all else in those internal, voluntary, and free acts whereby man sets the course of his life directly toward God ... However, the social nature of man itself requires that he should give external expression to his internal acts of religion; that he should participate with others in matters religious; that he should profess his religion in community.[11]

In matters of religion and faith, the criterion of conduct is conscience. It is not religions that give salvation; they are only ways. It is God who offers freely salvation to the human person who responds in freedom. In this covenant relationship mediated by religion all human persons are indeed equal. It is not relativism to say: God calls me through the Church, but also God seems to be calling my brother or sister through another religion. They are not free, but obliged to respond to God's call along the way in which they feel God is directing them. But it is relativism if I say that it is a matter of indifference to me (or to another person) whether I am a Christian, a Hindu or a Muslim, because all ways lead to God. For each person only that way leads to God which God indicates providentially. It is a matter of experience, unless we are ready to accuse the majority of humanity of insincerity, that people are led to God in various ways in a mysterious manner known only to Godself. It is true therefore that all rivers lead to the sea, but not for the same person. The world is not a supermarket of religions where one can shop around for the best one. Religion is a matter of God's call: a vocation. Conversion to another religion is only justifiable when one hears the call of God. Some might find this legitimacy conferred on other religions difficult to accept. Yet if God wants to save all people and the majority of them, both at any given time and in history taken as a whole, live and die as members of other religions, to consider them illegitimate is equivalent to saying that God's will is ineffective, if we accept that God respects the human, social and historical character of people. On the other hand, religions are only ways. What is important is that they facilitate the encounter of God and the human person.

Can one compare the different religious traditions objectively? It could be an interesting pastime for scholars of the history of religions. But it is irrelevant to our purpose here. Somehow we do not seem capable of seeing two things without putting them in a sort of hierarchical order. Is virginity superior to marriage? For whom? If God has called a person to the married state, it is obviously the best state of life for him. There may be other levels—structural, functional and symbolical, rooted in history and culture—in which such comparisons are meaningful; but not at the basic religious level of divine call and human response.

For persons who are accustomed to abstract ideas of "truth" perceived "objectively," such a point of view may be upsetting. Without outlining a whole epistomology, I shall make just two observations. First of all religious truth is symbolic.[12] *Symbol* indicates a mediation, a sacramentality. "Symbol" is not opposed to "real." God relates to us and we to God in and through symbols. This is not merely because we experience God in theophanies that give God a name and a form in the context of a history, a tradition, a culture. It is in and through some such symbol that God is experienced. (One could discuss whether mystical experience manages to do away with all symbols.) Secondly, this experience of God in and through symbols is always an act of faith. Once again we should not oppose faith and truth. The truth of revelation is not one that can be scientifically demonstrated. One needs the eyes of faith to perceive it. One cannot talk about it objectively, independently of the perspective of faith. Every faith perspective is under the constant judgment of the Absolute which is mediated to it through the symbol. Every faith can judge everything else from its point of view. But it cannot claim to do so objectively, that is to say, in a way acceptable to some one else who does not share that faith. One could always be strongly positive about one's own faith. But one should be very careful in being negative about someone else's faith. When faith meets faith, objective language is no longer useful. I do not think that a world theology transcending all religions can be anything more than a rational abstraction, though a convergent sharing of faith remains possible. The denial of the possibility of an objective language does *not* deny the objectivity of the reality spoken of.

THE CHURCH AND OTHER RELIGIONS

What is the self-awareness of the Church in the midst of the religions? I think we can say that after the Second Vatican Council, no one would think of the Church and other religions in terms of presence/absence of salvation, or light/darkness. There would however be some who would still think in terms of divine/human, supernatural/natural. Apart from the fact that such dichotomies are no longer current in theology today, such an attitude is untenable after the repeated affirmations of God's universal salvific will and of a common divine plan for the world. Terms like implicit/explicit, partial/full are more common today. One sees the history of salvation as a straight line that moves from the Cosmic to the Mosaic and the Christian covenants. The process is one of explicitation and fulfillment.

While we cannot deny the special significance of the short period of history between Moses and Jesus, it would not be fair to narrow down salvation history to that small section. A special call finds its meaning only in relation to the whole. So we cannot understand the significance of this brief period of history without setting it back in the context of the universal history of humankind, which is also a salvation history, because God has willed and planned to save all.[13]

I think the Copernican revolution I spoke of in the beginning is to be located just here. Do we think of salvation as the reality of the new covenant slowly reaching out into a world that is outside or do we see salvation present and active universally—universal meaning both everywhere and at all times—in the context of which we seek to understand the significance of the new covenant and the special role of the Church?

What then is the special role of the Church in the history of salvation in relation to the other religions? The Vatican II Document on the Church speaks of it as a kind of sacrament: "By her relationship with Christ, the Church is a kind of sacrament of intimate union with God, and of the unity of all mankind."[14] I think that this idea of sacrament offers us a good point for reflection. One could immediately ask two questions: what is a sacrament? Why do we need a sacrament when we have the reality (salvation)? I would like to look for an answer to these questions by analyzing one of the sacraments.

One often hears an analogous question: "If one's sins are forgiven through sincere repentance, why go to confession?" What is basic in the process of salvation is the divine-human encounter. While the sacraments celebrate such encounters, especially in relation to the paschal mystery, they have no monopoly over such encounters. If a sinner sincerely turns to God, sins are forgiven. The rite of confession becomes meaningful only as a communal symbolic celebration of the encounter. If the encounter is not there, the rite itself is only an empty shell. Since the human person is a corporal and social being, the ritual may facilitate, enrich and celebrate the encounter. Both the encounter and its symbolic celebration may be found in different forms in other religions. The sacrament of reconciliation, however, as a celebration of the Church shares in the structural aspect of the Church, which in turn is linked to the paschal mystery. This is an awareness that when the Church as a community is present and active in a sacramental celebration, God is present and active there. This is not magical; nor does it dispense with the basic divine-human encounter. But it links it structurally and through tradition to the paschal mystery and thus provides an assurance. The human person is still free to respond or not. But God is committed irrevocably through the institution of the Church and through giving it the power to bind and to loose. This irrevocable commitment is symbolically evoked in the sacrament. But this irrevocableness itself extends to all the acts of God in history, by reason of the once-for-all paschal mystery.

The Church therefore is a sacrament that makes present, sensibly (i.e. in a way accessible to the senses) and through celebration, a basic divine-human encounter. It is related to the paschal mystery of Christ because the Church that celebrates is a community that is aware of being founded by Christ.

What are the implications of considering the Church a sacrament of salvation? It makes present a mystery that transcends it—a mystery that reaches out further, not being limited to the sacrament. It is ordained to the ever fuller realization of the mystery. On the one hand, it is a symbolic realization: this makes it a witnessing community. On the other hand, it is neither exhaustive nor exclusive, though it is committed to strive for the ever fuller realization of the mystery. It is aware that the mystery is present and active in the world outside its visible structure as a community, though it may not know how. The final criteria to judge the presence of the mystery whether in or outside the Church are really the fruits of the Spirit—the values of the Reign of God. But our main point here is that by considering itself a kind of sacrament, the Church is not simply identifying itself with the Reign which is seen as a wider reality. The term sacrament, while affirming a real relation, also indicates a limitation, a nonexclusivity.

I think one real problem in this whole discussion is the extension of meaning that we give to the term Church. Sometimes we mean by Church the visible hierarchical community with the structure of sacraments and creeds, with clear boundaries marked by baptism. At other times, we mean by Church, the Mystical Body of Christ, coexistensive with the Reign, made up of all the saved, partly visible and partly invisible.[15] To complicate matters, one easily moves from one to the other meaning of Church. When I speak of the Church in the first sense I know what I am talking about: it is a community that has a history, a tradition, a socio-cultural identity. When I speak of the Church in the second sense, I tend to get lost in the mystery. This usage can be a source of confusion in two ways. First of all, one tends to identify the Church-community with the Church-mystery. While the second includes the first, the first does not include the second, though it is related to it. So I could attribute aspects to the second that I would not attribute to the first. For the Church-community, it is legitimate to be aware of its roots in the mystery: but it is presumptuous on its part to identify itself with the mystery and to make claims based on such identification. Secondly, when the Church is face to face with other religions in which it also recognizes the action of God, a simple identification between the Church-community and the Church-mystery becomes really problematic. Within the context of the Church-community, one is certainly entitled to explore its depths in mystery. But when one begins speaking of the relationship of the Church-community with the world, with other religions and with cultures, it helps very much if one can be precise in the use of terms. For instance in the context of interreligious dialogue, inculturation, and mission, it would help to speak normally of the Church-community, aware of its historical and cultural limitedness as a pilgrim Church, specifying therefore the mysteric aspects when one evokes them, being conscious even then that its relationship with Mystery is special, but not exclusive. The other religions too have as their depth the same mystery. On the one hand, any simplification of this complex reality will cause confusion in expression. On the other hand, once other religions are recognized as ways of salvation in the plan of God, one can justifiably talk of the Church also as one among other religions, engaging in dialogue, ready to receive as well as to give.

The evocation of an analogous situation in the field of ecumenism may be helpful. At the Second Vatican Council, for the first time, the Church recognized other Christians as ecclesial communities,[16] yet at the same time, it affirmed that the one Church of Christ subsists in the Catholic Church.[17] Some would say that once other Churches are accepted as Churches, the word "subsists" indicates a special link—to be explored and specified—but not a simple identity. There are, however, others who think that "subsists" really means "is" and who therefore tend to look on every Christian as an anonymous Catholic. Here also we have a similar tension. It is not merely a difference in terminology. It is a difference in awareness, worldview, approaches and attitudes. Even Rahner's celebrated phrase, "anonymous Christians," is ambiguous from this point of view and unacceptable, since it can be interpreted to mean an implicit relationship, not only to Christ, but also to Christianity.

The limitations of the Church-community can also be perceived from another point of view. Sometimes one distinguishes between the pilgrim and eschatological realities of the Church. As a pilgrim, it is an imperfect and inadequate response to God's call. But even eschatologically, the Church is only at an "already/not yet" stage. The fullness to which it is called is in the future. The Christ event is certainly God's decisive word. In relation to the Mosaic covenant that preceded it as a preparation, it is the final word. But for the world, it is only the beginning of the last times. Following scripture, one could take the analogy of a relationship of love between a man and a woman. They fall in love and a period of courtship follows. At a certain stage there is a definitive commitment in marriage. It is the end of one process, but the beginning of another. In the course of the married life, the love grows, finds fruitful expression, ripens. In the ongoing dialogue of love between God and humans, God's offer and human response reach a high point in Jesus, in the unique manner of a God-man.[18] Jesus is the definitive yes of both God and the human person. But this central definitive act is significant only in relation to the whole drama of love that precedes and follows it. The Jewish Christians wanted to see Christ as the fulfillment of the Old Testament and stop there. But St. Paul opened the doors of Christianity to the Greco-Roman world, which saw also in Greek philosophy a "pedagogue." After 2000 years, the Church seems to stand hesitantly at another stage of openness to the whole world, moving towards a world Church. Mission is meaningful only because it is a move towards a fullness in the future. The Church, as it is, is a historically and culturally limited realization of the Good News—not to speak of its other more human limitations. Moving out of this limited sphere it does not proclaim itself, but the Good News. It is Jesus who has to incarnate himself anew in the various cultures of the world and thus lead the world to its fullness. The Church, as the bearer in history of the Good News and its partial realization, has a role of witness and messenger facilitating the divine-human encounter. In Latin theology, in the context of a juridical point of view centered on Christ, the Church may tend to consider itself as a kind of mediator between God and humanity. With the renewed affirmation of Christ as the only mediator in the context of Catholic-Protestant dialogue,[19] and with the increasing recognition of the role of the Spirit in the divine economy in the context of Catholic-Orthodox dialogue,[20] there is a more realistic view of the Church today.

THE UNIQUENESS OF CHRIST

To say that the fullness is in the future may still upset some. Is not Christ our fullness? Do we not have everything with Christ? Is he not the unique savior? Has he not saved all by dying for all? So we come to the Christological problem.[21]

We profess our faith, "Christ died for all." What is the meaning of this statement? There is a spectrum of theological opinions varying from the purely juridical to the organic. Some would say that Christ has made satisfaction for all. The graces he had amassed by his infinite sacrifice are given to all who sincerely repent. The other extreme would be that Christ has saved the whole of humanity by the very act of uniting himself to it; this happens already at the Incarnation. Some would speak of a corporate personality: Christ does not die and rise again instead of us, but all of us die and rise with him. Some others would stress the risen Christ: in virtue of his passion and death, Christ is now established with power before the throne of God as Lord and Savior. Rahner proposes the theory of real-symbol causality: it is real because it is a definitive commitment that unites both the yes of God and the human person in one person; it is of universal significance because it expresses both God's will to save all peoples and Jesus' solidarity with every one; it is symbolic, because it is a prototype of every divine-human encounter.[22] Whatever theory we prefer, we have to safeguard a certain number of things: that the freedom and historicity of every person's response is respected; that this possibility of response is available to people not only after Jesus but also before him; that the possibility is not tied to an explicit profession of faith in Jesus in the Church.

We are faced here with an event in history that has a transcendent significance. Those who wish to point to the centrality of Jesus and the Church in a narrow manner harp on the historical aspect of the matter and speak of the scandal of particularity. Yet it would seem to me that only insofar as we liberate the mystery from its historical particularity without severing the link, can we realize its universal significance. As a matter of record, in the New Testament, the progressive realization of the universal significance of the death and resurrection of Jesus is accompanied by the realization of the universal outreach of his personality as the cosmic Christ of St. Paul and the Logos of St. John.

It is traditional to speak of two approaches in Christology: from above and from below. Traditional Christology was from above and can become easily monophysite in tone, if not in intention. One speaks of Jesus as God and Savior and attributes to him what we should normally attribute to God, Three-in-One. We know that the Father is the origin, that the Spirit is the cosmic and active divine power and that the Son has a cosmic role as Word, which at a particular time in history becomes flesh in Jesus. Jesus is heir to a particular religious tradition, to a particular culture and to a particular historical situation. He grew up like others, was ignorant and tempted, sacrificed his life for the others and was raised up by God on the third day. He sent his Spirit on his disciples promising that the Spirit would lead them into all truth. Meditating on and living this experience, the Church progressively discovers the universal, and divine dimension of his personality. But in doing this, Paul and John do not simply attribute every thing to the historical Jesus but evoke the cosmic Christ and the pre-existent Logos. Later theological systematization emphasized not only the unity of person, but also the distinction of natures. Yet popular piety and popular theology have always been tempted to consider Jesus simply as God, neglecting on the one hand his humanity and on the other the Trinitarian aspects of the mystery. Professional theologians made this easy by proposing the theory of "inter-communication of attributes between the two natures of Christ based on the unity of person" (*communicatio idiomatum*). Thus one could proclaim, "God died on the cross." Yet if we wish to be accurate we will have to say: "The Son died in his human nature." Without such precision, in a Christology from above one could easily speak a monophysite language. Karl Rahner remarks:

> When we say that Peter is a man, the statement expresses a real identification in the content of the subject and the predicate nouns. But the meaning of "is" in statements involving an interchange of predicates in Christology is not based on such a real identification. It is based rather on a unique, otherwise unknown and deeply mysterious unity between realities which are really different and which are at an infinite distance from each other. For in and according to the humanity which we see when we say "Jesus," Jesus "is" not God, and in and according to his divinity God "is" not man in the sense of a real identification. The Chalcedonian *adiairetos* (unseparated) which this "is" intends to express (D.S. 302) expresses it in such a way that

the *asynchytos* (unmixed) of the same formula does not come to expression. Consequently, the statement is always in danger of being understood in a "monophysite" sense, that is, as a formula which simply identifies the subject and predicate.[23]

Today with a Christology from below, there may be a danger of reducing Christ to one among the prophets. But while being aware of this danger, we still have to protest against the abuse of the theory of *"communicatio idiomatum."* Wilhelm Thusing says with reference to this:

> The *communicatio idiomatum* can have the function of safeguarding faith in the unique aspect of Jesus as the absolute bringer of salvation and precisely for this reason it may not be suitable for all generations of Christians, because this way of expressing Jesus' "divinity" has no structural basis in the New Testament. The doctrine of the *communicatio idiomatum* was developed in a particular spiritual climate or context, in which the classical Christology with its ontic categories was current. Before looking for a basis for the communication of properties in the New Testament, then, the protological statements that are a pre-condition for this doctrine should be examined, their New Testament meaning should be checked and it should be established whether they are historically conditioned. It is, then, only in this particular spiritual context that the doctrine of the communication of properties could have been a legitimate and possibly necessary safeguard for faith in Jesus. Outside this spiritual climate, the only one in which this doctrine is intelligible, it can only lead to a monophysitic misunderstanding. It is also undoubtedly misleading for anyone who is not able to follow this way of thinking easily.[24]

I submit that we are not only in a new climate of thought today, but also before a new situation, namely the realization of the positive value of other religions, that demands from us not only a careful use of traditional language, but a new language.

It is not my aim here to develop a Christology. But I think we can speak of Jesus as limited historically and culturally and talk of his absoluteness, uniqueness and universality with the proper nuances that his complex personality demands—to the extent that we can understand the mystery. One often finds this humility and caution lacking. Speaking of the presence of Christ in other religions, K. Rahner suggested that he is present there through the Spirit.[25] Criticizing Rahner's talk of "anonymous Christianity," R. J. Schreiter refuses even the term "cosmic Christ" and prefers to talk in terms of the Word and Wisdom according to the sapiential tradition.[26] Even the scholastics reflecting on the re-enactment of the paschal mystery in the Eucharist spoke of the power of the risen Christ. The attempt of Odo Casel to introduce the idea of a mystery shorn of historical circumstances has not found much favor. This observation is just to indicate that it is not enough to say that Christ is present. When we ask "how?" the different nuances have to be taken into account. The Word became flesh. Jesus was a man like us in all things except sin. Even if he was raised up on the third day, what he said and did and the tradition he left behind him in the Church is historically and culturally limited. It does point to and make present the mystery. But it does that symbolically, and the concrete symbols themselves refer to historical events in the life of Jesus. By that very fact its tradition and symbolic expression does not transcend the historical and cultural limitations—no more than Jesus ceased to be a real human being with all the limitations that it implied while being united to the Word. That is the *kenosis*. The resurrection does not do away with this historical limitedness of his earthly life. He may be the universal man in virtue of his resurrection. But in historical and cultural terms, for the Church and for the people, this is a universality that has to be achieved, not given. This is the meaning of the contemporary talk of inculturation as a new incarnation of Christ in every culture. This implicitly accepts that the first incarnation was culturally limited. When Paul spoke of the *pleroma* of Christ, he spoke of something eschatological—a process which has started, but which will be achieved only on the last day. Any serious thought of the salvation of people who lived before the passion and death of Christ would also rethink, not the historicity of that event, but the universal significance, not of the event, but of its historicity.

Proponents of a Christology from below, on the other hand, may be tempted to reduce Jesus Christ to one among the prophets. These people tend to emphasize the revelation aspect of Jesus to the neglect of the saving event of his death and resurrection. If we take this event seriously, then either we believe it is a divine-human event of a unique kind giving a universal significance or we see it as a limited human event with only an exemplary significance. While I am all for moving away from ecclesiocentrism, to oppose theocentrism to christocentrism is to misunderstand our faith both in the Trinity and in Jesus Christ. Jesus Christ is then no longer an incarnation, a once for all event on which our whole sacramental system is based; he becomes only an *avatar*, a manifestation, like which there can be many. If God's commitment is not definite and irrevocable in Jesus Christ, then I do not see that Jesus is more meaningful to me than Moses or Isaiah. I do not see either how one can profess faith in "Christ who died for all" and envisage the possibility of a plurality of incarnations. I do not see the need for it either since none of the great religions besides Christianity claim such a uniquely meaningful event. If faith in the Trinity involves the belief that where the Father is, the Word also is present and active, how can one oppose the Word made flesh to the Father? So I do not think that one can talk of a theocentrism that would be opposed to christocentrism.[27] However, in the light of my thoughts above, I would distinguish between christocentrism and Jesus-centrism (taking Jesus, the humanity of the Word, not in his transhistorical risen state, but in his historical manifestation). On the other hand, just as Rahner says that God, though immutable in himself, can change and suffer in the other,[28] namely the human nature of Jesus, we can say that Jesus of history becomes universal savior, not in himself, but in the other, namely the divine nature, the Word, to which he is hypostatically united.

Just as we should not separate the two natures in Christ, we should not confuse them either. Such an approach will make it easier to confess, on the one hand, the universal salvific will of God as realized sacramentally in the paschal mystery of Christ reaching out to all peoples and, on the other hand, the historical humanity of Jesus and the Church that follows him, linked to the mystery, yet historically and culturally limited, subject to the historical process and oriented in a special manner to the fullness, not already given, except as the first fruits, but to be achieved, not only in and by itself but by the whole of humanity in free response to God present and active, not always through the Church. The eschatological fullness need not take the form of the Church either in the sense that it is seen merely as Church extension. While we have an assurance about the structure of this plan of God for the world, the concrete processes will have to be discerned in history. Insofar as revelation means the manifestation of a global plan of God for the world, it is over. God has said the definitive word in Jesus Christ. But the history of salvation continues and will continue till the time when God will be all in all.[29]

The new paradigm, that has already been evoked a number of times earlier, could be outlined in three points. God's universal saving will is present and active everywhere in various ways. It is a plan progressively realized in history. It leads to the unification of all things till God is all in all. The three high points that structure the process and therefore have a special universal significance are: creation, the paschal mystery, and the final fulfillment. In this historical process, the paschal mystery is a definitive moment of irrevocable commitment in which God's free offer and man's acceptance of divine self-communication meet in a single act—a single person. The Church is a continuing sacramental (symbolic) re-presentation of this definitive divine-human encounter, called by its very being to witness to and to promote the plan of God—the mystery—which it does not identify with itself. The Church has no exclusive claims on the mystery both in life and in proclamation. It does not offer easier or fuller salvation. God alone is the savior present and active in the world in ways often unknown to us. Because of the universal salvific will of God and the socio-historical character of the human person, the salvific divine-human encounter is also taking place through other religions and their symbolic structures: scriptures, codes of conduct and rituals. Though we believe that they too are related to the paschal mystery in ways unknown to us, they are not direct symbolic re-presentations of its historic realization as the Church is. In the context of the plan of God for the whole of the human race, the

Church is called not only to witness and to proclaim for God's salvation but also to collaborate with all persons of goodwill, humble and respectful of the divine mystery that is operative in the whole world. While we have the assurance that the mystery of unification of all things in God will succeed because it is God's own effective will, and while we are sure of our own call to witness and proclaim it to the whole world, we are ignorant of the concrete ways in which the mystery of God is leading all things to their fulfillment. We have no grounds to believe that the Church-community is the only form or even the only instrument of this fulfillment. Human sin — peoples' refusal to cooperate with God — not to speak of personal and historico-cultural limitations and conditioning, is a factor at all times and everywhere, not excluding the "pilgrim Church."

A LOCAL CHURCH

Let us now come back to reflections on the Church in Asia. Though my main concern here is to clarify the relationship between mission and dialogue, I cannot do this without some reference to the total picture. The first plenary assembly of the Federation of Asian Bishops' Conferences said: "The primary focus of our task of evangelizing at this time in our history, is the building up of a truly local Church." It describes further the local Church as "a Church incarnate in a people, a Church indigenous and inculturated."[30] An authentic inculturation challenges and transforms the culture. The Church in India, for example, must challenge the caste system. But unless the Church seriously engages in the process of changing the caste system, at least within itself, its power as a witness to the gospel is reduced. Is not a certain spirit of uncritical accommodation with current social realities indicative of a one-sidedly "spiritual" view of mission as the saving of "souls"?

The Mission Congress in Manila (1978), following Bishop Patrick D'Souza of India, asked whether, in an area where baptism meant alienation from the socio-cultural community, one could think of leading people to the baptism of desire without actually baptizing them. I think it is a wrong question to ask. The obvious thing to do is to inculturate that community so that people who become members of it do not feel alienated from the socio-cultural milieu. If the alienation is due to certain types of discrimination, then the community is actually called to witness to its convictions bravely. Baptism is not only an opportunity, but a challenge. If neither of these possibilities is feasible, then I think that it is better to leave those people alone. If we seriously believe in the socio-cultural character of religion, bringing people to the Christian faith and then asking them to remain in their own religious milieu would be to ask them to live in a situation of intolerable religious ambiguity. This request would be radical relativization of religions, including Christianity.[31]

INTEGRAL EVANGELIZATION

Pope Paul VI said in *Evangelii Nuntiandi*: "For the Church evangelizing means bringing the Good News into all the strata of humanity, and through its influence transforming humanity from within and making it new."[32] It would be wrong then to consider evangelization narrowly as proclamation leading to baptism and, what is worse, look upon other types of activity as merely means or first steps to proclamation.

The primary task of evangelization is the advancement of the mystery of God's plan for the world—the promotion of the Reign. The building up of a local witnessing community is certainly an element in this task, but not an exclusive element. The kind of activity that we actually have in a given place depends on the concrete circumstances, needs and possibilities.[33] We have to read the signs of the times and discern the Lord's call in a given situation, rather than go with an abstract list of priorities. The signs of the times include, for instance, the readiness of a given group of people to listen to the Good News.

Living in Asia in multireligious societies and undertaking the task of promoting common human and evangelical values, Christians are called to collaborate with the members of other religions towards providing a common religious and moral foundation for our developing societies. Whatever may be their absolute faith positions, the different religions can and do find a common perspective in the area of human values. Differences in their historico-cultural roots also make their approaches complementary in regard to the promotion of integral humanism. An awareness of the Church's own limitations in standing up for people in the past and the ambiguity of the contemporary record of countries which Asians identify as Christian would help us to remain humble.

WHY PROCLAMATION?

If other religions are also ways of salvation, why proclaim the Gospel and seek to baptize people? The need to help people avoid damnation motivated missionaries in former times. We do not today share their anxiety. Should that anxiety be an essential element in our enthusiasm in proclaiming the Good News? The motivation to proclaim the Good News is a combination of an internal urge and a call—one discovers and experiences the Good News and the joy of this experience drives one to share it with others. This internal drive is confirmed and strengthened by the call of Christ to go out into the whole world and be a witness to the Good News. One may also feel the urge to proclaim the Good News because of conviction that it has something essential and specific to contribute, according to the plan of God, to the growth of the new humanity. The Cross and the Resurrection, the new commandment, the commitment to a new

humanity to be progressively built up in history are perspectives that give
a new kind of meaning to human experience. Thirdly, the Good News can
hardly play its role effectively in the world unless it is visibly and socially
present in culture as a local Church, indigenous and inculturated. To build
up such a witnessing Church is also a task of mission.

The desire for baptism is a call of the Spirit, of whom the missionary is
only a witness and a messenger. In particular socio-historical circumstances,
this call may take concrete historical forms. But it is always an encounter
between two freedoms—the freedom of the Spirit and the freedom of the
hearer. I am only a facilitator. Membership in the Church is not an easier
or surer means of salvation. Baptism is not an opportunity, but a challenge
and a mission. A Christian, like Christ, is a person for others. One is called,
not only to live, but to witness. One's witnessing must be enthusiastic,
without anxiety and without aggressivity. It is unfortunate if we cannot be
enthusiastic with what we have, without disparaging or feeling a hidden
pity for those we look upon as have-nots!

Though a spiritual conversion or turning to God is at the root of baptism,
it would be wrong to think that baptism is a purely spiritual act. It is also
a very socio-political act. One could ask for baptism because one also sees
it as an option for a superior culture or civilization, or as an opportunity
for development, or as a protest against an oppressive group, or as an act
of socio-political solidarity. The crisis of the mission in Asia is not unconnected to the memories of a colonial past, to renewed nationalism, to the
perception of Christianity as foreign, and to the vulnerability of the
Christian community as small minority groups.

If the purpose of proclamation is not simply to save people but to build
up effective witnessing communities, then some of the present policies may
need revision. The Gospel must be preached to the poor and one should
not neglect what are sometimes called responsive groups. But on the other
hand, are the cultural elite being neglected? Are we unfaithful to the basic
insights of Roberto de Nobili and Matteo Ricci or even Francis Xavier who
asked for learned men to be sent to Japan?

Proclamation is not an all or nothing proposition. Even when we cannot
build up a Christian community, we can still communicate the values of the
Reign of God. We can really speak of the acknowledged Christ of the Hindu
renaissance in India. At the same time, we can understand the mysterious
ways of divine providence if we realize that such communication of the
values of the Reign has taken place not necessarily because of, but sometimes in spite of the Church in India. To take but one celebrated example,
Gandhi would trace the Christian influence on him to Tolstoy, to Ruskin,
to the Quakers in England, rather than to any Christians in India. This is
not to deny that the Churches are doing a lot of good work in India, but
only to point out that God's ways are not always our ways.

If the mystery of salvation depends basically on the encounter between
an individual and God, then all mediations are just that, relative—not in

relation to one another but in relation to the mystery — except the One Mediator who is part of the mystery itself. If the Church cannot claim any exclusivity, then what it can claim is a special message and, thanks to the special witness of Jesus, an assurance based on the paschal mystery, and a vision of the whole world moving to its ultimate unity when God will be all in all. Even this assurance is of a structural kind, as I have tried to explain above, and it is different from an assurance born of a personal spiritual experience. This special knowledge is not a privilege, but a mission. Awareness of the goal, however, does not give an awareness of the concrete ways in which God proposes to lead the world to this goal.

WHY DIALOGUE?

As soon as one no longer sees the relationship of Christianity to other religions as presence/absence or superior/inferior or full/partial, dialogue becomes the context in which proclamation has to take place. For even when proclaiming the Good News with assurance, one should do it with great respect for the freedom of God who is acting, the freedom of the other who is responding and the Church's own limitations as a witness. It is quite proper then that the Asian Bishops characterized evangelization itself as a dialogue with various Asian realities — cultures, religions and the poor.

When faith encounters faith, no other way but dialogue is possible if one respects the other's convictions. When a developed metacosmic religion meets a simple cosmic one, the relationship may not be equal culturally. But when one metacosmic religion meets another, dialogue seems the only possible way. Besides one cannot hold on to an absolute commitment of faith without relativizing the other from one's own point of view. Karl Rahner, in a rare moment, tells us the following story:

> Nishitani, the well-known Japanese philosopher, the head of the Kyoto school, who is familiar with the notion of the anonymous Christian, once asked me: what would you say to my treating you as an anonymous Zen Buddhist? I replied: certainly you may and should do so from your point of view; I feel myself honoured by such an interpretation, even if I am obliged to regard you as being in error or if I assume that, correctly understood, to be a genuine Zen Buddhist is identical with being a genuine Christian, in the sense directly and properly intended by such statements. Of course in terms of objective social awareness it is indeed clear that the Buddhist is not a Christian and the Christian is not a Buddhist.[34]

A faith commitment gives an absolute value not only to the Absolute, but also to the symbol that mediates that Absolute. Two believers who meet each other, even when they realize that the Absolute to which they are both committed is the same, do not on that account relativize the mediating symbols. That is why a sort of supertheology that would reconcile in a higher synthesis two absolute commitments is not possible, though it would always remain a rational temptation. One can escape this predicament only at the level of interpersonal relationship that respects not only each other's freedom and the sovereign freedom of God, and also enters into a convergent movement through mutual sharing of experiences leading to mutual challenge and mutual growth.[35]

Proclamation and dialogue are relationships between persons. In the last analysis, the plurality of free persons is the basis of a pluralistic world. Plurality demands dialogue and community. It abhors system. Plurality, freedom, dialogue and community should pose no problems for people who contemplate the Trinity.

CONCLUSION

I began the paper by speaking of a new paradigm. I have briefly outlined it earlier in the paper. Now as a conclusion let me briefly state some of the implications that I have tried to draw out of that paradigm.

First of all, we must accustom ourselves to a new way of thinking from below, reflecting from experience and reality and not from above, in the abstract, deductively.

Secondly, experiencing the positive value for salvation of other religions, we must give them a place in the plan of God for the world.

Thirdly, we must realize that the Church is a complex reality consisting of a historic, visible and a mysteric level, namely the Church-community and the Church-mystery. When we speak of the Church in the context of other religions, it would help to avoid confusion if we are careful to talk about the Church-community. The other religions also participate in the Church-mystery. The Church-community is historically and socio-culturally limited though it is part of the process of the growing Reign of God. The fullness is in the future, not in the past.

Fourthly, we should take seriously the Chalcedonian admonition neither to separate nor to confuse the two natures in Christ. We should rethink the principle of *communicatio idiomatum*. We must remember the *kenosis* and the socio-historical and cultural limitedness of the man, Jesus. Again the *pleroma* of which St. Paul speaks is in the future, not in the past. Our faith affirmation that Christ died for all, however explained, does not do away with the limitations of Jesus as man in history and the Church-community that is constituted by and witnesses to the tradition of the historical Jesus, even if its experience reaches out to the mystery.

Mission and dialogue are converging movements in the context of a common commitment to a new humanity that takes seriously the freedom and the creativity of people and God.

PART II

PLURALISM

5

The Symbolic Dimension of Christianity

The element in the Indian context that has increasingly engaged the attention of its theologians in recent years is the fact of religious pluralism and the need to find a meaning for it in the plan of God in the light of the Word. The plurality of religions was not a problem as long as Christianity was viewed as opposed to other religions as truth to falsehood or as legitimate to illegitimate. Moreover, the problem would still be not so acute if one sees in the other religions only some good and holy elements that need to be rescued, so to speak, and assimilated. While these elements are acknowledged and judged from one's own point of view, the religions themselves can be conveniently ignored. The problem of religious pluralism becomes actual only when it is acknowledged that God communicates himself to people, not only in, and almost in spite of, other religions, but also through them, so that they can be really spoken of as ways to salvation. Such an understanding of other religions has grown in the recent past and has come to be widely accepted by theologians in India today.[1]

Faced with this problem of the pluralism of religions, two easy solutions seem unacceptable to me. One cannot adopt an agnostic attitude to other religions and behave as if they did not exist. Neither can a committed believer in any religion accept all religions as different ways to the same goal, just as all the rivers lead to the same ocean. A third approach to a solution, generally accepted by Christians, has been the use of categories like less perfect-more perfect; promise-fulfillment; implicit-explicit; etc. A certain sense of the superiority of Christianity has always accompanied this approach, as if salvation is surer and easier in Christianity than in other religions. I find this approach unsatisfactory. Religion is ultimately dependent on personal relationships—of a person with God and with other persons. Many from the East and the West will reach God's Reign before the "chosen" people get there—this is true of the New as the Old Testament. "Choice" by God is not a guarantee but a mission. However, it is not my purpose here to examine and criticize in detail the categories used by the third approach. Rather, I shall present another approach and make a few critical remarks at the end.

THE SYMBOLIC DIMENSION

I think that the notion of symbol is very helpful in explaining this and other similar problems. Let me first describe what I mean by the term symbol and then show how it can be useful in understanding situations like the one described above.[2]

As soon as we hear the word symbol, a host of images spring before our mind's eye. We see first of all mathematical symbols, for example, x, y, 2. These stand for some known or unknown quantity. They stand for anything at all: persons, money, values, things, time etc. Secondly we have linguistic signs. These are conventional signs but not as arbitrary as mathematical symbols. In English the word cow refers to an animal of a certain type. If one speaks English, one has no choice except to use that word. But in French one will say "vache." There is no particular reason why that animal should be a cow or a vache. These terms are applied to the same type of animal by two different groups of people who refer to them in this way by a convention accepted and learnt when the language is learnt. When we say that smoke is a sign of fire, we are speaking of an *index*, which is still another kind of symbol. Smoke is caused by fire. There is a material connection between smoke and fire: where there is smoke, there is fire. Therefore smoke indicates — points to — fire. That is why we call it an index. We also have *poetic symbols*, which are based on metaphoric relationships. If we say that fire is a symbol of love, it is because fire and love share a common quality, namely ardor. What makes fire a symbol is this quality, or way of being, identified by a person with imagination. All these types of symbols and signs are used in the process of communication between people. Our normal talk about symbols, even in theology, hardly ever goes beyond these types.

THE SYMBOLIC ACTIONS

Yet there are a host of symbols that are very different. They are not merely communicative like the symbols listed above and sometimes self-expressive like the poetic symbols. They are concrete and experiential. Let me take an example. I meet a friend on the road. I salute him with a bow. It is a gesture that indicates an attitude of welcome, especially if it is accompanied by a smile. Suppose I hold his hand and press it — shake hands. The pressure of my hand not merely communicates a message, but makes him *experience* welcome — feel the pleasure I have in seeing him again. More than that, it is a mutual, shared experience and expression of joy and love. It is not merely an intellectual experience, but a human one, including the physical dimension. We are not merely telling each other of our joy; we are not merely feeling it; we are not only expressing it in words and signs; we are linking it in a human way that involves our bodies too.

Let me briefly analyze this symbol. First of all it is not merely a symbol, but a *symbolic action*. It communicates a message of love and welcome. But it also *does* something more. It creates in both persons an experience. It creates an atmosphere of welcome, love, etc. This is a simple gesture. But all social and religious rituals are such symbolic actions. Thus a banquet celebrates and creates community. A rite of initiation effectively makes one a member of the group. The rites accompanying a funeral reiterate social and kinship ties. The symbolic action is a *human* action. The human person is a spirit in a body—or rather enfleshed spirit. Whatever we do and experience finds bodily expression. It is then that we find a total way of being and acting. Language in itself abstracts, alienates. In universalizing its concepts, it disembodies them. But symbolic action enfleshes meaning; it concretizes concepts; it makes communication into a human experience. It is from this point of view, for instance, that we should find a new dimension in the mysteries of the incarnation—enfleshing of the Word—and of the eucharist—the Lord becoming present to us in his body.[3] I shall say more of this later. The symbolic action is also a communal action. It is an action of a community that actualizes and concretizes interpersonal relationships. The person who is being initiated into a community enters into a set of new relationships with the others in the community of which he or she becomes a new member. The new member takes on a certain number of duties and obligations towards the group. The new relationships are ritually expressed and lived in the symbolic action.

What does this symbolic action symbolize? A great many things. I would like to mention here four of them, the last of which is the most important for my purpose, but which can be fully grasped only in the context of the others. The first dimension that a symbolic action evokes is the actual life-situation of the community and all the social and cultural inter-relationships it involves. The ritual of marriage reaffirms kinship ties through the manner in which the various relatives contribute to and take part in the celebration. A rite of initiation, besides making one a new member, gives some idea of the kind of group of which we become members and the type of structure and interrelations that exist in it. The special teaching offered and the rituals see to this. A similar analysis of all the rituals may be made. Every ritual reflects in some way the social and cultural structures that animate the community that celebrates it.[4]

The second dimension that a symbolic action evokes is not contrary, but complementary to the first. Rituals often manifest elements of anti-structure. For example, the image of the community that an observer would get while looking at certain types of rituals like pilgrimages to Pandarpur or Sabarimalai (or Lourdes), the Holi festival (or the carnival), or the eucharist is not the image of the community as it is and hence a faithful reflection of the current structures that make it function in view of the proximate goal it has set itself. It is rather the image of the community as it ought to be, or is called to be or would like to be. On these occasions, taboos of all sorts, distinctions of caste and status seem to disappear and the idea of universal friendship seems to be asserted and lived ritually and experientially. This seems to be a clear affirmation of a dimension of reality that is ever present, though prevailing needs and structural distinctions make us forget it. There is also an element of hope in the future realization of this ideal community.[5]

It is in this context that a third dimension enters in the case of religious symbolic actions. The affirmation of an ideal community is made in terms of a religious faith, which makes the rituals open out to a transcendent dimension. Religious faith not only affirms this community as a future ideal but aims at making elements of this third dimension clear. Initiation rites in most societies not only make the individual a member of a community; they also confer on him fellowship with the gods. Baptism not only makes the recipient a member of the Church, but also a child of God through a rebirth in the Spirit. Similarly, the eucharist is not only a symbol of community and brotherhood lived and manifested in a common meal; it is also a communion with God and a sharing of his divine life which brings together the community sharing the meal. It is this religious dimension that is often the basis of the anti-structural elements spoken of in the previous paragraph.

The fourth dimension of meaning of communal symbolic actions, and the most important one for my purpose here, is its representative character. Let me start with an example. A man and a woman, happily married, love each other. This mutual love animates their whole life. If finds expression in a variety of ways: a loving look, a caressing touch, an affectionate word; in the work the man does for supporting himself and his family and in the house-hold jobs that occupy the woman; in their companionship, mutual appreciation, self-sacrifice for each other, etc. There are a thousand ways in which love is manifested, expressed and experienced. All these are symbolic. But the act of love is something special. It is a pure and simple expression of love. It is not love expressed through some other type of activity. It is love itself in act. It involves the whole person, body and soul — a total self-gift. It is sensible because it involves all the senses. In it love acquires a visibility and becomes tangible. It is representative: it is not the only act expressive of love, while other acts are not so expressive. It expresses it in a particular way: it is somehow related directly to love itself. Yet it has no claims to exclusivity. It sensibilizes an experience that is ever present in every little act. Love expressed in an act of sacrifice or experienced in a moment of separation may be deeper and stronger. The act of love need not be the high-point of the experience of love. It need not be superior to or more authentic than other expressions of love. But its expression is specific, in the way described above. Let me retain then two characteristics of this special symbolic action. (1) It gives a particular expression to an experience that is constant, and extends beyond this particular act both in space and in time. In this it is not exclusive, but representative. (2) At the level of expression, though there may be a thousand ways of expressing love in symbolic actions, this is a particular, specific one. this specificity is in the order of expression and not in the order of intensity of experience. Both these characteristics make it symbolic of all the other symbolic expressions of love. Like the tip of the iceberg indicating the great mass submerged below the water level, it points to, in its visibility, a reality that may be lived and expressed in a great variety of ways, more or less adequate from a symbolic point of view.

SACRAMENTS AS SYMBOLS

The sacraments are precisely the kind of symbolic actions I am talking about. Normally when we talk of them as symbols, we think mostly of the spiritual dimension. Recently we have started talking about their social or communitarian dimension. I think we should now begin talking of their place in the totality of Christian life. Taking the sacrament of initiation as an example, it is not enough to look upon it as a symbol of rebirth in the Spirit, making one a son or daughter of God. It is more than an admission into the Church, the body of believers in Christ. It is a living expression of a reality of rebirth, of dying and rising that is happening continuously throughout one's life-time. This continuing renewal finds living expressions in one's life in a multitude of ways. All these actions are symbolic. The rite of initiation symbolizes and indicates all these by visibilizing symbolically the process of rebirth as such and not as indicated by some other action.

This dimension comes out much more clearly in the eucharist. The eucharist symbolizes communion of life. It is a sharing in the life of God given to us in Jesus Christ. This sharing unites all those who participate in it into a community. Communion in love and life either with God or with others is not an exclusive feature of the eucharist. We can express our love for God and unite ourselves to God in a variety of ways through prayer and good works. But in the eucharist God comes near to us in the symbol of food that makes present his incarnate person. We have remarked above that it is through the body that the closest union can be achieved, between human beings. In the eucharist, God comes to us in a body, and that too as food, so that a real and total assimilation and identification is possible. Similarly our love for our neighbor may find expression in the smallest act of love, of help, of service. But what union can be closer than the union of two in the love and life of God—like two branches of the same vine? Thus we see that the eucharist is a special way of living and expressing a reality that is co-extensive with Christian life. Note that I am not saying that our union with Christ and with the other is deeper and more intense than in other circumstances of life. Christ may be encountered as intensely and authentically in a poor and a suffering person as in the eucharist. But the way in which the encounter takes place is different in each case and the way of the eucharist stands apart. The eucharistic banquet is a symbolic expression of communion pure and simple, not mediated by any other symbolic action. Helping some one in need, for example, is directly symbolic of an attitude of service, which indicates or involves love. But sharing a meal is simply an expression of fellowship, communion and love. This is why it can be symbolic of all other ways of expressing love, more or less indirectly. The love is the same; but the ways in which it finds expression are many and one of them is particular, unique, specific. The perfection of love or the intensity of the experience does not depend on the ways in which it is lived and expressed. An experience mediated by a more expressive symbol need not necessarily be a deeper experience. I am repeating this idea because of the constant tendency in the past to confuse levels of experience and expression and to be liberal with value judgments like more–less, perfect–imperfect, present–absent, etc.

SYMBOLIC DIMENSION OF CHRISTIANITY

It is in the context of the notion of symbolic action and its various dimensions of meaning that I would like to understand the problem of the pluralism of religions. No serious theologian today would think of Christianity as the only true religion while the other religions are false. No true believer would look upon Christianity as merely one among many religions. I would also be hesitant to assert that in the order of life and experience, Christianity is better, more perfect, superior, easier, or more effective. I think that the specificity of Christianity lies in its symbolic character with regard to other religions.

In the light of what I have been saying above regarding symbols and symbolic actions, this brief affirmation regarding the symbolic character of Christianity with regard to other religions should be expanded and understood in the following manner. The saving act of God or God's loving self-communication to people has no limits either in space or in time. It is universal (1 Tim. 2, 4). The Spirit of God is present and active everywhere and at all times. The liberation achieved by Christ's resurrection is for all peoples. This liberation is actually operative in the world through a whole variety of symbolic actions. Some of these may belong to different religious traditions. Others may be "secular" — action for human development and liberation are recognized today as integral aspects of evangelization (cf. Mt. 25: 31-46). Christianity, from one point of view, is one of the symbolic ways through which God's love becomes present to people and active in them. It has no claims to exclusivity. The believers of other religions are saved in and through their religions. Let me clarify, in passing, that the saving act is one and the same; only the symbolic mediations of this action are different. While the symbolic action that is Christianity is not exclusive, it remains something particular. This particularity is made up of two factors. First of all the saving presence of God in Christ and in the Spirit becomes visible and tangible not merely in some indirect, though symbolic, way. It becomes visible and sensible in them—directly. Every way is symbolic, because it is human. But the symbolization in Christianity is direct while in other religions it is indirect. This distinction is applicable within Christianity itself. It is the same Christ one encounters when one gives a cup of water to a thirsty person and when one participates in the eucharistic banquet. But Christ is not present to the person in the same way. In both cases his presence is symbolic. In the first case, it is the thirsty person. In the second case, it is the sacrament of the body and blood of Christ and the community. But in the second case Christ is present in a particular way. He is there himself, with his body. He is not more present here than elsewhere. But the mode of his presence is different. That is why within Christianity itself the sacraments, and especially the eucharist, are specific symbolic actions—they are Christianity-in-act. The same distinction holds good between Christianity and other religions. If we look only upon the symbolic actions of ordinary Christian life, these are not very different from similar symbolic actions in other religions. What is specific to Christianity is the direct, though still symbolic, way in which the mystery of God's self-communication in Christ and the Spirit becomes present to us. It would perhaps help to look back to the analogy of the act of love to understand what I am trying to say.

The second of the two factors that make up the specificity of Christianity is related to the first. Because of the special direct relationship that exists between experience and expression in the symbolic action that is Christianity, it becomes symbolic of all other not so direct (symbolic) expressions of the same experience. The mystery that is present everywhere and at all times, finding expression in a multitude of ways, has become itself visible, tangible, sensible.

To repeat again what we have been saying in other contexts: this specificity of Christianity does not by itself make it a better, superior, surer or easier way to God.

There is nothing new or original in saying that Christianity is sacramental or symbolic. What is new is the use of this concept to understand and explain the relationship of Christianity to other religions. Normally the term sacrament is used only to explain the relationship through symbolic action between God and the human person. I am using the same term to explain the relationship between different symbolic actions expressive of the same experience, one of which stands apart from the others at the level of expression.

CHRIST AS SYMBOL

What I have said here about Christianity has christological implications. I cannot go into them here in great detail. But a few indications would not be out of place. When we usually speak of Christ as sacrament we think only of his symbolic mediation of our relationship to God. Christ is the sacrament of God. Many nuances will now have to be introduced. "Christ" is no longer a simple concept. We speak today of the historical Jesus and the Christ of faith; we talk of the Christ of history and the cosmic Christ or Christ of mystery. All these terms refer to the same person, but not to the same dimension of his personality and action. When we normally speak of Christ in relation to Christianity, we speak of the Christ who was born in the flesh, living today. How does he relate to the cosmic Christ? He is the same person, to be sure. But we have to do with two different dimensions linked in some way to the two natures of traditional theology. The relations between these two dimensions will remain as much a mystery as the relation between the two natures, namely the mystery of the incarnation itself. But in the light of my argument above regarding the eucharist and Christianity, correspondingly I would say that the Christ of history is the symbol of the Christ-mystery. The word symbol, of course, is to be understood in the rich sense I have given to it above. In the life and action of the man Jesus, the mystery of Christ present and active everywhere and at all times (Eph. 1: 3-10) becomes visible, tangible, sensible. It is a living expression of Christ—mystery—a particular and specific expression. The unknown Christ is active everywhere and manifests himself in a great variety of symbols. But he becomes humanly and bodily present and active in Jesus Christ. Jesus Christ, therefore, is symbolic not only of man's relationship to God, but also of the multitudinous other expressions of the same mystery everywhere and all times.

CONCLUSION

In a situation of religious pluralism, we were first accustomed to speak in terms of true/false or presence/absence. Then we began speaking in terms of more/less, perfect/imperfect, or preparation/fulfillment. These approaches do not really take into account all the facts. I am suggesting the category of symbol. Taken in a purely objective, physical sense, the concept of symbol is empty and can be of no use in this context. But understood in a human and personal way as symbolic action, it seems to suggest a new way of posing the problem and of looking for a solution. I think that the term symbolic action translates into contemporary terminology the idea of first fruits in the Bible. This relationship needs to be explored. The close relationship between Jesus Christ, Christianity and the eucharist in terms of expression–experience is also remarkable. We cannot really speak of the one without the other. The symbolic dimension with its stress on expression goes beyond a mere cognitive differentiation in terms of explicit/implicit, known/unknown. The tradition of scholasticism has been too much occupied with essences and has not paid sufficient attention to different ways of being, of living and of experiencing. Once the importance of the ways of experiencing a reality is understood, no one would ask, "If salvation is available to every one why should any one be a Christian?"

6

Theological Bases of the Pluralism of Religions

The pluralism of religions in India, as in the world as a whole, is a fact of experience that needs no demonstration. That it is also a problem would be evident to any one who looks at the newspapers. This problem could be analyzed at a socio-economic level as the struggle for economic or political advantage between two groups of people who find in religion an easy and an emotionally powerful factor of group identity. However, religions can be exploited in this manner only because, even at a strictly religious level, they tend to form closed groups protected by boundaries constituted by rites of passage and to look upon those persons who do not belong to their group not only as outsiders, but as pagans or infidels. One cannot say that all Christians are yet free of the attitude embodied in the well-known axiom: *extra ecclesiam nulla salus* ("Outside the Church, no salvation"). Even if such an attitude of exclusivism may not be fashionable today, a positive recognition of the "other" seems often to go with an affirmation of one's own superiority in relation to the other, however this superiority may be spelled out—whether as "fullness of truth," "certainty of salvation," "the more perfect way," or "the specially revealed." One notices an atmosphere of tolerance in areas of the world that are secularized only because religion as such is not taken too seriously or is relegated to the strictly private sphere.

Attitudes to other religions and to the pluralism of religions have undergone a radical change in the Catholic Church in the last twenty years. After the Document on Other Religions of the Second Vatican Council (1965), perhaps the most important public event which underlined this new attitude is the coming together of various religions to pray for peace in Assisi in October 1986. Though it was carefully explained that they were not praying together, the very fact that they came together to pray implied on the part of the Roman Catholic Church an acknowledgment of the legitimacy of the other religions. That acknowledgment was significant. Marcello Zago, one of the organizers of the event, explains in his commentary:

At Assisi, the welcome given to the religious representatives and people being present at the prayer offered by the various religions were in some way a recognition of these religions and of prayer in particular, a recognition that these religions and prayer not only have a social role but are also effective before God.[1]

A CHANGE OF ATTITUDES

Such a positive attitude towards the other religions was the result of a slow evolution in the experience and reflection of the Church. Not to mention here in detail the pioneers of interreligious dialogue in Asia, the Second Vatican Council also laid a solid foundation for later development. This foundation consisted in a triple affirmation: God's salvific will is universal and extends to all peoples in ways often unknown to us;[2] all peoples share a common origin and a common goal in life, namely, God;[3] the human quest for God, given the social nature of the human being, cannot be limited to the secret freedom of each individual's conscience, but rather it finds visible, social expression.[4] More sensitive and open to the reality of the other religions, the Asian Bishops saw in them "significant and positive elements in the economy of God's design of salvation" and acknowledged: "God has drawn our peoples through them."[5]

Pope John Paul II, in his dialogues with other religious leaders across the world, has stressed this theme of the unity of humanity in the plan of God and has developed its consequences for dialogue and collaboration. Speaking at Madras in February 1986, he said:

By Dialogue we let God be present in our midst; for as we open ourselves in dialogue to one another, we also open ourselves to God. . . As followers of different religions we should join together in promoting and defending common ideals in the spheres of religious liberty, human brotherhood, education, culture, social welfare and civic order.[6]

He spelled out the theological bases of this call to dialogue and collaboration in a speech that has been considered his defense of the event of Assisi. Speaking to the Cardinals at Christmas, 1986, he said:

In the light of this mystery (of unity), it becomes clear that the differences of every type, and first of all the religious differences, belong to another order, to the extent that they derive from the design of God. If it is the order of unity that goes back to creation and redemption and is therefore, in this sense, "divine," such differences—and even religious divergences—go back rather to a "human fact," and must be overcome in progress towards the realization of the mighty plan of unity which dominates the creation. There are undeniably differences that reflect the genius and the spiritual "riches" which God has given to the people (cf. *Ad Gentes* 11). I am not referring to these divergences; I intend here to speak of the differences in which are revealed the limitation, the evolutions and the falls of the human spirit which is undermined by the spirit of evil in history (*Lumen Gentium* 16).[7]

The important point in this affirmation of unity in diversity is the acceptance of religious divergences, which are not the result of human limitation or sin, as God's gift to peoples. What are the theological implications of this affirmation of the fundamental unity of the salvific plan of God for the world and the acceptance of the positive role of other religions in it?[8]

A HOLISTIC PERSPECTIVE

The first point I would like to stress is the goal of the divine plan. It is not merely the saving of the souls of everyone, but a gathering, a reconciliation, a unification of all things, not only of all peoples but of the whole universe.[9] This has been spelt out in terms of development and liberation. One uses the symbol of the Reign of God to indicate this holistic reality. It has not only spiritual, but human, social, cultural and political dimensions. This means that God's salvific plan reaches out not only to every human person, but to all dimensions of their life and history. When people are called to realize this plan of God in their lives, this call to collaboration reaches out to every aspect of their lives, not merely to the religious dimension.[10] In the same way, all peoples, of every race, culture and religion, are called to come together to constitute the Reign. While we have frequently stressed the holistic view of evangelization, we have not sufficiently reflected on the implications of God calling all peoples to the unity of his Reign.

Such a holistic perspective would lead us to affirm that the whole of history is a history of salvation.[11] The presence and action of God is there everywhere and at all times reaching out to every human being. The usual distinction between the natural and the supernatural seems irrelevant in this perspective. This does not mean to say that the history of salvation is not a history—that is, a succession of events—or that this history is not articulated into a pluralism of interacting units of religions and cultures and movements or that, while God is never absent, he may be present in various manners or degrees. Particular units may also have specific roles with relation to the whole; the specificity of these roles, however, has to be clarified with reference to the whole. But all these differences are ordered to an overarching unity, which is more basic and divine than the diversities.

Therefore mutual interaction, dialogue and collaboration among the various units are not only necessary, but inevitable. To resist such dialogue is to resist God's plan for the world.

ROOTS OF DIVERSITY

Even though the plan of God for the world is one and though it is the same God who is present and active to bring this plan to a fulfillment in history, diversity may arise from many sources. When God manifests God's self, it is done in the particular context of a historical situation, in a particular culture and language.[12] The human persons who receive such a revelation perceive it and express it from their limited personal, social, historical and cultural point of view.[13] Such an expression still needs ongoing interpretation according to varying historical situations—and this condition could be another source of diversity.[14] A deeper cause for diversity could be God's own positive will to communicate in a variety of ways not only to manifest the richness of God's being, but also to take into account the cultural and historical diversity arising out of the freedom and creativity that are God's own gifts to peoples. The fact of their being ordered to an eventual unification can only underline the reality of their diversity. That is why statements like, "All religions are the same" or, "All religions say the same thing" or "All religions are only different names for one and the same reality" are basically meaningless. To see the various religious traditions as different ways to one God, however, is meaningful.[15]

Every religion, while it is different from the others, is also limited: not because the Reality that it mediates and makes present is in any way limited, but because its capacity to experience and to express that experience is limited. With regard to the experience, we can go one step further and say that the capacity is not only limited, but also ambiguous. The human person or community is not only historically, culturally and humanly limited; it is also sinful. This condition will not only limit its capacity to experience God; it could make the experience itself ambiguous. Structural realities like the sacraments might guarantee an objective communication without ensuring an adequate subjective reception. The distinction between validity and fruitfulness provided for such eventualities. With regard to expression, the necessary use of symbols, which hide as much as they reveal, also make for uncertainty. One does reach the Reality in and through the symbol. But the symbol is always between the self and God and needs ongoing interpretation. A religion involves a public social expression of the experience and for this reason one cannot dispense with symbol.[16] This double limitation at the levels of experience and of expression—not to speak of God's own positive will of which I spoke in the last paragraph—makes every religion relative: in relation not to what they positively express but to what they leave out. The relativity is primarily in relation to the Absolute, though horizontally this would involve also a relativity with regard to other similar partial manifestations of the Absolute. The Absolute is really experienced in and through the relative. But this need not lead us to absolutize the relative. Some of the relative experiences and expressions may be more adequate to the Absolute than the others. Given the fact that God is one and God's plan for the world is one, all relativities are ordained to each other so that they could be considered mutually inclusive. The fundamental divine unity of which Pope John Paul II spoke therefore is not simply the least common denominator: rather it is already pluriform, and mutually complementary. This would lead to a revision of our ideas of revelation. In general one could say that where there is some divine self-communication, there must be some revelation, even if the nature and extent of it cannot be determined a priori. But it cannot be denied a priori either.[17]

Christianity is not exempt from this limitation. God indeed is absolute and so is Christ in his divine aspect. But this does not enable Christianity—the visible Church—to escape the various limiting factors that I have outlined above.[18] Theologians have no difficulty in accepting a pluralism in the Church both syncronically and diachronically.[19] I think that, *mutatis mutandis*, the same reasons for pluralism hold good with regard to religions in the context of the unity of God's plan of salvation for the world. The kind of unity in question is different and so will be the type of pluralism. The limitations of the Church with reference to the Reign are commonly accepted today.[20] Unless we take the position that the other religions are only partial manifestations, not only of the Reign, but also of the Church, there seems no reason not to accept the Church's limitedness in relation to other religions. At least when we are talking of the pluralism of religions, it is good to use the word Church only to refer to the visible community that is distinct from other religious communities and not to a mysterious reality that includes all the saved. To someone who has a linear view of salvation history and to whom therefore all other religions belong to a pre-Judaic economy (and for whom the Church is seen as their fulfillment) this point of view would seem unacceptable. Such a person would consider the other religions in the Christian era as in principle illegitimate. But what right have we to declare illegitimate religions that still continue to play a positive role in the plan of God for the salvation of their adherents?[21]

RELIGION AND LIFE

The phenomenon of the pluralism of religions would be easier to understand if we consider religion, not primarily as a creed or an institution, nor as only an experience, personal or communitarian, but as a symbolic structure that mediates a living relationship between the person/community and the Absolute. This view supposes a dynamic orientation to a future liberation and fulfillment, which takes into account the double freedom (of the human person and of the Absolute) that is involved. One can call this in biblical terms a covenant relationship.[22] Pluralism of religions is best seen as a pluralism of relationships, which, one would think, is inevitable — unless one is ready to consider the believers of other religions either ignorant or insincere. The only effective argument against this is the fruit of holiness that one can see in people like Gandhi. This is the reason people who have living experience of other believers see other religions more positively than those who theorize about other religions in the abstract. The affirmation that God is one and has one plan for the world implies that these relationships are ordered to a unity: a unity that is rooted in God, but is not given at the level of experience and expression and that has to be achieved in and through dialogue leading to mutual enrichment and a convergent growth towards fulfillment.

The significance and need for collaboration among religions would become clear if we understand the central, specific, role of religion in the life of people, which includes also other dimensions like the cultural, the economic, the social and the political. Religion deals with the dimension of meaning in life, with origins and ends, with ultimate goals and values. Within this context, however, the other dimensions of life have a certain autonomy with their own intermediate goals, values, methods and principles. Religions are called to play a constant prophetic role, challenging and inspiring the other dimensions. But religions cannot take their place. The process of "secularization" in recent decades has led to a differentiation of these various dimensions. This process has led in some places to the privatization of religion so that one's religious beliefs and attitudes do not really matter in social and public life.[23] But such an outcome is not inevitable. At the same time, the fact of pluralism of religions would discourage considering theocratic societies as a meaningful option. The only meaningful possibility seems to be to make sure that the differentiation does not become a dichotomy. This means in practice that a group of people, though belonging to different religions, can live together in one civil society. They could pursue common human and spiritual values on which they all agree and which they find meaningful, each with reference to his or her own religious tradition. Dialogue at a religious level could enrich and enlarge the religious basis for such commonly agreed values.[24] In the light of what I have said above with regard to broader perspectives of salvation which includes development and liberation, the pursuit of these common human and spiritual values in the area of social, cultural and political life is neither a strictly religious activity nor is it purely "secular" in the sense of being a-religious. Emergence of such a common free space for socio-political life seems a necessary condition for any meaningful experience of the pluralism of religions.[25] However, the real difficulty for pluralism does not lie at this socio-political level, but at the strictly religious level, in which all great religions, at least implicitly, claim to be superior or even exclusive. For Christians, such claims are linked to the person of Jesus Christ. A properly theological answer to the question of pluralism will have to consider such exclusive claims.

THE UNIVERSALITY OF CHRIST

It is the traditional affirmation of our faith that Christ is the unique and universal mediator of salvation. How do we understand this affirmation in the light of the positive place we give today to the other religions in God's plan of salvation? A lot has been written on this and it is not my intention to give here a survey of opinions on this question.[26] Most catholic and conciliar Protestant theologians today accept a positive role to other religions in salvation. This positive role is often justified by some in terms of theocentrism.[27] A few speak of an economy of the Spirit side by side with the economy of the Word in Jesus Christ.[28] Most such theologians argue for an inclusive perspective, but in doing so they propose a Logos Christology, whether transcendental or eschatological. The transcendentalists take an a priori approach and affirm that the salvific will of God operates through Christ reaching out to all who respond to him whether they are conscious of his mediation or not. Others see in the Christ-event a beginning—the first fruits—of a process that continues and will reach fulfillment on the last day. Even where Christ is not visibly acknowledged, his Spirit is seen continuing his hidden work and leading all things to a unity.[29] Some, from the background of Indian tradition, suggest a distinction between the historical Jesus and the Cosmic Christ seeing Jesus is the Christ but also seeing that the Christ is not only Jesus. Christ may also be mediated by other symbols in other religious traditions. This perspective is not simply theocentric. Rather, it takes seriously the Trinity and the role of the Word in the history of salvation. By saying that Jesus is the Christ, it takes the Incarnation seriously. While acknowledging the possibility of other symbols and mediations of Christ, the specificity of Jesus is also affirmed. The complex reality of Jesus as the Christ represents for them a guarantee both of the pluralism and of the unity of God's plans.[30] All these different approaches seek to make a place for pluralism within universality.[31]

Personal and Structural

Do we not set ourselves apart by speaking about Jesus as the Incarnation of the Word? I think much depends upon the perspective in which we understand it. Jesus himself came as a suffering servant, having emptied himself of everything that might be a title to special honor. A call to serve in the company of Jesus need not be seen as a title to any honor or superiority. Secondly, in discussions like this, there is always an interplay between personal and structural approaches. Religions mediate a salvific dialogue between God and the human person. God reaches out to every human person in ways unknown to them. For a particular person the way in which God is actually reaching out to him or her historically is the best way. From this point of view, comparing ways among themselves is pointless.

God's self-communication in love which is salvation is conditioned, not by the generous gift of God which is infinite, but only by the loving response which could be more or less intense or whole-hearted. The symbolic mediation may be more or less adequate and it may affect the levels of expression and communication. But from the point of view of God's self-communication, the actual way in which God is offering God's self and the person is responding in conscientious freedom is quite adequate.

In dialogue, each one is sharing one's experience of salvation. One can only witness to the way through which God has called one and all the riches that one has found in it. For that person this will have an absolute—that is obliging—value. Yet one can be aware of a certain relativity in the heart of that absolute imperative, if one is also conscious of the distinction between God who obliges and the concrete way in which this obligation comes to an individual. One can make this distinction meaningfully only when one encounters some other person who seems called along a different way. Once this distinction is made, one would be aware of the possibility that, living in history, God may call people to walk along different paths. Choosing paths (religions) therefore is not simply a personal option made after a comparative study, but a response to God calling anew. In dialogue a person looks at others and their experience and hears their witness from one's point of view. But that point of view now has a space in which to accomodate the points of view of others with respect—if not always with understanding—but committed always to listen to God who is calling. Such sharing should lead to mutual challenge, enrichment and common thanksgiving. A person in dialogue is not making a comparative study of creeds or doctrines, but is witnessing and listening to the mystery of God active in history, in the lives of peoples.

Talk of a superior way is meaningless except in the context of a salvific dialogue between God and a human person or community. The focus of dialogue is not the Ways (religions), but the mystery of God's self-communication to human persons. This is the mystery of love and freedom and conscience. At this level one need not hesitate to confess one's deepest experiences and convictions, because one does not engage in discussion, much less in polemics, but in doxology—thanking and praising God—and in praxis—opening oneself to and responding to the God who is calling.

Are we looking at religion purely in terms of interpersonal relationships between God and the human person? Is not the incarnation a more authentic self-communication of God? What about the significance to universal salvation of the paschal mystery? I think that the faith affirmation that all are saved by the death and resurrection of Jesus need not radically upset the kind of perspective that I have been discussing above. First of all, this salvific act has universal extension not insofar as it is a human, historical act, but because of the divinity of Christ. However its universal outreach may be explained,[32] it is not a special gift entrusted to the Christians, but a mysterious reality that is universally present and active in ways unknown

to us. The Church conserves, celebrates and proclaims the real memory of
this event, without possessing fully or controlling it. As such, the Church
has a special prophetic role in relation to this Mystery, but it cannot attribute to itself the centrality or the definitiveness or the normative character
of this Mystery. Precisely because this Mystery is universal and as such
manifests itself in a variety of ways, no one manifestation can claim to
ultimacy. The presence of the Mystery in the world is discovered as a
pattern, a structure of the various manifestations that are mutually related,
not only because they are all manifestations of the same Mystery, but also
because they are all tending to a unification that is God's will for the
universe. This pattern can be experienced and discovered only through
dialogue. The various elements of the structure are held together like a
field of forces. We are within the field, not outside or above it. Being where
we are, we can discover how we are related to everybody else and it is
precisely in discovering these relationships that we can also discover how
all are related to the Mystery. It would not be proper to set up any particular element of the structure as the norm or center. The true and only
norm is the Mystery that is at the same time transcendent and immanent,
acting from within and yet prophetically attracting to growth and judging
from without. Some of this prophecy and judgment may precisely be mediated through the other manifestations of the Mystery, namely the other
religions. The principle of judgment, at the level of history, then, would not
be one of non-contradiction with reference to a presumed norm, but that
of *analogia fidei* in a wide sense. This analogy can be discovered and applied
only through dialogue. The Church may be conscious of being the fulfillment of Judaism. But the problem has been, I think, to have extended this
pattern to the Church's relationship to all other religions on an a priori
basis, thus considering them pre-Judaic. I think that this view of history is
more responsible for our problems with regard to interreligious dialogue
than any perspective of faith. What we need then is really a new theology
of history that would accept the other religions as positive elements in the
salvific plan of God for the world.

DIALOGUE AS CHALLENGE

With this new awareness, whatever be our certainty in faith with regard
to the universality of the mystery of Christ, we should not—without more
careful distinction—make similar affirmations regarding the pilgrim
Church. At the historical level, ultimacy and fulfillment are eschatological
realities of the future. The Church may be aware of a special relationship
to this end. But with reference to the other religions, the nature of this
special relationship and its implications can be spelt out only in the praxis
of dialogue, and total clarity will be available only on the last day. Christ
is indeed the center and fullness of all things, but that Christ is not simply
the Jesus of history, but the Christ of the *pleroma* who, reconciling all things

in himself, offers them to the Father in the Reign that is God's promise to all peoples. This Reign will be the *pleroma*, the assembling of all the gifts of God in history in a catholic unity, and not the universalization of the particularity of the Church.

If we do not reduce Christ to Jesus, an acceptance of pluralism among religions and consequent dialogue and collaboration among them is not only possible and meaningful, but necessary. Actual practice of dialogue would also clarify and greatly enhance our understanding of the perspectives that make it possible. I do not think that we have to accept either a false equality of all religions, or surrender any of our faith convictions. But our faith convictions could be broadened to make space for dialogue. And in doing so, we would discover the great structure of God's salvific plan for the world of which we form a part, but which will continue to remain a mystery challenging our continuing and believing commitment and search.

We should not be under the illusion that an atmosphere of interreligious dialogue will solve all religious strife. Apart from political, social, and cultural factors that may be responsible for this strife at the strictly religious level, personal convictions and social symbol systems will certainly clash. But such clashes can take on a prophetic dimension and become creative tensions if there is a common commitment to search for transcendence and fullness in God.

THE INDIAN TRADITION

A spirit of active tolerance is very much the Indian tradition, whatever may be the communal conflicts that are afflicting us at the moment. The *Rock Edict XII* of Ashoka, extolling concord and mutual learning and appreciation among religious people, is well known.[33] The Vedantic perspectives of the Upanishads affirming the unity of all things in Atman-Brahman on the one hand and the distinction between the Real and the Unreal on the other made possible a discrimination between basic oneness and phenomenal multiplicity. In personal terms we have the inclusive declaration of Krishna in the Gita: "Even those who in faith worship other Gods, because of their love they worship me, although not in the right way."[34] The principle of *adhikaratva* by which the symbol of one's worship corresponds to one's psychological and spiritual needs make acceptance of the practice of others easy. Though some modern Hindus speak in a relativizing tone about all religions being like rivers leading to the same sea, we do have people like Gandhi and Radhakrishnan who were sensitive both to the differences and the underlying unity. The latter declared: "God wills a rich harmony and not a colorless uniformity."[35] The secular democracy of the Indian Constitution, which is not a-religious, but open equally to all religions, provides this broad outlook with a legal framework. It is rooted in this tradition that a contemporary Hindu prefers not conquest and coexistence but an active understanding "in the service of a truth which will perhaps never shed its mystery but to which each tradition bears witness and is in this united with each other."[36]

CONCLUSION

The ultimate human and theological base to accept and to take positively the pluralism of religions is to experience one's limitations. One would then learn to be aware of the mysteries of history, to respect the freedom of God and of the human person, to discover the *advaitic* structure of all being, and to be committed to the pursuit of the unification of the whole world. In one sense, this challenge is not particularly a religious problem. It is in building up a human community of freedom, fellowship and justice that religions would or should discover themselves in dialogue. Just as inter-religious strife often takes place for social and political reasons, it is a discovery of community at the human level which should lead to a fruitful conversation between believers of different religious traditions.

7

The Pluralism of Religions and the Significance of Christ

A growing positive attitude to the possibility of salvation in and through other religions seems to undermine traditional faith in Christ as the unique and universal savior. If we are helping Hindus and Muslims to grow in their own faith, are we not being disloyal to our mission to proclaim Jesus Christ as their savior? Who is Christ for us? How do we understand him and his role in salvation, particularly in relation to the other religions? We are asking these questions not in the abstract, a priori, but in the context of our experience of other religions in India. We are living in a situation of religious pluralism.[1] There is a wide acceptance today of the idea that people are saved not only in spite of, but in and through their religions, because God has reached out to them in the context of their life, community, and history. This realization is not so much the conclusion of an argument as born out of a living experience of other believers. The question is how we are to reconcile this universal salvific will of God with an individual act of salvation in the death and resurrection of Jesus.

I shall try to answer this question in four stages. I shall, first of all, outline rather schematically and critically the present stage of discussion on the question. Then I shall specify my own method of approach. Thirdly, I shall present some new perspectives that must guide our search for an answer. Finally I shall indicate my response to the question. I shall then point out in the conclusion some implications for action. I am aware that this is a difficult question and I do not claim to have found *the* answer to it. I will be satisfied if I have clarified the question a little more and localized more precisely the mystery.

SEARCH FOR A NEW PARADIGM

Authors who have studied this problem in recent times are accustomed to speak of three broad paradigms that classify the answers usually given by theologians: exclusivism, inclusivism and pluralism. As there are many excellent surveys of these trends,[2] it is enough for me here to present them schematically in order to provide a context for our reflection. We should, however, keep in mind that such schemes tend to ignore nuances in particular theoretical positions.

The *exclusivists* say that no one will be saved unless that person confesses explicit faith in Jesus Christ as the savior. Other religions may have many good things in them as the best fruits of human reflection and effort. But they do not mediate salvation. The Church is the only way to salvation.

The *inclusivists* accept that there may be grace and revelation in other religions, so that they may mediate salvation to those who believe in them. But the salvation they mediate is salvation in Jesus Christ. Even if the other believers may not be aware of the fact, they are "anonymous" Christians, related to the Church in some hidden way. Jesus Christ and the Church are then considered the fulfillment of the other religions, and Jesus Christ is the center of the history of salvation.

The *pluralists* find this inclusive attitude a patronizing one. They prefer to say that all religions are ways to the Ultimate, each in its own manner. As Christ is the way for the Christians, so is Buddha the way for Buddhists and Krishna or Rama for Hindus. They opt for a "theocentric," as opposed to a "christocentric" perspective of history.

I find all three paradigms unsatisfactory. The exclusivists are simply negative to all other religions and they ignore the broad Christian tradition that has accepted the possibility of salvation for people outside the Church — even though this may have been explained in various ways. After the Second Vatican Council and the event of Assisi, October 1986, when the Pope came together with the members of other religions, to pray for peace, no Catholic can be an exclusivist.

The inclusivist position is the one most common today. In the context of other religions, its ecclesiocentrism is a problem. To say that someone is an anonymous Christian when one explicitly rejects membership either in the Church or belief in Jesus Christ as unique savior seems presumptuous. Other religions, while they are respected by inclusivists, are placed in a relation with Christianity as "partial" to "full" or as "unconscious" to "conscious." This is an improperly a priori Christian solution to the problem.

The pluralists, on the other hand, do not take the "otherness" of other religions seriously. Real differences, even contradictions, among the religions are played down, while the search for an underlying unity ends up with a lowest-common-denominator rubric such as liberation or human development or the unity of the human race proposed as common to all religious traditions. One could, of course, develop a theology of religions that is soteriocentric because all religions seek to lead to liberation and salvation is a more unifying element than even God. The problem, though, is not to find a point of agreement among religions, but to prove that they are different ways to the same goal. Specificity of faith commitments is not considered. For example, Christ can be considered simply one among many ways only if he can be reduced to being a mere man. For those to whom Christian uniqueness is a myth, the God-incarnate is also a myth.[3] Just as Christians will not recognize the Christ of faith in the pluralists' presentation, neither will Buddhists find their Buddha, nor Hindus their Krishna. Paradoxically, pluralism itself becomes a form of nominalism reducing radically different expressions of religiosity to the same reality or experience. Such a rational conceptual approach looks on religions as systems of doctrine or practice that one can compare from some imaginary vantage point outside all religions and thus ends in simplistic abstractions.[4]

A METHODOLOGICAL FRAMEWORK

The context of our discussion is a community of people living and working together, sharing a common culture and socio-political structures, but belonging to different religions. The role of religion is to be a prophetic, interpretive force in the life of the people. Where there are many religions they have to play this prophetic role in dialogue. We favor neither a secular society without religion, nor fundamentalistic communalism where religions become a political force. Even at the religious level our task is not only to witness actively[5] to our faith (as some evangelicals do), but also treat other believers with respect and tolerance and collaborate with them in common socio-cultural and political tasks like the promotion of peace and development, freedom and human rights. We have not only a mission to witness to our faith, but also a responsibility as members of a human community. A school, for instance, is not a propaganda institution, but should render public service to the community and has responsibilities that a parish church may not have.

Our approach will not be an a priori one. I do not start from a self-understanding as a Christian and beliefs about means of salvation, from this point of view judging from the outside other religions and their role in the history of salvation. Our approach here will be dialogical. We listen to the other believers, and are challenged by their faith and life. Even if we do not actually dialogue with them, we have to be present to them in mind and imagination as we reflect on the meaning—for our faith—of this multi-religious situation. It is in the context of this relationship that we seek to rediscover our identity.

The horizon of our search for understanding is our own faith perspective. We are not engaged in a historical or phenomenological study. We are not studying religions objectively as systems of doctrines or behavior. We do not pretend to adopt a neutral, suprareligious perspective. Since our horizon is our faith and we are dialoguing with other peoples of faith, our approach is not rational or scientific in the normal sense. Searching as believers we cannot escape the "hermeneutical circle." We have to explore a vision to which we are committed in faith; and we cannot look at it from outside this horizon.

We are not searching for an abstract universal scheme that will somehow unify all religions. We are not engaged in an evaluative, comparative study. We are searching to make place for other believers in the perspective of our own faith, while respecting the identities of the others without somehow reducing them to or interpreting them in terms of our own. This is the reason why an approach in faith is not opposed to an attitude of dialogue. Neither accepting that we are simply different, nor trying to reduce the other's identity to one's own, we seek to make space for the other in the context of our own faith, leaving to the activity of dialogue the discovery of the concrete articulations of the interrelationships, because we believe that God is one and has a single plan for the universe which includes all these various manifestations. These methodological elements will become clearer as we proceed with our reflection.

ELEMENTS OF A NEW PARADIGM

Relationship and Structure

If we take a merely phenomenological approach we see religion as a system of doctrines, rituals, and rules for behavior. But religion is more basically a saving relationship between God and the human person. In the context of human life in community, God calls and the human person responds. Conscience and freedom have an essential role in this process. There is an interplay of two freedoms which is a source of pluralism. For instance, God for Christians is Parent, Son, and Spirit. However this plurality in God may be understood, it guarantees a plurality of personal relationships with God. Since the affirmation of God as Parent, Son, and Spirit is not an a priori declaration, but the expression of the pluralistic experience of God in the history of salvation, this possibility of pluralism is of more importance than an abstract unity of the Godhead or of the Ultimate. While it is legitimate to talk of unity in pluralism, any attempt to reduce pluralism to an abstract unity is a rational temptation.[6]

The saving relationship between God and the human person is lived in the context of a culture and of a history. These will certainly influence the concrete forms in which the relationship finds expression. The concrete forms of expression not only symbolically mediate the relationship, but also give visibility to it and in some way constitute it. These forms of expression in scriptures, rituals and organizational structures constitute a tradition. The experience of relationship is lived through them even if it transcends them. When I love a person, it is not simply an abstract feeling—I give it symbolic expression. I live my love in and through this expression—even if my love is not reduced to this expression. This expression is not simply a medium of communication nor an instrument. It is rather my love in act.

While, on the one hand, I can live the intensity of my love even in inadequate expressions of it, on the other hand, I will have to confess that my expression is inevitably limited by culture, history and my own personal inadequacies. In addition, my response may not be all pure and true—there may be such factors operative as mixed motives and hesitations.

In this network of relationship and expression that is the core of religion, one can point to a pair of dialectical poles that constitute a field within which the relationship is lived—namely, the *Absolute* and the *relative*. The personal relationship as commitment in faith has an unique and absolute character about it, particularly because it is a relationship to the Absolute. The symbolic expression of it is culturally, historically and humanly conditioned and therefore relative. The Absolute and the relative are not two different things, but two poles of one relationship—like the spirit and the body intrinsically linked in human personality. I am not talking here of the obvious pair—the Absolute (God) and the relative (the human person). I am, rather, talking of the absoluteness of faith as commitment to the Ultimate and the relativity of its expression in religion. Human fault and error contribute further to the relativity. It is in and through the relative that the absolute relationship is lived. Even when God becomes human in Jesus, God cannot but become part of the cultural context of the Jewish tradition and language and in the historical context of the time in which Jesus lived. But the relative expression does not relativize the absolute relationship. In an earlier paper I distinguished between faith as experience, faith as celebration and faith as reflection.[7] Aloysius Pieris distinguishes between core-experience, collective memory and interpretation.[8] Panikkar speaks of Christianness, Christianity and Christendom.[9] The poles I am talking of here will be experience on the one hand and the other two aspects taken together on the other.

If we look at various religions as structures of expression, we may speak about the more or less developed; the tribal and the great; the popular and the elite; the mystical and the prophetic religions. These classifications are meaningful at a certain level. But we cannot legitimately thus compare religions as simply relative to one another because they have no meaning in themselves apart from concrete relations between members of the respective traditions. Each religion is capable, in its own historico-cultural situation, of giving expression to an absolute relationship. Therefore religions are relative to this absolute relationship and not to one another. Authentic dialogue is not between religions, which are seen as complementing one another, but between persons, who may mutually enrich themselves. Conversion is not the result of a choice of the best that follows a comparative study of religions but the response to the manifestation and call of God in and through a particular tradition. Sinful or imperfect elements in a religion are always to be judged in terms of the Absolute which it mediates in its expression.

At a phenomenological level, concepts like revelation, scripture and prophet, may have a certain basic common denotation. But it would not be proper to make that the sole basis for a comparison, since they are fully meaningful only within a tradition, not in the abstract. In the context of the ongoing relationship between God and a community, a particular person may be given by God a prophetic role; the community may recognize that person as a prophet; other believers in dialogue within that community may recognize this prophetic role in that community. Nevertheless such recognition does not automatically imply an affirmation that prophets have the same role for *every* community. We could say the same thing about the scriptures and the foundational symbols of a community. Many people reading the Bible may recognize Jesus as a great man whose teaching and example have universal relevance. But only a Christian in his faith confesses him as the incarnate Word.

If we take the dialectical relationship between the absolute and the relative poles of religion seriously, then to say that all religions are only different expressions of the same experience is not correct. It is also a fashion to affirm that at the mystical level one is beyond name and form, and that mystical experience is the same in all religions. It is true that at the root of any authentic religious experience there is the same God. But to conclude from this that it is the same experience is to ignore, on the one hand, the various ways in which God can manifest Godself and, on the other, the various cultural and symbolic ways in which the human person lives such an experience. Given the spirit-in-body nature of the human person, one can not question the possibility of an experience of the Absolute beyond name and form as much as the possibility of the experience itself being beyond name or form or identification of it as the same experience as those common in another tradition.

The main point I wish to make here is that we are not interested in a comparison of religions as systems which can be objectively analyzed, but in a dialogue between believers who are able to make an absolute commitment of faith in and through their religions to the God who is manifested in various ways.

It Is God Who Saves

We are accustomed to speak of the salvific value of religions. This is obviously inaccurate. It is always God who saves, not religions. People may be saved *in* and *through* a religion, but not *by* it. Religions are but mediations that do not substitute for but only make present God's saving love. Some would say that it is faith which saves, not religion. But such a distinction is questionable in the light of what we have seen in the previous section about the two poles of religion. This ever present action of God in salvation is sometimes obscured by the way we speak. For example, the Latin church has always had an anxiety to affirm its legitimacy in ontological terms. One speaks of the Church as a sacrament and sacraments are described as causes. The priest is said to be acting "in persona Christi." Active statements like "I absolve you," and "I baptize you," are preferred. Such a manner of speaking may obscure a presence of the Spirit and of Christ in sacramental celebrations in which the role of the church is only ministerial and not representative. The Orthodox tradition is much more sensitive to the continuing action of God through his Spirit which the Church prays for. The difference is seen clearly in the famous dispute concerning the key moment of the eucharistic prayer—the institution narrative or the epiclesis. This overall orientation may tempt the Latin church to reduce God's action to the Church's action and to make the Church's mediation essential, while the Orthodox tradition makes place for God's continuing action not only in, but also outside the sacramental and ecclesial system. This is the principle of "economy."

Speaking of the primacy of God's action in salvation will also help us not to isolate God's action in Jesus, but to set it in the context of the totality of God's action in the world seeking to communicate Godself to human beings which embraces the whole process of history from creation through redemption to its ultimate consummation. We see in the Old Testament how the people starting from their experience of liberation from Egypt through an intervention of God move to recognizing Yahweh both as the creator in the beginning and as the re-creator of the world in the last times. We see the same process in the New Testament, particularly in John and Paul. The experience of Jesus leads them to the discovery of the Word (John 1:1-14) and of the Cosmic Christ and the Spirit (Eph. 1:3-13; Rom. 8). Such a total perspective will dissuade us from opposing creation to redemption as natural to supernatural. A global view will also discourage us both from a dichotomous approach to the religions as Church and non-Church (exclusivism) and from an easy irenicism that sees religions as different human efforts towards the one God (superficial pluralism). We would better respect the pluralism of religions in history and seek for their articulation into a unity according to the plan of the one God. A historical perspective would also make us see this unity not as a system that is already given, but as a unification that has to be achieved, built up, realized both by the Spirit and by us, precisely through dialogue and mission.

Speaking of God's action in salvation is a reminder to us that in the realm of religion nothing is purely human. God is always present and active in creation and in history.[10] This is the meaning of the universal salvific will of God. This presence is articulated in various manifestations that are ordained to a unity. This does not mean that all manifestations are the same or of the same value. It does not mean either that the human response is not conditioned by sin and imperfection, or even by refusal. But it does mean that we must always have a global perspective. God manifests Godself in various ways to various persons and groups in sovereign freedom. Such manifestations are not arbitrary, but ordained to the global plan of God for humankind. A particular manifestation may be more or less important to God's plan. This can be discovered only through revelation and a posteriori in history. There is no problem in recognizing the differences between tribal, folk, and great religions. But even such religious development need not be seen as the result of purely human efforts.

While every divine manifestation is a personal or community experience, some of them, if not all, may also have a social implication. For everyone, the manner in which God reaches out to that person is adequate for that person's salvation.[11] But God's manifestations, as God's gifts and charisms (see 1 Cor. 12:4–11), may have a significance for the human community. Such a gift gives the person or the community a particular mission (role) in history. Such a role and the gifts ordained to it are a call and a responsibility; they are not titles for honor or for a feeling of superiority. No religion is closed in on itself. It is always called to be an open structure. Ultimately one is judged by the depth and the generosity of one's response to the call of God and not by the special gifts one is given for the sake of the community. A Christian is not more favored than a follower of a tribal religion at this level, but the Christian *is* aware of a connection to God's mission of which the tribal is not aware.

Jesus Is the Christ

One of the problems that we face when we speak of Jesus as the Christ in the context of other religions is reductionism. In the past, the Catholic tradition—in spite of the Chalcedonian definition that Jesus Christ is true God and true human being and that these two aspects should neither be confused nor separated—tended to focus on his divine aspect, even when it spoke of the sufferings of Jesus. Today there is a move to rediscover and emphasize his true humanity. It is obviously difficult to hold these two aspects of the mystery in tension. In the New Testament we see the first disciples experiencing the man Jesus and through reflection on his life and action, especially his death and resurrection, and growing in their understanding of his divine aspect. The complexity of this personality of Jesus is expressed in various ways in the New Testament and later. Today we might need to find new ways of expressing this mystery. But if we simply reduce Jesus to being a human person, however extraordinary, then the questions of theological uniqueness and eschatological universality do not arise.

The first question that we have to ask when we talk about Jesus Christ is: Who is Christ *for us*? Are we talking of the *Word* in whom everything was created and who was at the beginning enlightening every one coming into the world (John 1:3–5, 9) or of *Jesus*, the Word incarnate, who emptied himself and took the form of a servant and died on the cross (Phil. 2:6–11) or the *risen Christ* who is transhistorical, no longer bound by space and time, present and active among us but whose action in the Spirit we cannot limit to our own little efforts (Acts 10), or the *Christ at the end of time*, the pleroma, in whom all fullness will dwell (Eph. 1:23)? It is the same person, but a person who is in the process of history while simultaneously transcending it. We should not forget this dynamic complexity of the person of Christ or that part of the complexity is the diversity of the relationships he displays in virtue of that complexity. The divine and the historical human poles of this complexity are sometimes specified with the terms "Christ" and "Jesus." Jesus is the Christ, but the Christ is not only Jesus.[12] The Jesus of history is limited by his humanity, culture, and history. This was his choice. But it was in this Jesus that the action of God—Parent, Son, and Spirit—becomes manifest. The Christ will reach fullness only on the last day when all things will be reconciled.

When we speak of the historical Jesus, distinguishing him from the Christ, we refer to the historical, not the risen Jesus. After the resurrection, Jesus becomes transhistorical or cosmic. He is no longer in time and in history. But we—the Church—experience this risen Jesus who lived and died in history in and through the memory that has been handed down to us—in the community of disciples, in the scriptures, and in other ways. Already the resurrection is a transhistorical event. This memory that we have of Jesus that leads us in faith to experience the mystery of his person is humanly, historically, and culturally limited and conditioned. It is in and through this historical memory that we experience Jesus. But at the same time we are aware that the risen Christ and his paschal mystery is present wherever God's saving grace is present. This presence does not obviously pass only through this particular historical memory that we celebrate. This is what we mean by saying that the Christ is more than Jesus. But to be complete, we must at once specify that here we are speaking of the Jesus of history, and not of the risen Jesus. We need not speculate about the precise nature of the risen humanity of Jesus, but we can talk about his humanity in history. That is why it will be helpful if we talk about the historical Jesus or the Jesus of history and not simply about Jesus or the humanity of the Word. Distinction between the historical and transhistorical stages of Jesus' humanity does not mean separation. We do not mean to say that Jesus in history was a mere human person who becomes divine in his resurrection. We are, instead, before two manifestations of the same person. But the process that leads dynamically from the one to the other— the life, death, and resurrection of Jesus—is a real process and not just "play acting." The risen humanity is what it is because of the historical life and death of Jesus. At the same time, however, the distinction between the historical and the risen manifestations of Jesus helps us to understand the specificity and limitations of the Church-community, whose tradition goes back to the memory of the historical Jesus. The paschal mystery itself is made present to the community in and through the symbol of the Last Supper. In the past, when we spoke of Jesus or of the Church as the sacrament, we referred to the *real* experience of God that they mediated. Now we should become aware that this mediation is primarily *symbolic*, though no less real, and refers directly to a historical memory in and through which we reach out to and experience the mystery. By not identifying the memory and the mystery, in whatever way we may understand the special connection between them we make space for other possible symbolic mediations. We know this is possible even within our own tradition—we may encounter Christ in the poor as much as in the eucharist, though not in the same way. The former encounter may be even more crucial to our Christian life.

When we speak of the theological universality of the Christ we have to take into account the whole cosmic breadth of the action of Christ and not limit it to its manifestation in the historical Jesus. It is true that we should not separate the two poles of the same person. But the relationship between the two will be discovered, not by universalizing the particularity of the historical Jesus but by setting it in the context of the universal action of the Word. The disciples intuit the divine dimension of the personality of Jesus precisely by realizing the universal significance of his salvific act in his death and resurrection. We can say that it is insofar as he is divine that the historical actions of Jesus acquire a universal significance.[13] But this universal significance cannot be fully understood if we do not place it in the context of the universal action of the Word.[14]

This universal action of Christ cannot be localized in a point of time in history, because it will not be complete till the last day when Christ will be all in all. The universality of Christ, therefore, includes all God's manifestations in history. While we Christians see a special, even unique place and role in this history for God's action in Jesus we cannot simply universalize this.

Our perspective here will depend on how we see history in relation to eternity. Eternity is transcendentally contemporaneous with time. When we speak of the divine we cannot speak of before and after. It is *tota simul*— everything at the same time—as the scholastics used to say. Yet when the divine enters history this same divine action has to take place in history— in temporal succession. But when we speak we often confuse the two levels. At the divine/eternal level, the phrase "Christ saves" has universal resonance. The action transcends time, there is no before and after. And yet in time, at the human/historical level, there is a succession and a dynamic progression. The term "eschatological" sometimes indicates this with its dynamic of "already" and "not yet." We cannot separate eternity and history. Yet eternity embraces and transcends history and must not be identified with one particular event however central it may be in the historical process. Correspondingly, history *concretizes* the eternal, without historically particularizing it.[15]

This eternal vs. historical dynamic is true of all divine actions, but is particularly so of God's action in Jesus. If we are not careful we will be talking in two registers in a confused manner. Thus talk about universality is meaningful at the divine/eternal level. When we talk about the Word/ Christ we are talking at this level. This universal action of God in Christ is realized in time through a history—in a dynamic progession of actions that constitute a unified structure. These concrete actions have a universal significance and relevance as parts of this structure. But affirming this is different from universalizing the historical/particular, making it historically universal. To come back to our earlier formulation—Jesus is the Christ, but the Christ is more than Jesus. The mystery of Christ includes all the other manifestations of God in history. Therefore we cannot reduce it to its manifestation in the historical Jesus. Much of our talk about Jesus as Christ keeps on playing simultaneously on two registers about the strength of the unity of the personhood of Jesus Christ—eternal/historical, divine/human—without a clear differentiation. I am trying to point to the differentiation between the divine and the human/historical in that person and to the implications, not only for the way we speak, but also for the way we understand God's action in history.

Our faith affirmation—though it has its foundation in the historical—transcends history. Our encounter with other religions, for instance, is at the historical level of experience. But our theology of religions—while it takes account of this historical experience—is an affirmation of faith "from below," and not "from above." We can also look at the problem from a slightly different point of view. We often tend to talk at an objective, ontological level without taking into account the historical, personal level in which we live and act. It is not helpful to affirm the objective universality of Christ and draw a priori historical conclusions from it without trying to understand the concrete manner in which people actually reach salvation outside the Church which confesses faith in Jesus as the Christ.

A similar differentiation, to which we are accustomed, is between the economic and the immanent Trinity. The Triune God is identical, whether immanent or economic. But there is a story of God's manifestation in history through Word and Spirit that leads us to understand and articulate relationships within the Trinity. It would not always be helpful to speak simply of God or Trinity acting without differentiating the actual person involved in a particular manifestation. It is the Word that becomes flesh. It is the Spirit that descends on Jesus at his baptism in the Jordan.

Starting from this articulation of the economic Trinity, many theologians speak about the differentiation between the manifestations of God in Christ and in the Spirit and see in this differentiation the possibility of understanding the universality of the mystery of Christ. Christ is universal because the Spirit is universal.[16] He is present and active everywhere even when Christ is not acknowledged. Some would even speak of the "absence" of Jesus in the economy of the Holy Spirit.[17] Some, saying that the Spirit is the Spirit of Jesus Christ, seek to reduce the action of the Spirit to that of Jesus Christ. It is the risen Christ that sends the Spirit. The link is certainly there. But the Spirit is not Jesus Christ. Its mediations are real and need not lead to faith in Jesus Christ in the context of history. Here we have another opening to other religions from a Christian perspective. While this articulation between Christ and the Spirit is valid and instructive, I have chosen in this paper to focus on the articulations in the person of Jesus Christ himself.

How do we see God's action in Jesus? The image that seems most helpful to understand the event of Jesus is the biblical one of the covenant. For a Christian what is special about Jesus is that in his paschal mystery has been manifested God's loving self-communication to all peoples. The passion and death of Jesus show that this relationship is not something natural, automatic or physical, simply because Jesus is God-human, but a human transformation that every one has to undergo in freedom through dying and rising. In raising Jesus to new life God has made a commitment to — an enduring covenant with — humanity. This does not mean that the other manifestations of God in history become useless. They lead people — in their respective cultures — to their personal commitments. As in marriage the formal, public commitment does not take away the value of, but valorizes the expressions and communications of love both before and after the formal covenant, God's covenant in Jesus valorizes all his other manifestations. The covenant in Jesus has a cosmic significance precisely because of the divine (Christ) in him. The whole of salvation history is held together by the cosmic aspect of the mystery.[18]

Sometimes we speak of Christ as the final Word, as the norm by which to judge everything else. There is certainly truth in this claim. But the question is which Christ we are talking about. It is true only if we think of the divine aspect of Christ. The Word is the norm. On the last day Christ will be the pleroma, the fullness. But the historical Jesus is Christ's kenotic form. Jesus promises to send the Spirit who will lead his disciples into all truth (see John 16:13). The fullness of Christ is in the future when God will gather together in him all the riches that he has communicated to the world. Therefore such statements must be understood, not historically, but eschatologically — in a dialectic of already/not yet. Only such a vision will enable us to understand that, in a real sense, Jesus *becomes the Christ in fullness in the process of salvation history*, and thus it is also our task to promote this becoming through mission and dialogue.

The church is the witness and the servant of the mystery. It lives the mystery through the memory of the tradition it has received from its manifestation in the history of Jesus. But it should also be sensitive to other manifestations of Mystery in the history of humanity. Its mission is to proclaim and promote the mystery of the kingdom in its fullness and not itself. The Church's preferred manner of mediating this message must be, following Jesus, *kenotic*.

A Servant Church

Part of the problem that we face when we discuss questions concerning the universality of Christ is the image of the Church with which we operate.

The church is a visible institution with a creed, rituals, and organization. In this sense we can see it as one religion among others. But sometimes we also think of the Church as a mystery, the Mystical Body of Christ, that includes all who are saved. Whatever be the justification of such language, it is not helpful to think of the Church in this manner in the context of other religions and of history. If we consider the Church as a religion, then we cannot attribute to it the uniqueness and universality that we attribute to Christ. While people attain to salvation outside the Church, the Church itself is a pilgrim, limited by culture and history.[19] It confesses Christ who is the Truth. But it does not possess him and its own understanding of him is limited by the historical memory it has received. The gospels speak to us about Jesus, but do not claim to offer an adequate expression of him despite their multiple attempts.

We often have an image of salvation history as the growth of the Church till the whole world becomes the Church. I do not know where this image comes from. The Bible rather speaks of the remnant, a community that is persecuted which looks forward in hope for the Lord's coming.[20] I think that the image of the Church as the servant, proclaiming the mystery of the Reign of God, ready to offer its life as witness, may be more authentic than the one of a triumphalistic army conquering all before it. Its service is precisely that of helping the unification of all humankind by promoting a human community of dialogue and collaboration. Its task is to proclaim Jesus and his mystery, more in action than in words, so that others too are challenged by him and turn to God—"converted." Some may be called to join the community of his disciples. Others may undergo real change while remaining in their own religions. The concrete way in which the transformation and unification will take place is a mystery that is known to God alone. All we can do is to be faithful witnesses in action, not only to the mystery of God's love, but to its self-sacrificing manifestation in Jesus.

A person, ideally, ought to become a member of the Church not merely to be saved, but because the believer feels called to participate in the mission of the disciples of Jesus. It is a call to a service, a particular role in history—not an honor or a reason to feel superior. One is not saved "more" or "quicker" because one is Christian. The measure of salvation is the freedom and generosity of God. We may recall the parable of the workers sent to the vineyard at various hours of the day (Mt. 20:1–15).

A Vision of History

One traditional view of salvation history sees it as a progressive narrowing down from creation to the Mosaic covenant to Jesus after whom it opens up again through the growth of the church. It is a linear view of history, stressing the discontinuity between nature and grace, and between before and after Christ—and envisages other religions as distinct from the divinely authorized history of salvation. This vision is narrow and unsatisfactory. It does not take into account the fact that God is the Father and Mother of all. God's election of a people or of a person is not exclusive, but sacramental and symbolic. The cosmic activity of the Word and the Spirit are affirmed by the Old and the New Testaments precisely on the basis of the particular experiences of God's saving action in a person's or people's life.

An alternate vision affirms a saving plan of God that embraces the whole world and all peoples. It is not cosmic in the sense that it is simply identified with nature and history but because it includes the whole cosmos and history, while taking into account the key element in history—human freedom. It is an interplay between the freedoms of God and of human persons, between call and response. In a sense it is very personal. But it is also communitarian. Election, representation, solidarity, and mission are creative and structural elements of this history. The covenants between God and the human person are played out in the context of cultures and traditions. Both freedom (of God and of the human person) and cultures are factors of pluralism. But this pluralism is integrated within the one plan that God has for the world. The unity of the plan of God is a unity of relationships, neither of identity nor of simple plurality. Relationship implies a plurality of roles and functions within a totality.

A role that one may be called to play in a community is a service; it is not a personal title for honor. In the community itself, a role is ordained to the functioning and the building up of the community; one is not superior to or better than another—all are necessary. From a rational perspective we cannot think of relationships except in terms of a structure whose elements are somehow related as more or less, as superior or inferior. We are accustomed to think that priests are superior to the people or that religious are following a more perfect way of life. We used to think that "objectively" virginity was superior to marriage. Today we are struggling to overcome such stereotypes. To a person who is married, marriage is the best way of life. Priesthood is a role of service in the church, just as the lay people have their role. In the religious sphere the model for pluralism is the Trinity, which is a totality of relationships and not a structure of more or less. The ideal of the Church as a communion of persons and communities is also struggling against older hierarchical or structural models.

God's plan for the world is a network of relationships. We are aware of how God has been manifested to us and what mission God has given us in the world. We are not aware of how God may have been manifested to the others. Nor do we comprehend, much less do we dominate, the plan of God for the world. What Christians can do in this situation is to affirm and live their own identity, witness it in word and deed, and enter into a relationship of dialogue with others. It is in listening to others and in discerning together that we may progressively discover the plan of God as it unfolds in the course of history.

In faith we Christians affirm that God's saving action reaches out to all peoples in ways unknown to us. We confess in Jesus, the Christ, the universal savior. We experience in our dialogue with others that God has also been active in them. We look forward to the transformation and unification of all things in heaven and on earth when God will be all in all (1 Cor. 15:28). With this hope we enter into relationships to contribute to the building of a new heaven and a new earth. Dialogue is the manner in which we witness to what has been revealed to us of Mystery while we respect the ineffable transcendence of Mystery.

THE SIGNIFICANCE OF CHRIST

In the light of our reflections above, the profound meaning of affirming that the Christ is the universal savior is that God is really the savior of all peoples. He is not the God of a particular people. God's action is not limited to a particular historical and cultural tradition. Christ has broken down such walls that divide. Once we have recognized Christ in Jesus, we see with the New Testament, particularly with John and Paul, that Christ and his Spirit are active everywhere. Our task is not to carry Christ where he is not present, but rather to discover him where he is, sometimes in mysterious ways unknown to us. The process of this quest is not a material-scientific study of culture and history, but a listening in dialogue to the people in whom we perceive the salvific dialogue between God and the human person taking place. As we listen to the experience of others, it is also our privilege to actively witness to our own experience of the mystery of Christ in Jesus and its relevance to the contemporary world. We feel that we are sent as witnesses on a mission. However we must not be astonished to find that others, too, may claim such a mission.

We must resist the temptation to reduce the universality of Christ to the universality of the visible, institutional Church. We witness to a mystery with which we cannot simply identify ourselves. We often speak about the link that the Church has with the Reign of God. We do not often reflect on the distance that separates the Church from the Reign. One reason is that we tend to think too juridically in terms of power and representation, and not in terms of freedom and relationship—that is, in personal terms. It would be helpful to reread in this context St. Paul's reflection on the Jews in relation to the mystery of salvation (Rom. 10–11). One could say that the limitations of the Church in culture and history make place for the other religions in the plan of God for the world—just as the going away of Jesus seems to make place for the Spirit in history in the reflection of John (John 16:7).

I spoke in the beginning of three paradigms in contemporary theology of religions—namely exclusivism, inclusivism and pluralism. The paradigm I am trying to evolve will find a place between inclusivism and pluralism. It is inclusivist insofar as it reflects in the perspective of the Christian faith in the mysteries of the Trinity and of the Incarnation and their ongoing action in history. But because of the differentiations I have made between the Word and the Spirit, between the Jesus of history and Christ, and between Christ and the Church, the inclusion is only at the level of the mystery of God and Christ whose universality we affirm in faith. It is pluralist, not merely at a historical, phenomenological level of the religions, but also at the level of the plural manifestations of God in history, through the Word eternal and also incarnate and through the Spirit. Therefore the pluralism is already at the level of religion as experience. In faith I affirm that this pluralism is structured into a unity. All believers, because they believe that God is one will have to affirm this. But this unity is eschatological, and both the concrete shape and the actual realization of this unity transcend history.

I would like to present this as an *advaitic* perspective that seeks a mediation between the one and the many, not denying either, but making them the poles of one complex reality.

The goal of mission is to make our own contribution to the realization of the plan of God for the world. This requires listening to the others, reading the signs of the times, building up community, promoting freedom, fellowship and justice and witnessing to the hope that is in us (1 Peter 3:15). To proclaim the universal salvific will of God in Christ means not just to talk about it, but to make it happen. We must also proclaim—realize—the Good News of Jesus. This means that it is not enough to talk in general about the values of the Reign, about justice and development, and about peace and freedom. Jesus was involved with the life of the poor. He particularly opted for the poor and the oppressed. He chose the way of the cross, of total self-giving, even unto death. He sought solidarity with people, particularly in suffering. He lived the reality of communion symbolized in the sharing of food as his own very being. It is significant that this aspect of the suffering Christ, who identifies himself with suffering humanity, seems to attract people like Gandhi and many Indian artists who are the pioneers of Christian art in India, though they do not belong to the Church.[21] To narrow down such a broad and rich mission to increasing membership in the church seems a pity. Even such "conversion" is God's work, not ours. A Church open to the world and to God's mystery will have open frontiers and be less worried about its identity and propagation than about the Reign of God.

CONCLUSION

People are afraid that to affirm pluralism is somehow to fall into relativism—that is, to see all religions as the same and to condone pure relativism. If we look at pluralism not in the abstract or in material terms but in personal terms of freedom and relationship, then we will see its richness on the one hand and on the other the need to affirm and witness to one's own identity. I am happy to be a Christian. God has called me to be one.

I have discovered the mystery of God's universal salvific will in Christ through Jesus. Jesus has shown me the way to promote this mystery in the world in the particular way of being on the side of the poor, ready to give and to share even unto death. I proclaim this message as more than ever relevant to today's world. But I also respect the mystery of God's free relationship with other free human beings. Other religions do not exist apart from other believers. I respect pluralism as the manifestation of the freedom and personhood of God and of the others. I am not anxious to somehow structure them into a system. As a matter of fact, at the level of religions as institutions, pluralism often becomes a problem.

Respect should find expression in various ways according to the context. If I am simply a member of a multireligious community, I can be satisfied with dialogue and witness. But if I run a hospital, just as I would claim the right for the Christians to be ministered to by their chaplain, I should at least be open to allow others the appropriate means to find support in their own religions in a critical period of their lives. Similarly, if I manage a school, I have a responsibility to provide every one an opportunity for an integral education. The school is not merely, or even primarily, a religious institution; it is a service to the community. One may see it as a good occasion to witness to one's faith and to contribute to the building up of the Reign, but one has also a responsibility to see to the faith education of the members of other religions, especially if reflecting on their faith can have a purifying and prophetic effect for them. This responsibility seems even more obvious and acceptable if we properly understand the universal saving act of God in Christ.

PART III

EVANGELIZATION

8

Evangelization in Asia: A New Focus?

Evangelization was the theme of the first plenary assembly of the Federation of Asian Bishops' Conferences in Taiwan in 1974. The bishops described it as the building up of the local Church. This activity finds expression in a three-fold dialogue with the local cultures, with the religions and with the poor of Asia. The International Congress on Mission, meeting in Manila in 1979, stressed again "the continued building up of the local church as the focus of the task of evangelization today, with dialogue as its essential mode."[1] This building up of the local church is the task primarily of the local church itself: this is what is new in this "new age of mission."[2] The bishops of Asia have been initiated to this three-fold dialogue by the many meetings of the Bishops' Institutes for Missionary Affairs, Religious Affairs, and Social Affairs.

This view of evangelization was certainly a very welcome development. Not much earlier, evangelization used to be identified exclusively with the proclamation of the Good News leading to conversion. Caritative or developmental work for the poor, called social work, and dialogue with other religions were seen as preparatory stages to evangelization. Inculturation was seen as a more adequate means of communicating the Good News in a manner easily intelligible to the hearers of a different culture. Sometimes these were considered means which one used when direct proclamation was not possible; they were said to be indirect evangelization. Today one speaks of them as integral dimensions of evangelization. The 1971 Synod of Bishops recognized this with regard to the promotion of justice: "Action on behalf of justice and participation in the transformation of the world fully appear to us as a constitutive dimension of the preaching of the Gospel."[3]

Evangelii Nuntiandi spoke of the evangelization of culture:

What matters is to evangelize man's culture and cultures . . . the Kingdom which the Gospel proclaims is lived by men who are profoundly linked to a culture, and the building up of the Kingdom cannot avoid borrowing the elements of human culture or cultures. . . . In turn, they have to be regenerated by an encounter with the Gospel.[4]

In a speech to the Secretariat for Non-Christians, John Paul II said in 1984: "Authentic dialogue becomes witness and true evangelization is accomplished by respecting and listening to one another."[5] These dimensions of evangelization had been affirmed in an integral manner by the Asian Bishops as a three-fold dialogue.

CHANGING PERSPECTIVES

Such an evolution in the way one thinks about evangelization is not principally due to a sudden discovery of a new situation in the "mission" lands. That the Church needed to adapt itself to the local culture had been realized by Matteo Ricci and Roberto de Nobili. That the people to whom the message is proclaimed are poor is no new discovery either. On the contrary with its schools, hospitals and social projects, the Church has often given the impression of being a development agency rather than a spiritual presence. Even the discovery of the "seeds of the Word" outside Christianity is as old as the Fathers of the Church. What is new is a change in the worldview of Christians. I think we can underline three changes as more important in the development of a new awareness with regard to evangelization: a new idea of salvation, a new view of history and a new perspective on the world.

We realize today that salvation is not simply the saving of "souls." It is liberation and fulfillment for the whole human person-in-community. Beyond human community, it reaches out to transform the cosmos. It does not rescue human beings out of a sinful world. Rather it heals and transforms all the structures—socio-economic, political, cultural and religious— of personal and community life. This is the image of the new world that we get from the Prophets and St. Paul. This is what Paul VI means when he says that the

Church evangelizes when she seeks to convert, solely through the divine power of the Message she proclaims, both the personal and collective consciences of people, the activities in which they engage, and the lives and concrete milieux which are theirs.[6]

This holistic view of the human person and the world also challenges another familiar dichotomy between this world and the next. The Reign of God that Jesus proclaimed is not merely a reality of the future—"a pie in the sky"—but is something that we are called to realize here and now. The forces of transformation—"the power of the resurrection" (Phil. 3:10)— are already at work. We can create a world of peace, fellowship and justice, precisely because it is our sins that have been the cause of injustice, hatred and war. The Church is the "first fruits" of this new humanity and is sent into the world, in the power of the Spirit, to witness to and to work for the Reign's realization. The war between good and evil is being fought on this earth, here and now. There will be nothing new in the future if the transformation does not progressively take place now. Taking for granted the ever present help of the creative Spirit, it is the human community that builds up its future, even if its efforts will be fulfilled much beyond its imaginings by God at the end of time. This is the mystery of the Incarnation. Jesus did not come to liberate us from this world. He came to give us the assurance that God is with us and that the creative Spirit is effective. The mystery of redemption is a mystery of God empowering the human person-in-community to realize his Kingdom progressively in this world, even if its full realization is eschatological.

This brings us to the realization that redemption is not God's "after-thought"—not a "supernatural" intervention into a "natural" world. This is the third dichotomy—natural/supernatural—that we must transcend. The whole of history is the interplay between the freedoms of God and the human person. The whole of history is under the plan of God that St. Paul calls the "mystery" (Eph. 1:9). The Spirit and the Word are there from the beginning. This activity of the universal salvific will of God does not exclude special manifestations at particular places and times through particular persons or peoples. There is a growing conviction today that such special divine manifestations may also be discerned in other religious traditions. This is why the bishops of Asia recognize in other religions "significant and positive elements in the economy of God's design of salvation" and assert: "God has drawn our peoples to Himself through them."[7] The "signs of the times" witness to God's continuing activity in our world. These manifestations are significant only in the context of the universal salvific will. Insofar as they are manifestations of the same God—our common origin and goal—they are related to each other in some structured way. It is one of the challenges of evangelization to discover, through dialogue, such inter-relationships in the light of faith.

VARYING IMAGES OF EVANGELIZATION

It is in the background of these new perspectives that various images of evangelization are still in tension affecting our approaches to the tasks of evangelization. Around the time of the Second Vatican Council, while some saw mission in territorial terms as establishing the Church where it is not yet present, others saw it as a continuing activity of the Church wherever it is. The process of dechristianization in the Christian countries and the need for their re-evangelization or second evangelization made people hesitate to limit the meaning of mission to "foreign" missions. One remembers the famous question: "France, a mission country?" There was a tension

between a theological view of mission as the prolongation of the mission
of the Son from the Father continued through the Spirit and present in
the Church, making the whole Church missionary[8] by its very existence and
constitution and a more sociological and geographical view of mission as
extending the frontiers of the Christian world, with a priority to making the
Church present everywhere.

Some would see the movement of salvation history as a linear one of
God's special interventions in history narrowing down to Jesus Christ as
the center and then opening out again through the Church in mission to
embrace progressively the whole world. Others would see the Church as
the servant, with visibility and assurance, of a cosmic process so that salvation history is rather a convergent meshing of many strands with the
Church being the central thread — somewhat like the cornerstone of an
arch, to change the image.

Some see evangelization as a proclamation of the Good News. They
speak a language of communication: the Gospel is the text, whose living
reality becomes the context and the interpretation and expression of the
meaning or relevance of the text to the context, which is not seen as a
perennial message formulated in the abstract — a creed — that is proposed
for the intellectual adherence of the hearer as being the "truth," but rather
as a living reality to be re-interpreted and contextualized in a given historical context. This new emphasis is welcome. But one may be tempted to
remain at the level of communication of ideas and messages. The message,
of course, calls for action when it is accepted. But action is a consequence
rather than an integral dimension of the message. From this perspective,
for instance, evangelization could be discussed in terms of cross-cultural
communication. Contextualization is certainly more than communication.
But one may be tempted to remain at the level of a message that is made
meaningful, with the hope that appropriate action will follow.

A perspective that integrates ortho-doxy with ortho-praxis sees evangelization rather as the building up of a community which witnesses more with
its life than with only words. Building up of the local church as the focus
of evangelization integrates orthodoxy and orthopraxis. This is the perspective chosen by the Asian bishops. Taking into account the situation in
Asia, the Asian bishops analyze the building up of the local church in terms
of a three-fold dialogue with the culture, with the religions and with the
poor of Asia. The dimensions of evangelization in Asia are therefore spelt
out as inculturation, interreligious dialogue and liberation, all of them contributing to the building up of the local church.

The SEDOS Seminar on Evangelization adds to this list "proclamation."[9]
This addition is problematic. While the Asian bishops seem to have a holistic perspective in which inculturation, liberation and interreligious dialogue
merge into the one task of building up the local church as the focus of
evangelization, this totality is broken up by adding proclamation to the list.
While Asia sees inculturation, dialogue and liberation as various aspects

or dimensions or forms of proclamation of the Good News in concrete ways corresponding to various situations of reality, the addition of "proclamation" as a fourth term has broken up this unity and has made all of them various tasks that a missionary engages in according to the situation. One sometimes hears people identifying proclamation with direct evangelization, calling the other tasks indirect. Another difficulty with this view of evangelization is that it might appear to limit it to the "non-Christian" and the dechristianized countries. It might thus lose the wider perspective of the Church itself as mission.

It is not my intention here to advocate one or another view of evangelization described above. Each one of them has valid elements that need to be integrated in a wider perspective. I think that the time has come for the Church in Asia to move towards this wider perspective.

NEW FOCUS

As the Asian countries were emerging from a colonial period, the need to build up an indigenous Church was strongly felt. And given the reality of Asia, it was thought that this cannot be done without a three-fold dialogue with culture, with other religions and with the poor. I think that this focus needs re-examination. As a first step, let us look at the way that this three-fold dialogue finds integration.

Inculturation, interreligious dialogue, and liberation can be taken up as mutually involving dimensions of one and the same activity of building up the local Church. They can also be engaged in as separate, independent activities. One can struggle to liberate the poor in a "secular" way, marginalizing religion as alienating. One can dialogue with religious leaders and engage in theological discussions or share each other's riches of the Spirit without bothering about the poor. One can see culture either as the tradition of the past or as the creative dimension of the present involving literature, the arts and the sciences and promote dialogue with it ignoring both religious faith, especially in secularized cultural situations, and the poor. In this manner, inculturation, interreligious dialogue and liberation can be three separate, independent activities. I think that, at least in India, this seems to be often the case.

On the contrary, culture can be taken as the way people live and give meaning to their lives. Religion is not only an integral dimension, but even the deepest element in culture. Socio-economic situations and religio-cultural perspectives mutually influence each other. Thus one cannot really inculturate or transform culture with the values of the Gospel without dialoguing with the religious traditions that are the animating elements of cultures and without changing the socio-economic structures that keep people enslaved. One cannot liberate people from all that oppresses them without transforming their worldview and system of values and without dialoguing with the various religions so that religions do not remain forces for division and alienation but become prophetic sources of inspiration, and do so in collaboration with each other—particularly in multireligious societies characteristic of Asia. Interreligious dialogue is indeed meaningless and alienating if it does not lead to collaboration for the common promotion of human and spiritual values leading to holistic liberation and authentic inculturation. Inculturation, interreligious dialogue, and liberation are different kinds of activities with different intermediate goals. But they will be alienating if they do not influence and involve each other and lead ultimately to a holistic liberation of the human person-in-community. It is then that they become three integral dimensions of one activity that is evangelization.

As we begin to realize their integration, however, we also discover that their common focus moves beyond the building up of the local church. How do we describe the holistic liberation of the human person-in-community? I think it should be characterized as the Reign of God rather than the Church. That is why I would suggest that the focus of evangelization in Asia should be the Reign of God rather than the local church. This is not just a change in terminology. The focus can radically affect the way in which we engage in our evangelizing activity. One can dialogue with culture for one's own benefit, for the sake of indigenizing the theological, liturgical and structural self-expression of Christian faith and life—that is, building up the local church. One can also dialogue with culture in a multireligious or even in a largely non-Christian society in order to transform that culture, even partially, through the values of the Gospel without being able to "Christianize" the whole of that culture. One can have the one without the other. One can say that the best way of doing the first is to engage in the second.

Similarly, one can dialogue with other religions with a view to one's own growth by the assimilation of all that is good and true. One can engage in dialogue as a first step towards proclamation. One can use dialogue as a means of dispelling misunderstanding and prejudices and move towards collaboration in defense of common human and spiritual values. One can also dialogue in order to share with others one's riches and, by presenting a prophetic challenge, provoke them to grow. One can dialogue, finally, in view of providing a common moral and spiritual foundation to a common commitment to build a better world. John Paul II said to leaders of other religions in Madras:

> By dialogue we let God be present in our midst; for as we open ourselves in dialogue to one another, we also open ourselves to God . . . As followers of different religions, we should join together in promoting and defending common ideals in the spheres of religious liberty, human brotherhood, education, culture, social welfare and civic order.[10]

In the same way one can dialogue with the poor to build up the Church of the poor. One can dialogue with the poor to liberate them from the oppressive structures in a socio-economic sense. One can work at transforming the self-image and the world views (culture) that keep them enslaved. One can dialogue with the poor in order to provide for them in dialogue with other religions, a moral and religious dimension in a holistic liberation, that reaches out beyond the poor also to their oppressors.

Speaking of the building up of the local church as a focus of evangelization in a poor and multireligious society like Asia might tend to limit our perspectives only to such activities among those listed above that contribute directly to the building up of the local church. However, when one speaks of this three-fold dialogue in some detail, one does go beyond such limits. I would suggest, therefore, that if we make the Reign of God, rather than the church, the focus of evangelization, then that would and could embrace all the activities listed above, including the building up of the Church.

When many years ago, Raimon Panikkar wrote his book, *The Unknown Christ of Hinduism*, M.M. Thomas replied with a book on *The Acknowledged Christ of the Indian Renaissance*. In that book, Thomas showed how Christ and his Good News have influenced many Indian leaders of other religions to work for socio-political and religio-cultural reform though they did not become Christians. We have here a clear case of the positive impact of Christ and his Good News which falls short of the building up of the Church (as a visible community), but which transforms the culture and history of a people through making the values of the Kingdom present effectively in their midst. Such a transformation can certainly be an aim of evangelization. In the light of the ongoing march of peoples towards the new humanity of the last days—the Reign of God—such a transformation is something positive and worthwhile in itself, as a step in the building up of the Reign of God that Jesus proclaimed. We do not have to see it merely as a step closer to the Church. It is certainly more than the hidden activity of Christ and the Spirit—the unknown Christ of Panikkar. There is an explicit impact of the Good News of Jesus. It may be partial, but it is positive. It is evangelization—"bringing the good news into all the strata of humanity from within and making it new."[11]

We need not be afraid that a change of the focus of evangelization from the local church to the Reign of God will lead us to ignore the local church. Building up the local church as a witness to and the servant of the Reign will be an important and essential, though not an exclusive, element of this new focus. The Gospel can hardly transform society unless it is effectively made present by a community—the Church—that is committed to and involved in the historical process. It is precisely this involvement, leading inevitably to the three-fold dialogue with the cultures, the religions and the poor of Asia that will build up the Church and do so in the here and now of history—that is, build up a truly local church.

Building up the Reign of God is not simply building up the Church. The

Church is not simply the Reign of God. In the power of the Spirit, God is building up the Reign also in other ways through other peoples—in ways unknown to us, but which we are called to discern in dialogue. But the Church is aware of being the visibility—sacrament—in history of Jesus and his life, death and resurrection. It is aware that this very sacramentality is calling it to become a local Church everywhere. That is why, for the Church, "to be" is to proclaim, to witness, not only the Reign of God in general, but also as it becomes present in the life, death and resurrection of Jesus and as it continues in the community of his disciples. This community is called to build itself up, builds itself up and is built up by the Spirit, as a community in mission. That is why baptism is a challenge to be on mission and not merely an opportunity simply to be saved. It is precisely in view of the task that is given to it that the Church seeks new members and builds itself up in history. Taken out of this context of the Reign and the need to be an actively witnessing community, a call to baptism may become mere proselytism. On the other hand, to consciously refrain from calling people to discipleship and to witness is to proclaim an abstract, rootless, a-historical Reign and to be untrue to one's very identity as a witness—respecting always the freedom and mystery of the Spirit who calls as well as respecting the freedom and mystery of the person who responds. Who will be challenged by a witness that the one witnessing does not seem to be passionately committed to? How can we witness to a passionate commitment without inviting participation? Just as it would be wrong to ignore the wider perspectives of the Reign which Jesus proclaimed and we proclaim after him, it would be wrong too to ignore its specific manifestation in Jesus whose "memory" is the inspiration of one's life.

Building up the Reign of God is a wider cosmic reality. In the power of the Spirit, all are called to it in various ways known to God alone. In this constructive task, some may be challenged more particularly by Jesus and his Gospel without however hearing the call to discipleship and community (e.g. Gandhi). But someone who has heard this call and who has responded in faith cannot witness to the Reign without witnessing to the community, the Church. One does not, however, identify them or make them coextensive because one realizes that other believers are promoting the same Reign through their faith commitments. The demand to dialogue with them and to collaborate in building up the Reign does not in any way reduce the responsibility to witness to one's faith because the collaboration called for is *not* one based on the least common denominator, but on the mutual and collective enrichment born of authentic witness in dialogue, respecting the freedom of each one to respond to God's call in whichever way it comes to that person. A pluralistic context supposes not only respect for the identity and freedom of the other, but also loyalty to and affirmation of one's own identity. Otherwise, the dialogue will be inauthentic.[12]

Such a broadening of our vision and goal would free us to think and to plan many and more creative ways of proclaiming and realizing the Reign.

It will make evangelization an unambiguously outward-looking project. Inculturation, interreligious dialogue and liberation would acquire a new relevance and a more open thrust.

THREE MODELS OF EVANGELIZATION

Avery Dulles has written about various models of the Church and of revelation. A model is a framework of attitudes and approaches that structures a basic image or insight. Thus the Church may be seen as an institution, as people, as a servant, as a sacrament, etc. The models are not mutually exclusive. They highlight different aspects of the same reality. But from the point of view of attitudes and programs for action, it may be important which model is central in structuring one's perception and analysis. Looking at various approaches to evangelization, I would like to suggest three models.

The first model of evangelization is Church-centered. The aim of evangelization is to build up the Church. Proclamation of the Good News is seen as the predominant activity of mission. Other activities like promotion of justice or interreligious dialogue are seen only as means or first steps towards proclamation. The theological focus is on the historical Jesus, who is the incarnate Word and who founded the Church as the means of salvation and who sent it out into the world on mission. This model is the traditional one. The temporal point of reference is the past.

The second model of evangelization is world-centered. The focus is on God the Father and one's preferred mystery is creation. One stresses theocentrism as different from christocentrism. Pluralism is a fact of present experience, rooted not only in the differences of nature, but also in the diversity of cultures that are the fruits of the creative activity of peoples. Differences among human groups are a result of the varying gifts of the Creator. The Church may be said to have a symbolic, even a normative role in the history of salvation. Dialogue is the principal activity of evangelization. Even proclamation becomes an aspect of dialogue. The temporal point of reference is the present, because creation is seen as an ongoing activity involving the people of every generation as co-creators with God.

The third model is Reign-of-God-centered. The diversity of peoples and religions is recognized. The unique intervention of God in Jesus Christ is also acknowledged. But the plan of God is leading everything towards a final fulfillment to which all are called. As a dynamic and creative process, history becomes important. Life looks not to the past, nor to the present, but to the future. All are called to transcend their present state in growing towards a fulfillment that will be the work of the Spirit. The Spirit of course does not ignore the work and role of the Father and of the Son. But he is creative, making all things new. In doing so he integrates in a holistic manner all that is good and true. Evangelization centered on the Kingdom is dynamic, future-oriented, rooted in reality and history, integrative and holistic. It is the building up of a new humanity. It is leading the world and all peoples to their fulfillment. Proclamation is of this fullness which can only be realized in the mutual self-gift and the consequent mutual enrichment of dialogue. "Liberation" refers to the necessary remedial action, in the light of the sinful structures that have been built up by human beings; but it somehow misses the positive aspect of fulfillment or realization. Creation and redemption find their final realization in the new heaven and the new earth.

BUILDING UP A NEW HUMANITY

That the Church's mission involves the building up of a new humanity is not a new insight. What may be new, however, is making it the primary focus of evangelization. Speaking of the Church as a community of faith, the Federation of Asian Bishops' Conferences says: "It constantly moves forward in mission as it accompanies all humankind in its pilgrimage to the Kingdom of the Father."[13] The Asian bishops stress "the Church's responsibility in the world, in the public spheres, in the construction of a more fully human future for Asian peoples."[14] The Seminar on the Indian Church in the Struggle for a New Society says about the Church:

> Her mission requires that she herself embody in her own life and structure the Kingdom values of freedom, fellowship and justice. It also requires that she contribute to the promotion of those values in the ordering of human society. The struggle for a New Society is therefore a constitutive element of the Church's evangelizing mission.[15]

In a sense this says nothing much more than did the Synod of Bishops of 1971.

In contrast what I am suggesting is a shift of focus by which building a new world or the Reign of God is not seen merely as one constitutive element among others of the Church's mission of evangelization. Rather it is the main focus around which the other tasks—inculturation, dialogue, proclamation—are grouped, mutually integrating and influencing each other. I suggest also that it is in building up the Reign that the Church will build itself up as a Church-at-the-service-of-the-Reign.

If we now place ourselves at the point of this new focus and look at the three-fold dialogue with culture, with religions and with the poor, we will see them in new ways. I shall limit myself to a few indications here, with particular reference to the situation in India with which I am most familiar.

The need for the Christians in Asia to become indigenous and inculturated is precisely so they can be more effective because they are more involved in their attempt to transform the Asian reality. The Christians cannot really hope to transform reality without getting involved in public affairs. I use the term, "public affairs" as being broader than "politics."

Normally when we speak of inculturation, we seem to think only of the Church "ad intra." We think about indigenization in liturgy, in theology, in spirituality, in our way of life. It is necessary that the churches in Asia become really local churches with regard to their life and self-expression. But what seems more urgent is that they should be involved with the on-going life of the people and make every effort to transform it in view of the Reign of God in the power of the Spirit. It is in doing this that the Church also will become a truly local church and find an authentic self-expression that is neither archeologizing (looking to the culture of the past) nor alienating (looking to the culture of the elite).

After a study of Asian Christian social protest in recent history, Parig Digan concludes that one element that inhibits the Church from playing its prophetic role in transforming reality, especially in situations of injustice, is a minority complex that leads it to self-defensive attitudes.[16] This complex may even be stronger if the Christians are not only numerically small but also belong to minority ethnic groups—as happens in some areas. If this analysis is true, the Philippines is the only country in Asia where the Church can play any significant role in public affairs. We have seen this happen there recently. Does this mean that the other churches in Asia because of their minority status are condemned to inactivity in the field of public affairs? Does this mean that the only way out of this difficulty is an increase in numbers? Such a conclusion is not obvious to me. First of all, numbers are not the only inhibiting factor. One could be a minority of one and yet play a bold prophetic role. I think there are many other inhibiting factors that need to be explored and tackled. Secondly, unless we confuse religion and politics, a religious minority group need not always be a political minority.

Where a state is closely linked to a religion, minority religious groups become effectively also political minorities. But where a state has constitutionally a secular character, as in India or Indonesia, for instance, the religious affiliation of the citizens, apart from being a personal or collective inspiration, need not be determinative of their political options as such. A person belonging to a minority religious group may belong to a majority political party. Persons of all religious faiths can work together in the defense of common human and spiritual values. Unless special religious beliefs or rights are affected, one's minority status in the field of religion need not affect one's political status, even if a democracy need not be immune to group pressures. Communal politics based on religion are a threat not only to rights of religious believers as such. They are also a danger to all other human and civic rights. Unless religious communalism in the public life of a country is taken for granted, a religious minority group need not necessarily be a political minority group.

BECOMING A CHURCH OF ADULTS

I do not wish to belittle the difficulties that the Church as a minority group of people may be encountering in assuming an effective, participative role in public affairs. But I think numbers are not the only factor and certainly not the decisive one. Two other interrelated factors have been highlighted recently in India. Reflecting on the visit of Pope John Paul II, Paramananda Diwarkar writes:

> An observer who followed the papal tour and made friendly comments ended nevertheless by saying "It is clear that John Paul II is a strong Pope, a fighter for what he believes in, while the Catholic Church in India is quite the opposite." Whatever be the measure of truth in this statement, would it be impertinent to suggest that John Paul is effective because he is free to be himself, while the Church in India is not... We are not a young Church, except in the sense that we have never really grown up.[17]

The Church in India does not feel itself to be a responsible adult, free to decide, to take initiatives and to act. But what are the causes for this? One could easily speak of the centralizing tendencies in the Church. The Church itself seems to have realized this during the Extraordinary Synod. By speaking of the Church as a communion and by encouraging further reflection and study of concepts like subsidiarity a way is being opened to a renewed awareness of the Church as the communion of local churches. Let us hope that this new awareness will lead to appropriate change of structures. However I think that it would be a mistake to throw all the blame on the centralizing tendencies. Doing that would be a concrete indication of our adolescent state. How ready are we to act as a local church? We speak constantly of inculturation. But what stops us from inculturating our spirituality, our way of life, our local administrative structures? Liturgy is admittedly a sensitive area. But what effort have we made to use the freedom, even if limited, that we do have? The new rituals of the sacraments, for instance, do indicate some elements in which an episcopal conference can propose cultural variations. We have not made use even of these small provisions. Because of the ritual and cultural differences in the country and because of the difficulty of adopting a national policy in the matter, liturgy was made an area for the regional bishops' conferences to animate. One expected a period of creativity, at least in some areas of the country. But what has happened so far? This is just one example to show that we do not yet seem to be ready to take our responsibility seriously. We cannot say, for instance, that participative structures like the synod of priests or parish councils are functioning widely and meaningfully in the country. In short, we are not functioning like an adult Church, even when and where we can.

One reason for this, among others, are the structures of dependence, some of which we have internalized. On the occasion of the visit of the Pope to India, some members of the other religions, who did not seem happy with the visit, took the occasion to point to the foreignness of the

Church. Such foreignness is often identified in terms of being part of a well-structured international organization and hence suspected of being controlled from abroad, and of being dependent on foreign funds and personnel.[18] Belonging to a world religion with transnational structures is not in itself blameworthy or a disadvantage. It can even be helpful in crisis situations. The concrete forms such organizations take are conditioned by history. Let us hope that the progressive emergence of the structures of communion in the Church would lead to a responsible local church. But such an evolution of new structures would not happen by itself without some responsible and creative initiatives from the local churches. Secondly, fraternal aid is useful and sometimes necessary. St. Paul took up a collection from his Asian Churches to help the Church in Jerusalem. It becomes detrimental when we are hindered from being responsible for ourselves and made to project an institutional image much beyond our means and discourages prophecy for fear of losing such aid. Self-reliance is a sign of responsibility and maturity and is not opposed to responsible mutual aid. Thirdly, foreign personnel at the service of the local churches are a living sign of catholicity and communion. At the same time, we should be conscious of the sensitivity of newly independent countries in a postcolonial period. The Church is often linked with the colonial past. Even today the Church, with its educational and medical institutions, appears to be the bearer of modernity that is confused often with Western culture. Some Christians might even appreciate such identification; it might even be one of the motives for some to opt to become Christian. In the context of a tension between tradition and modernity such institutions will be welcomed certainly by the elite, but also by the poor, who see in them means of upward social mobility. Their services will be made use of willingly. But here is the ambiguity: they are not admired for the Gospel that they witness to, but for the material and moral values that they represent—values identified as useful, though foreign. While the people themselves try to integrate such values in their own way in their lives, these institutions and those who run them, if they have not attempted such integration, will continue to remain foreign in their eyes. Is that the image that an inculturated Church wants to project?

I think that the basic question concerning inculturation is whether our Church is a truly local church, responsible and mature, free and creative, in communion with other local churches and with the Church of Rome or is it a Church that is unfree, and dependent, not so much because of external controls, though these are not absent, but because of internalized bonds. When we work with the poor for their liberation, we speak of the need of liberating them not only from economic and political structures of oppression, but also from the cultural structures like a poor self-image, worldview, values and relationships which keep them bound. The Church needs such a process of cultural transformation. This is a more urgent task than inculturation in the liturgy. The latter will never happen adequately without the former. As the recent experience of the Philippines Church has shown, one becomes an indigenous local church by acting like one, by becoming one with the people, making their concerns one's own, struggling with them towards freedom and fulfillment—or in other words, towards the Reign of God. Talk about inculturation will remain abstract till the Church has the courage to get involved with the lives, the struggles, and the hopes of its people.

PROPHECY AND INSTITUTION

Another difficulty that may stand in the way of real involvement with the people, especially on the side of the poor and the oppressed, for any prophetic and liberative activity that is more than charitable is the image we project of the Church. We are still very much an institutional Church, not the People of God. The institutional model of the Church is a valid one. But an institution evokes immediately ideas of a structure and a leadership. The leadership becomes the focus of the institution. For many in the Church and for most people outside it, the Church means the bishops and the priests who officially represent the institution. The relationship between the Church and the world is analyzed in terms of the Church as an institution and the state: one speaks of the two powers, the spiritual and the temporal. In the past two centuries in Europe, the states have tried to become secular progressively and to assert their independence from the Church. The Church itself is attempting to stay out of practical politics and yet claim the freedom to speak or act prophetically. The laity are encouraged to get involved in the world. The form of their involvement varies from Catholic Action movements controlled by the hierarchy through Christian Democratic parties to more independent forms of involvement. The paradox of the situation is that by taking a political stand they will not be recognized as representing anyone but themselves. It is the clerical leadership that is always identified as "the Church."

I do not intend to discuss here the complex issues of Church and state, religion, and politics. If the local Churches in Asia are serious about their "dialogue with the poor," they have to clarify to themselves these issues. Here I shall limit myself to three observations.

Does not the community of Christians have not only a religious identity as a Church or churches but also other social and political identities? In the so-called Christian countries of Europe with secular Governments such a question may sound strange. But in Asia the images still seem confused. In such a community with various identities, could there also be a variety of leadership roles? Could the leadership role of the clergy be seen as limited to the religious sphere? Could the laity have real access to leadership in other spheres of the Christian community? Have we to accumulate all leadership in the Christian community in the clergy?

An actual case may easily illustrate the kind of issues I wish to raise.

We are aware of the public stand taken some years ago by the Bishops' Conference of the Philippines on the morality of the elections. Let me say that I appreciate and admire their bold and clear stand. But their prophetic stand also brought some questions to my mind. When should bishops speak as bishops, that is, as official religious leaders of the Christian community? The ministry of teaching entrusted to them may demand that occasionally they speak authoritatively on a matter of faith or morals that may also have practical and even political implications. Such teaching involves the community because it is authoritative. They then speak as bishops with their full religious authority. I think that the statement of the Philippine bishops to which I refer above does not belong to this order. But there could certainly be occasions like this when bishops speak with their personal and moral authority as public figures without involving their strictly religious authority. They no longer speak for the Church, nor to the Church. They need not wait for unanimity in such matters as if it were an official statement and they were afraid of showing public disunity. I think that if the Christian community, the bishops, leaders of government and others were aware of such distinctions, bishops may tend to be more prophetic and forthcoming. What would have been the image and the impact if the condemnation of the elections came from a group which included, besides bishops, prominent lay leaders and public figures, not involved in party politics? What would have been the image and the impact of the condemning group if it included also prominent members of other churches and other religious traditions like the Muslims? What is significant is that no such broad-based groups seem to exist.

In the multireligious societies of Asia, where the Church is in a minority, this may be the only way in which the Church can speak freely, boldly, effectively and prophetically. It is in this manner that I understand what John Paul said in February 1986 during his pilgrimage to India:

In the world today, there is a need for all religions to collaborate in the cause of humanity, and to do this from the view-point of the spiritual nature of man. Today, as Hindus, Muslims, Sikhs, Buddhists, Jains, Parsees and Christians, we gather in fraternal love to assert this by our presence. As we proclaim the truth about man, we insist that man's search for temporal and social well-being and full human dignity corresponds to the deep longings of his spiritual nature. To work for the attainment and preservation of all human rights, including the basic right to worship God according to the dictates of an upright conscience and to profess that faith externally, must become ever more a subject of interreligious collaboration at all levels. This interreligious collaboration must also be concerned with the struggle to eliminate hunger, poverty, ignorance, persecution, discrimination and every form of enslavement of the human spirit. Religion is the main-spring of society's commitment to justice, and interreligious collaboration must reaffirm this in practice.

COLLABORATION OR WITNESS

Such a project of collaboration however may encounter two sorts of objections. First of all, one senses a danger of losing one's identity as a community of Christians. There need be no such danger. That is why we speak of collaboration. In the pluralistic societies of Asia, we have to promote secular states that respect human rights and do not discriminate in terms of religion, race or language. A known danger in this area is the use of religious sentiment as a cementing factor and motive-force in politics; thus we have Buddhist and Muslim States. Many would like to make India a Hindu State. Such confessional states inevitably reduce other minority religious groups to the status of second class citizens in practice, because these minority groups cannot make any contribution from a religious point of view to the common good. Such situations are ideal grounds for the breeding of communal conflicts, since the minority groups, unless they are too small and powerless, would fight to assert and defend their identity. We should rather promote secular states that treat all religious groups with equal honor. In practice this might mean special provisions to protect the minorities from the majorities.

More positively, we have to promote societies where pluralism in religion is seen as a source of richness contributing to mutual growth rather than as a source of tension. Creating such an understanding will be one of the goals of interreligious dialogue. One can collaborate meaningfully with others and contribute to collective wellbeing only in so far as each religious group remains itself and is able to make not only its political, but also its religious contribution to the community. Therefore the call to collaboration and dialogue as a means towards it is not a call to discover an easy common ground based on the least common denominator; properly understood, dialogue, even at a practical level, must lead to mutual enrichment around common values. Each religious group must bring to the understanding and support of these values the religious traditions and orientations specific to them. In this manner we will have not a flattening of identities, but an enrichment. That is why I am not talking of mutual tolerance or peaceful coexistence, but of active collaboration. This is also the ideal situation to proclaim or to witness to the specific values, ideals and vision that one believes in, in a positive way, and not in opposition to something else. Such a situation can also clarify the relation between religion and politics. We have to show that religion is really relevant to politics so that it is not seen as alienating. At the same time, in the context of rising religious fundamentalism, we have to show that politics should not be too closely identified with one particular religion. This means that religious faith must find expression in political choices and activities; but religion as an organization or institution has no strictly political role.

A corollary of such an attitude would be to revise our notions of what we consider Christian. We Christians have a way of appropriating everything to ourselves. Any good person is an "anonymous" Christian and we lay claim to everything good and holy anywhere. On the one hand such affirmation may witness to our faith in one God, Lord of all things. On the other hand, it is not respectful of other believers, their traditions and what the Lord may be doing in them. One way of showing our respect for other believers and their traditions is to be able to spell out what is specific to us—not only in terms of our creed, nor of some values that we have and that we claim that others do not have, but in terms of aspects of life and values that our faith seems to reach out to in a particular way. The life and work of Jesus, his death and resurrection have certainly a specific way of looking at poverty and suffering, death and life. These are the basic questions that a religious person keeps asking. The community that carries the active memory of Jesus brings to the common struggle for the Kingdom a special light and power. We will have to spell these out carefully. Probably we will be able to clarify our specificity to ourselves and to others only in living dialogue with others who believe differently from us.

One does not really reach the fullness of evangelization if one does not witness in word and deed to this specificity. One should be careful in talking of witnessing to the values of the Gospel. Every Christian must fight for justice as an authentic expression of faith. But fighting for justice is not a peculiarly Christian activity. There are many others of goodwill, even nonbelievers, who do so. It does not help to say that they are Christian without knowing it. It would be more honest to ask ourselves whether there is a way or manner of fighting for justice that would show to everyone that, while we are fighting for justice with and like others, we are still witnessing to the Christian faith. And such witness is perceived only in a personal encounter. Once this is realized, then we may discover that some types of works and institutions are more transparent than others to such personal witness.

CONCLUSION

The evangelizing Church that I envisage would be an open, pilgrim, dynamic community committed to the building up of God's Reign of freedom, fellowship and justice. The Church cannot evangelize or creatively transform society and culture without getting involved with the living reality of the people, especially the poor—that is, without being political both in a broad and a narrow sense. Such involvement will have to be Christian witness without being ecclesiastical. This need to be Christian without being ecclesiastical will lead us to discover the role of the people in the Church and new types of leadership. This will give rise to a new image of the Church whose visibility is not that of the institution and its custodians but of the people, the focus of whose activity is the Reign of God in the world and whose primary means of achieving this is action to transform the world.

If I may refer back to a question I raised above and that was raised at the time of the Council regarding the meaning of mission, I think that it is time that the Asian Churches took a clear option for understanding themselves as being on mission in the world, not primarily to build the Church up, but to build up the Reign of God. In this context let us accept that we are numerically small but ready to transform the world from within as leaven, free from temptations to power that might come from numbers.

We must of course keep our identity and our communion in our faith and around the Eucharist. But we should not allow this fellowship to separate us from the people around us with whom we live united culturally, socially and politically and even religiously in dialogue. We need not too quickly adopt the strategy of basic ecclesial communities. They are normally integral in their approach, including socio-political dimensions. They may function well in Catholic countries. But in multireligious societies we have to explore alternate strategies that adequately respond to our multiple social obligations and avoid anything that could be divisive.

Going beyond easy dichotomies like sacred-secular or clergy-lay, we should rediscover the plurality of identities that every community has in the contemporary world and the plurality of structures, roles, charisms, and leadership that correspond to these identities. Such a realization may lead us to a new ecclesiology of the People of God in the world, based rather on *ad extra* concerns than *ad intra* problems. The Church will continue to be a mystery, but one in the service of a greater mystery through which God wishes to bring "back to himself all things, both on earth and in heaven" (Col. 1:20).

9

Inculturation:
Perspectives and Challenges

The Good News is a seed that sprouts anew in each culture in which it is planted. It is not identified with any one culture but it is capable of animating all cultures. It incarnates itself in each culture, giving it a new meaning and unity, a new orientation and openness, transforming it in the power of the Spirit and leading it to the catholic (universal) fullness of the new creation. In this way, the Good News finds a new expression highlighting newer aspects and resources of its liberating message and the culture has a new principle of life that not only gives it a new identity but leads it to the universal fellowship with the disciples of Christ.

The theological basis of inculturation is two-fold. On the one hand, the Incarnate Word who became flesh (John 1:14) is not only the model and justification of inculturation, but demands it. God has chosen this way of sharing his life with people by transforming them from within as leaven. On the other hand, the plurality of cultures leads us to perceive the Church not as a monolith, but as a communion of churches. The Word itself remains the principle of unity amid the enriching multiplicity of forms in which the creative Spirit gives it expression.

What I have briefly indicated above is widely accepted in the Church today. I shall therefore turn my attention in the following pages to certain practical problems which arise when the task of inculturation is taken up seriously.

THE CONTEXT OF INCULTURATION

Inculturation today is not a simple encounter between the Gospel and a new culture. The Gospel comes to these new cultures as already embodied in a particular culture. The encounter, therefore, is really *between two cultures.*

The process becomes a double one: discovering the Gospel in the form

121

in which it comes embodied through the process of interpretation and re-expressing it in new cultural forms. This might sound like a work of translation. Yet the Gospel is not primarily a series of statements, but a complex of attitudes, ways of thinking, living, acting, celebrating and structures of common life. Similarly, culture is not merely a language; it is a worldview, a complex of symbolic expressions, a way of life. Hence what is required is a re-embodiment of the attitudes and values of the Gospel in new cultural forms.

As an encounter between cultures, inculturation gets caught up in a network of *intercultural problems*. On the one hand, the cultures that the Gospel encounters in Asia are ancient, highly literate, developed and self-sufficient ones which are quite proud of themselves. The Gospel is not making much headway in its dialogue with them. On the other hand, the Gospel has come to Asia as a culture considered colonial, threatening freedom and self-identity. This culture is seen as modern, attractive insofar as it is the bearer of science and technology, but problematic insofar as it disrupts traditional worldviews and ways of life. The situation becomes more confusing when the Christian minority is attached to the foreign culture as provider of a distinct and supposedly superior identity (because of its links with modernity). In this complex situation, inculturation is no simple process. Every choice and initiative is looked at, resisted or accepted by various groups of people for various conscious and unconscious reasons.

This complexity is further intensified when we consider that inculturation is not an abstract encounter between two systems, but a dialogue between groups of people, who are the bearers of these cultures. This adds a psychological dimension to the problems indicated in the previous paragraph. An aggressive nationalism rejects the Gospel as bearer of unwanted attitudes and values of a foreign culture. Meanwhile, small communities of Christians, suffering from the insecurities of living as a minority community, oppose the very project of inculturation.

Every culture is actually a complex of subcultures. The elite, the middle-class, the poor, workers, the urban proletariat, youth—all have their sub-cultures, each with its specific characteristics and tensions. An ethnographical approach to culture might try to avoid this complexity. For example, someone interested in Indian culture, instead of learning it in living contact with the people, starts a study of written and other documents and expressions and seeks to build up a general composite picture of Indian culture, attitudes, values, movements and worldview. Thus a systematic picture of a classical culture in all its richness emerges. Its only inadequacy will be that it corresponds to none of the contemporary subcultural expressions and thus in a way, it becomes irrelevant for purposes of inculturation. This has been a common failing in the past in Asia.

Culture also includes religion as one of its elements. Religion is the animating principle of a culture. Culture is like a body, with religion as its soul. The very possibility of inculturation supposes that this link, though organic, is not absolute. But still the link is intimate so that inculturation is not a mere translation but demands a reincarnation. Therefore, the gospel encountering a culture, necessarily encounters also a religion. This encounter can be open and formal in interreligious dialogue. It can be very indirect in encountering cultural forms which are not religiously neutral, because religion is one element, the most important, of the worldview which the culture expresses. Therefore the good and holy elements which the Gospel preserves in a new cultural synthesis will necessarily include religious ones, with a new significance, in a new context, as part of a new totality. This problem was not faced squarely in the past. Starting with Ricci and de Nobili, only those elements that could be shown to have a purely social and secular significance were adapted into Christian life. This attitude is still prevalent in Asia. It is shown, for instance, in slogans like "Indianization, but not Hinduization" that we often hear in India even today. This view of culture as merely secular and of other religious elements as objects to be avoided is not only inadequate, but unreal and untrue. Interreligious dialogue is an integral part of inculturation.

THE PROCESS OF INCULTURATION

Thinking narrowly of the proclamation of the Word, inculturation is spoken of as the adapted presentation of the Good News in a language and in symbols which can be intelligible to the people to whom the Good News is being proclaimed. Such a presentation is necessary. But inculturation is more than that. It is transformation of the life of a community of believers from within by which the Good News becomes the principle which animates their attitudes, worldview, value system and action — in short, their whole life. This inculturation is the very process of Christian living. From the ground of this authentic life will spring a new way of worship, a new way of theologizing and new patterns of relationships and behavior. Therefore, only an inculturated life — praxis, experience — can be the source of an inculturated spirituality, worship, theology and proclamation. The starting point and locus of inculturation is the community. It is in the context of its life that the encounter between the Gospel and culture takes place. The community's experience of its problems, its search for significance and relevance in life is the starting point. It is to this situation that the Good News is addressed. The community needs to interpret the Good News, reaching across the cultural forms of its proclamation and making it relevant to the situation here and now. Such interpretation leads to discernment, commitment and action. This moment of interpretation and involvement is the creative moment of inculturation. Once such a process of an authentic Christian living starts, it finds natural expression in symbol and celebration, in a worldview and way of life. The material for this expression does not come from a vacuum but it is the stuff of the life of the community. As history and life march on, inculturation also will be a dynamic continuing process.

It is also a constant process of death and resurrection. The community is constantly challenged by the Word to liberation through conversion. It has to die to itself, to its limited vision, inadequate attitudes and imperfect values and constantly strive towards a closer fidelity to the Gospel. As the seed dies in the ground before it germinates, the Gospel too remains true to itself and effective only insofar as it dies constantly to its limited historical expressions and becomes relevant to the life situation today through interpretation. The missionary must disappear in the manner of John the Baptist in order to free the Word from the bonds of the missionary's own culture so that it may act and transform, animate and create ever new and relevant forms.

In such a dynamic perspective, experimentation becomes necessary, normal and accepted, with all the uncertainty and possibility of failure that go with experimentation. Not to risk is to condemn oneself to safe immobility and to become quickly irrelevant.

It should be clear from all that I have been saying that the primary agent of inculturation is the living community. It is not the work of an elite or of the leadership who create a new culture in their laboratory, so to speak, and then communicate it to the people. Experts and leaders have a role of facilitation, certainly. But the active agents are the people. It is they who live and build up their future. It is they who relate their faith to life, creatively express it in spirituality and worship and proclaim it with their deeds as well as their words, provided they are not hindered from doing so by higher authority. But many recent attempts at inculturation in Asia have been the work of the specialists, resulting in various tensions, for example, in India.

The link between the idea of the living experience of the community being the starting point and locus of inculturation and the idea of basic ecclesial communities may be pointed out here. This link seems to be the only way to solve the problem of relevance and of coming to grips with the complexity of the cultural situation of any given community. Such linkage would avoid inculturation itself from becoming another alienating process.

AREAS OF INCULTURATION

In this section, I do not intend to offer an exhaustive list of areas which inculturation must transform. I wish only to highlight a few important ones: spirituality, worship, ministry, catechesis, theological reflection, culture and proclamation.

When we look at the Asian context in which the Gospel has to be proclaimed, two elements immediately stand out. These are its poverty and its religiosity. If the Gospel is not proclaimed as a Good News of liberation from poverty and oppression as well as a form of personal spiritual fulfillment, it will fall on deaf ears. The kingdom which the gospel proclaims and promises is a human community of fellowship and equality, of love and service, of justice and sharing (Rev. 21:3-4). It reaches this goal not only through a change of structures, but also through a conversion, both of individuals and groups, which leads them to growth, freedom and fulfillment. Just as the Church may find an ally in various secular movements in its pursuit of justice, it will find help and collaboration in the various spiritual traditions of Asia, their methods of prayer and psycho-physiological techniques (e.g., Yoga, Zen), and their symbols and rituals that give expression to popular religiosity, in its pursuit of self-realization.

Spirituality is a way of living one's faith in the world. Inculturated indigenous spiritualities will be differentiated—like the spiritualities of various religious orders—not by the human and Gospel values and attitudes common to all of them, but by variations in emphasis on particular values, in the use of techniques of prayer, in ascetical practices, in symbols and themes of popular piety, in sacred places and times. Such variations will emerge naturally from a close association and dialogue with indigenous spiritual tradition. Familiarity with Asian Scriptures that document the spiritual experience of peoples, with spiritual masters and their writings, and with the saints and their mystical outpourings in sacred songs must be promoted. These various sources could nourish our prayer and reflection. A guided initiation to and experimentation with various Asian methods of prayer and asceticism must be encouraged.

One area to which special attention should be paid in Asia is the development of a relevant spirituality for the people. The elite follow various spiritual traditions coming from the West. They also experiment with Asian spiritual resources and methods. But the common people are neglected. They follow a mixture of a minimum sacramental observance with popular devotions and various indigenous practices inherited from their past that do not lead them beyond a cultic level to a deeper Christian life. This shallowness is one of the principal obstacles to inculturation. People are attached to all sorts of externals and feel threatened by any change whatsoever. Their spiritual life, instead of being a source of dynamism and creativity, becomes a force for alienation and stagnation.

Worship is a celebration of significant moments in the life and growth of individuals and of the group as a whole by a community of believers. It is an expression of their faith and life in symbols—a ritual re-enactment of the mysteries that constitute the basis of their lives. In this area, a two-fold approach is needed. On the one hand, we have to discern the variable and invariable elements in the sacramental rituals of "divine institution" and create new forms of celebrations centered around the invariable elements.[1] On the other hand, we have to give a new Christian significance to seasonal and national festivals, and to the social celebrations of a people. In spite of the opening given to the development of radically new forms of worship by the Second Vatican Council,[2] most of what has been done so far in Asia has not gone beyond the externals of music, gesture and atmosphere. The leaders of the local church seem hesitant to lead; the experts feel that their initiatives are not encouraged, and the central role seems to be one of control favoring uniformity through translation. A certain elitist approach from above to inculturation in worship could also be one reason for the stalemate in this area.

An inculturation of ministerial and organizational structures is an indispensable part of any inculturation process. Yet this area has been neglected in Asia. Organizational structures are simply transplanted from evangelizing Churches without any attention to the local needs and situations. A Asian Colloquium on Ministries has made proposals within the existing framework but it has hesitated to pose radical questions, like married ministers in far-flung mission areas. Even the limited suggestions made at the colloquium have yet to be taken up at any level of the Church.

Catechesis is no longer seen as the transmission of a body of doctrine in an appropriate language. It is an initiation to values and attitudes, to a way of life, to a worldview, to characteristic patterns of behavior. It is a guided insertion into the ongoing dynamics of the life and problems of the community. The pedagogy will have to be experience-based. Its aim will be to guide the individual to a growing appropriation of faith, in freedom. It becomes the responsibility of the whole community. Nonformal methods of discipleship seem more suitable for this purpose than formal instruction, though this has its place too.

Theology is the element of reflection that guides interpretation and discernment in the process of inculturating the Gospel described above. Theology, ideally, is not an academic science. It is a reflection born of praxis. It will follow a dialectical method, the poles of the dialectic being experience on the one hand and the Christian perspective handed down in a living tradition on the other. It searches for the significance of the experience in the background of the plan of God for the world as revealed to us in Jesus Christ. It seeks to understand that Mystery in the context of the questions and problems raised by a relevant Christian life. In this way theology will become more a critical reflection, offering an ideology for involvement; it will be an inspiring vision. It will lead not only to transforming action, but to celebration. Such theology will not simply be a translation in a local language of eternal truths. It will not be merely a comparative study that reveals elements similar to Christian ones in other religions. It will not be limited to an appropriation of what are perceived as good and holy elements. It will be creative reflection born of the dialogue of faith with the life of a community in all its cultural and religious complexity.

In the Asian context, the pluralism of religions has provoked a serious reflection on the need and motive for evangelization and on the theology of religions. We have to go beyond this to develop a theology of pluralism itself. Though the need for development and liberation in most Asian countries has encouraged a theology of liberation, the specific Asian context in which non-violence, self-realization and renunciation are special values, suggests a theology of liberation for Asia different from the one developed by the Latin American Churches.[3] An inculturated theological reflection must necessarily be done in a local language. Language is not a neutral medium. It is a way of perceiving and speaking about the world. The use of a local language or medium in a wide sense involves also the use of local symbols and methods of reflection. This will also save theology from being a highly abstract technical science accessible only to an elite. Theology must become popular, relevant to the life of the community here and now.

The Good News needs to be proclaimed not only in a medium (language, symbols, etc.) that conveys the message effectively to the people. It must also appear relevant to their experience, problems and questions. Gandhi said that to a starving man, God comes in the form of bread. Thus to the oppressed, the Good News comes as a promise of liberation: whereas to the oppressor, it proclaims judgment. It calls everyone to conversion from selfishness to self-giving. In India, for example, can we proclaim a Good News that does not seek to liberate the hearer from the evils of caste and communalism or that does not give strength to fight against injustice and corruption?

In most countries in Asia today we have local churches. Hence the problem is not one of how to proclaim the Good News in a language and in a context that is foreign. The problem rather is how far the Gospel has been inculturated, become part of the people's life in a creative way so that their proclamation can be not only through words but by example, so that the Good News is seen not only as good in itself but relevant to today's situation.

The proclamation will also have to be wary of being overdependent on the mass media of communication which are controlled either by the state or by the rich and the powerful—and are often geared to create needs and to the diffusion of middle-class values. There is a growing awareness of the greater importance and impact of group media in making basic communities reflect and in challenging them to conversion.

One area from which the Churches in Asia are comparatively absent is that of culture. I am using the word here in its narrow sense to indicate the arts, the aesthetic and creative aspects of social groups, the recreational activities of leisure, the world of the imagination and the emotions. Where are the great Christian writers, artists, poets and musicians who are not only known among the Christians but who have made or are making an impact through their creative work at a national level? It is the creative people whether at the elite or at the popular level who create new symbols, channelize and propagate new values and attitudes, give a name and a form to new goals. A program of inculturation without a serious effort at cultural formation in this sense will reduce culture itself to a mere tool or a technique. The community will remain marginal in the country. This danger is particularly acute in countries where the Christian community is a small minority—such as it is in most Asian countries.

ATTITUDES FOR INCULTURATION

I do not intend to make a large list. I shall be satisfied with indicating four of the more important attitudes. These can be cultivated.

The first is mature freedom in the Spirit. This freedom is based on a deep faith rooted in the Lord, which does not seek easy security in laws, structures and institutions. It is open to the future. It is the source of self-confidence and identity which are essential for creativity. It is ready to take risks, correct mistakes and go out to the others in sincere openness and dialogue.

Secondly, acceptance of pluralism as a positive value is another necessary attitude. Uniformity is a cheap way to unity. The richness of the Good News demands to be explored and expressed in a variety of forms. This variety is not a mechanical multiplicity, rather, it is a source of enrichment. Where there is pluralism, there are bound to be tensions. Yet tensions can often be a source of growth if they are met with creative freedom.

Readiness to die in order to rise again is a third indispensable element of growth. Otherwise one becomes immobile and stagnant. But this demands great humility. This death, as I have pointed out above is demanded of every one: the Gospel as embodied in a particular tradition, the missionary coming from a foreign culture and the local community with its culture. A new creation will not be possible without death. Dying is a concrete way of total self-giving.

Finally, a sense of faith (sensus fidei) as a constitutive element of a living Christian community guides interpretations and discernment, evaluates experimentation and growth, identifies and checks possible abuses and promotes unity. It is not something that emerges out of mutual sharing and discussion in the light of a common commitment. Rather, it is a process, it is a sign that the Spirit is present in the church.

INCULTURATION AND THE TASKS OF THE CHURCHES

Inculturation is primarily the task of the local church. In the light of what I have said above, I can specify inculturation further by saying that it is the task of the basic communities. It is the task of the people. But they must be free to experiment, to create and even to make mistakes. The task of the leaders is to create this atmosphere of freedom and trust, and facilitate the emergence of the creative forces of the people. They also have a role of guidance and coordination. Inculturation cannot be imposed from above; it must be a process of growth from below. Therefore the function of the leaders is not to initiate and to enforce, but rather to direct and to coordinate. What is said today about conscientization and development can also be said about inculturation. The people at the grassroots are their own best agents of inculturation. The leaders can only play the role of catalyzers. Possible mistakes will be corrected by a "sensus fidei" of which the leaders remain the spokespersons under the guidance of the Spirit.

The role of the universal church is to promote intercultural dialogue and coordination in such a way that a variety of cultural expressions converge towards a unity in communion. The temptation to impose uniformity must be resisted. The autonomy of the local churches must be encouraged. There must be a decentralization of power. The unity aimed at must be a unity of faith, of mutual sharing and service, a unity of fellowship. Fraternal collaboration between local churches is to be encouraged but without detriment to the autonomy of the local church. Financial aid must be handled carefully so that it may not be detrimental to a creative autonomy or alienate the local church from its roots by promoting an artificial expansion based on foreign funds. Such fraternal collaboration must be had in an atmosphere of dialogue where one is ready to learn, open to new perspectives, prepared to receive as well as to give.

It is not for me here to elaborate on whether the local churches in Asia are aware of their responsibility and freedom. My own experience in India is that they do not seem to be thus aware. The past is still weighing heavily on them. There is insecurity, fear, resistance and suspicion. Are these truths also representative of other Asian churches?

One area that demands special attention is the formation of the leadership in the Church. If the formation in the seminaries is not inculturated and if the lay leaders are not formed to participate actively in the life of the community in all its aspects, inculturation will remain an unattainable ideal. How can the seminaries give an inculturated formation if the professors are all trained in Europe and America, in cultures and contexts quite foreign to their life and work? Cultural exchange and openness to the world are good. But they will benefit creatively only those who are already well rooted in their own culture.

CONCLUSION

If evangelization aims at building up local communities and churches which are alive to their situation, and involve themselves in the active realization of a new humanity, inculturation would just happen by itself. Any other way of inculturating the Gospel would be artificial and eventually alienating. To inculturate is therefore to build up an authentic, living local church.

The problem with most Asian churches is that they are local churches that still need to be inculturated. Inculturation then becomes doubly difficult and encounters psychological and sociological obstacles quite unconnected with the Gospel or the Church. I have indicated some of these in the first section. Yet if they do not wish to remain marginal as little foreign enclaves among their own people, they have no choice.

The most urgent task before the Church today is to create a climate where local churches can *feel* and *be* free and responsible for their own life in all its aspects. After centuries of a rigid uniformity, it will not be easy to do this. But without this climate, the local churches will not grow. Only when they grow, will the universal Church become really a communion of churches.

10

Modernity:
The Indian Experience

The experience of modernity in India is a complex one. The sources of this complexity are the rich and ancient culture of India which is reacting with the forces of modernity, sometimes in unpredictable ways, the colonial-postcolonial history that is coextensive with the history of modernization and the multireligious and a multicultural situation which contextualizes this modernity. But before I go into this Indian experience, I feel the need to discuss the phenomenon of modernity from my own point of view, because I find some of the usual presentations of it unsatisfactory.

The idea of "modernity" itself seems questionable, if it is taken as more than a convenient term to refer to a set of contemporary phenomena. To call ourselves modern with reference to all the past ages seems pretentious, because every age sees itself as "modern" compared to the previous ages. Anyway the term is widely accepted and I shall also use it, but in a value-neutral manner.

AMBIGUITIES OF MODERNITY

Modernity is characterized by the growth of science and technology. Science seeks to understand observable phenomena in terms of a cause-effect structure that makes possible prediction and control. Technology discovers not only the means of effecting such control, but also the means of production, by making use of the laws of nature. Productive technology gives rise to industrialization, sustained by the ability of amassing capital. Industrialization leads to urbanization resulting in a reorganization of social relationships. Another important aspect of modernity is the facility, rapidity and extent of communications. This may eventually be a more significant element of modernity than science and technology, because attempts to understand nature and efforts to use it for one's own needs are not new in human history.

All these elements of modernity are neutral in themselves. They can be used or abused. Science promotes a rational approach to life and reality. But one may be tempted by rationalism to deny transcendence and to believe that reason can explain everything. Technology can be used to fight disease, poverty and hunger through production and control. One might be tempted to a magical conviction that one can control everything and feel a sense of power. Industrialization can maximize production and satisfy needs. It can also create needs through advertisements, promote acquisitiveness and consumerism and be guided solely by efficiency and the profit-motive. Social mobility can facilitate personal development and freedom. It can also create an atmosphere of egoism and competition. Communication can cultivate relationships among peoples. It can also produce means of mass alienation and control. It is important to realize that there is an element of choice in every case. The use or abuse of modernity is a moral problem. People who have learned to assert their freedom in religious matters, for example, have become slaves to industrial and commercial structures before which they feel helpless. Yet they will live with, even defend, these structures as long as their consumer needs are not threatened.

In the field of religion, a crucial result of modernity is said to be secularization. The typically "modern" person has no room for the sacred in thought or life. Religion no longer provides the legitimation for socio-cultural and political institutions. Religion is no more the over-arching meaning system of life, but limits itself to ultimate concerns, while other areas of life and society have acquired their autonomy. S. S. Acquaviva, after discussing various surveys of religious practice in Europe, concludes:

> All that can be said with certainty is that the decline of the sacred is ultimately connected with the changes in society and human psychology. . . . There seems to be no place for a conception of God, or for a sense of the sacred, and ancient ways of giving significance to our own existence, or confronting life and death, are becoming increasingly untenable.[1]

THE THEORY OF SECULARIZATION CONTESTED

This thesis has been widely contested by sociologists.[2] Most people agree that in recent history, there has been a growing differentiation among social institutions and that religion no longer has the dominant role. There is also agreement that persons feel more free to choose, even in the field of religion, so that the religious institution (like other institutions like the family, etc.) does not have the same hold on people. But phenomena like the new religious movements seem to indicate that while the religious institution may have been affected, people have not become less religious.[3] On the contrary, the pressures of modern life on the one hand and the continuing relevance of questions like the meaning of suffering, of life and death, make

religion even more relevant and urgent.[4] Faith has never been the conclusion of an argument and while it may have become more personal, it is not
more difficult to believe today than in earlier ages.[5] Yet it is true that the
ideological and religious pluralism characteristic of modern society coupled
with the breakdown of traditional social structures have changed the conditions in which a person has to choose to believe. Faith is no longer
transmitted through socialization into a religious community. It has to be
proclaimed and be responded to in every generation. This task is further
complicated by the fact that pluralism tends to relativize particular religious
institutions.[6]

Even the reduction in the practice of religion seems to be a phenomenon
peculiar to Western Europe. Surveys in the United States of America,
which is as modern and developed as Europe, show that there has been no
significant variation in religious affiliation or practice. Michael Hout and
Andrew M. Greeley conclude a study on Church attendance in the USA
during the period 1940-1984 saying: "Contrary to the received wisdom in
the social sciences and the mass media, we could find no evidence for
religious secularization as measured by attendance at religious services in
the United States during the past half century."[7] Sociological studies have
also shown that even within Europe, the pattern of institutional differentiation varies widely according to the nature of the religious institutions
(Protestant or Catholic) and its place in the socio-political context(Church-
State).[8]

WHY IS EUROPE SECULARIZED?

These observations indicate that if Western Europe is "secularized," it
may be for reasons that are peculiar to Europe. I shall list here briefly these
reasons as seen by a non-European. First of all, there has been a philosophical tradition in Europe of positivism, empiricism, materialism and
rationalism that has grown side by side with science and technology and
has consistently denied transcendence.[9] This philosophical tradition is not
present in Asia, for instance. Even in the USA the dominant philosophical
tradition is pragmatist and utilitarian that could exist very well with puri-
tanism and liberal capitalism. The European philosophical traditions have
created such a pervasively secular intellectual atmosphere and a popular
disinclination to disagree with this culture of unbelief that many people
who have religious experiences are unwilling to talk about them. It is worth
inquiring how much this influence is a sort of intellectual climate and how
far it corresponds to the life and experience of the people. David Hay and
Ann Morisey, presenting a survey among adults in an industrial district in
England regarding possible experiences they have had that could be considered religious, conclude:

We would hypothesize that to chart the decline of the western religious institution as the one true indicator of secularization may be to

misrepresent what is going on. An alternative account, hinted at by our findings, is that religious interpretations of human experience are by no means disappearing. . . . Perhaps what we have been investigating is not so much "invisible" or "implicit" religion as religion "kept secret" in what is perceived as a hostile environment.[10]

Secondly, in Europe there is also a cultural tradition, inherited from Greece, of a dichotomy between the sacred and the secular, the natural and the supernatural. It is significant that theologians often counter this by using the more holistic approach to the person and the world which is characteristic of biblical anthropology. Rather than a harmonious relationship between the secular and the sacred that are articulated into a totality, to a tendency to subordinate the secular to the sacred is opposed the attempt to make the sacred immanent in the secular, not only secularizing the sacred, but eventually leading to atheism, since such a sacred is no longer needed.[11] This dichotomy can become a conflict when the sacred and the secular become institutionalized in the Church and the state, as two powers in society.[12] One consequence of this strong institutional aspect of the Church is that people who do not practice their religion are often anticlerical and anti-Church, rather than antitheistic. One does not see these conflicts in the USA, because from the beginning it is based on a clear differentiation between the Church and the state. However, the religiosity of the American people manifests itself in public life in a sort of "civil religion."[13] In a multireligious society religious affiliation and practice becomes an important source of identity in the community.[14]

What seems clear from this brief analysis is that secularization is not an automatic consequence of the modernity brought about by science and technology. Socio-cultural factors also play an important role in determining whether the people are ready to show themselves to be religious. This does not mean that modernity does not pose many and great challenges to faith today. But we have to look for them in individual and collective selfishness; the unrelenting pursuit of a good life that never says it has enough; in unbridled competition and consumerism and consequent risk of failure and despair; slavery to impersonal technocratic and commercial structures; a lack of social concern, which is shown particularly in the unjust exploitation and oppression of the poor and the alienated in society, many of whom take to destructive behavior, either towards others in violence or towards themselves in drugs. These are grave moral and religious problems. Concentration on secularization may mislead us into thinking that the main problem is at the level of consciousness and meaning (faith), rather than at the level of praxis (morality). The decreasing level of social awareness and concern for the other, as shown in voting patterns in western democracies, seem to be of more immediate concern than secularization. Helping people to a faith commitment in an atmosphere of pluralism is another challenge. The struggle today is not against atheism, but for inculturating the faith on the one hand and, on the other, for making the people see the relevance of the faith for and in their lives.

IS INDIA SECULARIZED?

Is India secularized as a consequence of the impact of modernity? If I say that it is not, people have a knowing smile as if to say: it will come; it is bound to come; of course, India is still developing, etc. On the contrary, I shall argue that available evidence indicates that India is not only not secularized, but that modernity has contributed to a revival and consolidation of religion. One of the reasons for this is certainly the cultural and religious tradition of India which is very different from that of Europe. However, this will not save India from the moral and religious problems that industrialization, urbanization, affluence and communications bring in their wake. These are the real challenges for evangelization in India today.

Let me first take the problem of secularization in India. A survey among scientists belonging to different religions working in four different urban centers in India has shown that over 80% have some sort of religious belief and at least occasionally practice their religion.[15] Another survey among peasants, who were being organized by Marxist parties for their struggle against their landlords, makes the surveyor conclude:

People's organization does not necessarily have a very secularizing effect on people even though the ideology under which they are organized may have an atheist bias. Most people tended to feel that their trust in the gods was either strengthened or not affected in the struggle; certainly it was not weakened.

There was a strong feeling of reliance on the gods in the people despite their consiousness of their own power to organize. . . . This reliance on the gods was also frequently interwoven with ritual precautions at critical points in life and with such practices as banning evil spirits and using horoscopes.

The gods are ambiguous, they bless and they punish. They send diseases and also rains, they protect or withhold blessings, they give reasons to celebrate. They do not seem to liberate people but neither do they stand in the way of liberation. . . . They may worship God in a certain form but their understanding of God also transcends this form. . . . The presence of God is very much experienced as the presence of energy in nature, in things and in people. . . . Since the presence of God is energy, it is only natural if most people feel their trust in God is not weakened through political organization but either strengthened or not affected, at least it is not usually weakened.[16]

This citation shows that even unlettered peasants can have a faith that transcends symbols and articulates the sacred and the secular without opposing one to the other. They could integrate into their praxis the Marxist class struggle while withstanding its atheism.

Another survey conducted in the southwest of India, which is one of India's more literate areas, but among the people at a popular religious level, indicates that 90% of the people are religious.[17] But among these one can distinguish two groups. While one group interprets religious symbols in a traditional way, the other group has not abandoned these symbols but tries to reinterpret them in the light of modern values like freedom, equality, justice, etc. The open structure of the Hindu religious system makes such reinterpretation possible.

> There are two types of Hindus in India. One type understands itself and its identity solely in terms of religious traditions of the past. The other understands itself not only in terms of traditional values but also in terms of the values of freedom, justice and equality which India has set for itself to build its future.[18]

> In the study of Hinduism as a symbol system of meaning with which Hindus envisage the essential pattern and the ultimate conditions of their existence, we cannot take a static and uniform view since manifestly their conception of "nature," "self" and "society" undergoes certain changes. This is especially important since Hindus never defined their religiosity by a definite set of core symbols and fixed meanings in order to institutionalize their collective religious heritage. The ordinary people are conscious of this freedom of thought they enjoy to assimilate new meanings and symbols from whatever sources as long as it strikes them as sensible, and they continue to affirm their identity as Hindus, as they are born Hindus.[19]

M. M. Thomas, making a special study of the secular ideologies of India in the recent decades, makes the following significant comment.

> India is following an "open secularism" in its idea of the State. And the Indian idea of the Secular State is reinforced by the many political and social ideologies which are "secular" in the sense that they begin their thinking on man and society, not from the reality of religion or God, but from the scientific study of empirical reality. Nevertheless they presuppose each in its own way, a framework or the search for a framework, of the meaning of human existence, and a sense of the Ultimate which undergirds it.[20]

Similarly, after an extensive study of the modernization of Indian tradition, Yogendra Singh maintains that modernization may take various forms in different societies according to the variety of cultural and social structures that it encounters in them.

As for modernization in India, we find a growing trend that traditional role-structures are giving way to modern ones. But persons following these roles often retain categorical values of tradition instead of those of modernity. We have mentioned how caste itself is adopting many functions which properly belong to rational corporate groups. Generally, ritual order and religion which are essentially based on categorical values of a traditional nature do not show evidence of decline, nor is there an easy possibility of their disappearance in the near future. Since many of these categorical values differ from one society to another, there may always be a possibility of unique combination of traditional values with modern ones; the categorical values can hardly be falsified by scientific proof and hence the spread of science may not *logically* lead to obsolescence of traditional categorical values.[21]

I think this distinction between categorical and instrumental values is an important one. Others have spoken about the pragmatic and transcendental aspects of religion.[22] One could also speak about religion as lived and religion as reflected on. At the pragmatic level, religion responds to the needs of people. At the transcendent level, religion offers meaning and motivation. Science can make inroads on religion at the pragmatic level. It can hardly touch the level of meaning or of "the plausibility structures," in the terms of Peter Berger,[23] without becoming an ideology or philosophy. At that level it is no longer scientific. The modern world may place before people a plurality of religious meaning systems or promote an ongoing reinterpretation of the existing meaning system in the light of new experience. It might offer substitute meaning systems in terms of ideologies. It cannot do away with a meaning system altogether.

In summary, my point is, whatever may be the case in Western Europe, the link between modernity and secularization is not a necessary one that is universally verified.[24] What, then, could be the reasons that India is able to resist the forces of secularization that many judge so formidable?

THE INDIAN TRADITION

For centuries India has articulated the relations between the sacred and the secular in a way that has avoided a conflict between them.[25] For example, the way the life of each person was structured aided in this. One spoke of the four goals of life: *Dharma* (righteousness), *Artha* (wealth), *Kama* (pleasure), and *Moksha* (ultimate fulfillment). Each had its appropriate time and stage in life. Similarly, each individual was to progress in life in four stages: *Brahmacharya* (student), *Grihasta* (householder), *Vanaprasta* (forest-dweller), *Sanyasi* (renouncer). The question is not how closely these structures were actually followed but to note that there was an ideal framework within which a variety of styles of life could find a place and a justification. Similarly, the framework of the caste system, distinguishing among the priests, rulers, traders and servants, imposed a differentiation of social institutions for a well-structured society.[26] It is unfortunate that this system became rigid, based on birth rather than function, making internal personal mobility impossible and consigning a quarter of the population beyond the pale of the system as untouchable. But this framework for the differentiation of social institutions enables India to respond to modernity in a different manner from that of Europe.

India also has a long tradition of secular trends which it had learned to integrate in the mainstream of tradition. Thus Buddhism and Jainism, which started in the 6th century B.C.E., were in a sense secular religions because they spoke about ethics and not about God. But after initial successes all over the country, they were largely absorbed in the main Hindu tradition. Contemporary secular movements in the Tamil country in South India are rediscovering ancient roots.

> There are autochthonous roots to a strong this-worldly orientation, as propounded by modern Tamil leaders and thinkers. The indigenous roots are to be found in three main currents of the Tamilian heritage: in the considerable stream of non-religious literature besides the devotional and cultic tradition, in Tamil Wisdom literature of the type represented by the Tirukkural and in side-branches and off-shoots of the Tamilian *bhakti* movement, especially in the Siddha tradition.[27]

For nearly six centuries, first Muslim and then British rulers had made sure that there was a clear differentiation between politics and religion. Side by side with the rigid social system of caste, Hinduism has promoted very strongly the ideal of personal development and fulfillment. At least at the ideological level, this promotion relativizes the social structures. Indian culture has also developed a holistic approach both to the human person and to the world. Rationalism and denial of transcendence has never been a significant philosophical trend, and contemporary atheistic ideologies have not had any real impact even on people who followed their political programs. Pluralism of cultures and religions and a tradition of tolerance is also characteristic of India.[28] Hinduism is not an organized institutional religion and it allows a lot of internal pluralism as we saw above. These may be some of the reasons why secularization, according to the European model, does not seem to be a problem in India. On the contrary, as Milton Singer writes:

> The effect of the mass media has not so much secularized the sacred traditional culture as it has democratized it. ... There is a kind of built-in flexibility within the orthodox Vedanta position which permits an easy incorporation of a wide variety of changes.[29]

The problem at the moment in India is not the decline of religion, but its becoming a political force in the form of communalism. Communalism pretends that people who share a common faith also share common economic and political interests, which are different from those of the believers of other religions.[30] Religion is then made use of as a cementing force of a group that is fighting for its economic and political interests. When religion acquires such a socially cohesive role, it also tends to get fundamentalist, sharply distinguishing itself from other religions. Language (culture), race and caste can become similar communal forces. The challenge for the Church in this situation is to show, on the one hand, that religion is relevant to politics and, on the other, that religion itself is not a political force. In a multireligious society like India, it can only do this by helping, in collaboration with the other religions, to build a secular state, which is open and positive to all religions, which encourages the religious education and motivation of its citizens, but which refuses to become denominational or a-religious. This is the option that has been made by the Indian Constitution.[31] This can be achieved only through interreligious dialogue which does not limit itself to a sharing of experiences, but devotes itself to a common commitment to developmental and liberating projects. I think it should be possible to move beyond the civil religion model of the USA to an inter-religious model.[32]

In this context, first of all, the Church has to project the image of a religious, spiritual group of people and not merely that of a philanthropic organization. Secondly, the Church needs to develop a national outlook that goes beyond the defense of Christian interests. It has, of course, to keep and defend its identity to be able to make its specific contribution. But it should not remain inward looking. Thirdly, the Church has to be and to be seen to be Indian. In India modernization has coexisted for some time with westernization during and after the British rule. While Indian society is becoming modernized, its culture has withstood the impact of the West, and it is rediscovering its identity.[33] Yet the Church and its institutions seem to give an impression in the popular mind of being Western. This impression could marginalize it in the ongoing national movement and be detrimental to the religious and spiritual impact the Church could and should have. In its own institutions, especially the social and the educational, it has a good opportunity to promote interreligious secular involvement.

A SPIRITUAL HUMANISM

A second challenge of modernity to the Church in India is the development of a spiritual humanism. This affirms on the one hand the priority of the human person over the machine. Human rights take precedence over industrial structures. People should not feel powerless in the face of industrialization which advances according to its own logic. Production is useful only insofar as it is for the profit of the human person. Industry is an instrument: it is not a social institution that can claim a certain autonomy vis-à-vis religion. One must be careful in applying the principle of the autonomy of the secular to the merely material. On the other hand, the human person is open to the transcendent. This is why I speak of a spiritual humanism. Hence a consumerism that does not look beyond the immediate present is not worthy of the human person. Consumerism, more than being an offense against the other, is first of all an offense against oneself. It is against the realization of all that is human in a personal fulfillment, by limiting itself to the animal level. The Church, with the other religions, has resources in the Bible as well as in the Indian Scriptures and spiritual tradition to promote such a spiritual humanism.[34] People such as Gandhi, Tagore and Nehru offer concrete models for contemporary times.

A SOCIAL SENSE

The individualism of modernity has to be countered by the development of a social sense—a feeling for the other. A modernity that is merely consumerist and based on the profit-motive can foster individual and collective egoism. Against this we have to promote a respect for all persons, their rights, and their development. At the same time, we also have to cultivate the sense of the common good. In a big country like India with its pluralism of cultures, regions, languages and religions, the community can only be a structured one. Hence one cannot exclude group identities. But these group identities must never be exclusive, but always inclusive. Besides we must deliberately cultivate a pluralist sense of belonging so that one and the same person will belong to different groups according to his language, work, residence, culture, religion, etc. Personal freedom and social participation must go together. An important challenge in this area is the caste system. It is changing under the impact of modernity so that caste groups are becoming political forces. Promotion of further social mobility and pluralism characteristic of modernity may be one way towards the slow eradication of the caste system. We also have to move towards a meaningful democracy. A mechanical democracy, based simply on individual franchise, may easily lead to the oppression of the minorities and the poor unless their protection is guaranteed by a constitutional structure. A democracy without morality can be very oppressive. That is why the general manner of functioning of democracies globally is today not very reassuring, since it seems to be more the expression of the collective selfishness of the middle class majority than a search for the common good.

Justice, then, must be an important concern of the Church in the face of modernity. Especially in a poor, developing country, on the one hand, the Church has to aid in the promotion of development by using all the scientific and technological resources available. On the other hand, it has to struggle on the side of the poor against the growing disparity between the rich and the poor. Otherwise, with production, exploitation also will become efficient and pervasive. This concern for justice will have to show itself also in working for a just international order. Communications may have made the world a global village, yet this phenomenon has also made the disparity between the rich and the poor nations more pronounced.

Increasing industrialization and urbanization and the consequent competition and mobility is breaking up the traditional structures in the village and the family. While this might permit the flowering of the individual person, it can also bring unbearable tensions and lead people to anomie, deviance, violence and drugs. It is not enough to care for these consequences without questioning the roots that give rise to such phenomena. In a society that is undergoing transformation, these may be liminal phenomena. There may also be the signs of alienation inevitable in a consumer society that has no place for authentic humanism, sense of community and transcendence. It is by urging and making present these values that the religions and the Church can play a role in the building up of society.

CONCLUSION

The challenges of modernity are similar everywhere, though the concrete forms they take differ according to variations in social, cultural and economic conditions. In meeting these challenges, the Church in India first of all must realize their particularity in India and not parrot analyses that may be valid elsewhere. The Church must also make full use of the riches of the Indian humanist, social and spiritual traditions. It must also meditate on and share with other believers the challenges and the inspiration of the Gospel. It should build up model communities which can be symbols, witnesses and sources of encouragement.[35]

I suggest that the problems of modernity concern not primarily belief but moral praxis. Consumerism should concern us much more than rationalism. Industrial and commercial structures are enslaving human persons; that should cause more preoccupation and response than science and technology. Misuses of the media, especially by the advertising industry, are the prime sources of alienation today. I am afraid that talk about secularization may tend to limit itself to world views, history and philosophy. The crucial question today is whether it is a secularized worldview that is causing moral deterioration resulting in large-scale injustice or whether wrong moral commitments are seeking justification in secularized worldviews. Obviously this need not be a conscious process. But it should be brought to the level of consciousness through reflection.

11

People as Promise

The new heaven and the new earth held up as objects of our hope in the book of Revelation is described as a happy community with whom God himself will be "at home."

Now God's home is with mankind! He will live with them, and they shall be his people. God himself will be with them, and he will be their God. He will wipe away all tears from their eyes. There will be no more death, no more grief or crying or pain. (Rev. 21:3-4).

What strikes one here is that the goal is not pictured in material, cosmic or physical terms. It is a vision of a people, of joy and fulfilment, of fellowship with God. The end of history is not an earthly paradise; it is a happy and contented nation.

GOD'S PLAN AND PROMISE

This accent on people as the promise is right in biblical tradition. Calling Abraham to leave his land and his people, the Lord promises, "I will give you many descendants, and they will become a great nation" (Gen. 12:2). The promise is repeated again when Abraham did not hesitate to sacrifice his son Isaac: "I promise that I will give you as many descendants as there are stars in the sky or grains of sand along the sea shore" (Gen. 22:17). Jacob hears the same promise: "Nations will be descended from you" (Gen. 35:11). God makes his covenant with a people: "The whole earth is mine, but you will be my chosen people, a people dedicated to me alone, and you will serve me as priests" (Exod. 19:5-6). The theme recurs again in the prophets. Just a sample from Isaiah: "The new Jerusalem I make will be full of joy, and her people will be happy" (Is. 65:18).

The images of the banquet and the Reign of God bring out vividly in symbolic terms this picture of a happy people. The banquet is a symbol of fellowship, joy and celebration. Jesus speaks of the Reign as a feast (Cf.

Lk. 14:15-24). He tells his disciples at their last supper: "I will never eat it until it is given its full meaning in the Reign of God" (Lk. 22:16) The Reign itself is a human reality, "because the Reign of God is within you" (Lk. 17:21).

Though the festive meal and the Reign are human and living realities, still they have something static about them. One could very well imagine something that descends from heaven ready-made: "The new Jerusalem, coming down out of heaven from God, prepared and ready, like a bride dressed to meet her husband" (Rev. 21:2). The Jews certainly were looking forward to a Reign of peace, joy and prosperity ushered in by a victorious king after a war of liberation.

But a number of other images used by Jesus with reference to the Reign offer a more dynamic perspective. Jesus speaks of a seed that grows into a big tree (Mt. 13:31-32), of a field that yields a rich harvest (Mt. 13:3-23), of a vine that produces fruit in abundance (Jn. 15:1-5). These images underline a number of interesting factors. The Reign is first of all something that is growing. It is a historical process. The happy community which is the object of the promise is not only an end; it is a goal towards which history is moving. Secondly, this growth is not quantitative, from the outside, like the growth in numbers of an organization, but qualitative and organic. The goal is a fulfilment. It is something sought after, achieved, created. It is not what one gets, but what one becomes, what one makes of oneself, whatever be the role of other supportive elements. The creative Spirit of God works from within. Set in the context of cosmic history, the mystery of God's plan, the promise takes concrete shape in bringing together all things with Christ as head.

All things are done according to God's plan and decision; and God chose us to be his own people in union with Christ because of his own purpose, based on what he had decided from the very beginning ... You also became God's people when you heard the true message, the Good News that brought you salvation. You believed in Christ, and God put his stamp of ownership on you by giving you the Holy Spirit he had promised. The Spirit is the guarantee that we shall receive what God has promised his people, and this assures us that God will give complete freedom to those who are his (Eph. 1:11,13-14).

The promise, then, is both a gift and a task. It is the work of the Spirit (Rom. 8:18-23). But the Spirit only frees our own inner energies, making it possible for them to grow unhindered. As Paul says: "I keep striving to win the prize for which Christ has already won me to himself" (Phil. 3:12).

From this brief look into the Bible, I wish to select three areas for further reflection: God's promise concerns people; the realization of this promise is a process of growth; the growth is not only a gift, but a creative task. Let me explore the implication of each of these three statements.

HUMANIZATION

Development is a much abused term today. Everyone speaks of it. One hears of developing countries or societies and developed nations. One often notices that a humanistic perspective is often lacking in this talk of development. One speaks of it in material, economic, social and political terms; one often forgets that all these are meaningful only with reference to people. Scientific progress is taking strides today. The people are not only delving deeper into the atom. Their mechanical arms reach out farther into the universe. Their control over nature is steadily expanding to the extent of posing a threat to the ecological balance of nature itself. But what is all this material development for? What meaning has it for people and their life on this planet? How does it contribute to the development of people, of the human community? Have people, instead, become the slaves of their machines? Will the power released by science be used to destroy rather than to construct the human community? What is the goal of scientific progress: humanization of matter or mechanization of the human?

It is not rare to see people speaking of development in terms of the growth of the gross national product or of the augmentation of the per capita income. Industrialization is considered a must. Factories are constructed. Commerce increases. Multinational corporations are built up. More and more goods are produced and distributed. Correspondingly, urban slums are multiplied; rural areas are impoverished; the gap between the rich and the poor keeps on widening. The miracle of economic growth occurs despite the misery of millions. Brazil is a good modern example. One cannot refrain from asking: at what cost economic growth? The production of more and more goods for whose benefit? Exploitation of natural resources for the enrichment of whom? Who benefits from the vast network of international trade? Has economic growth become an idol that has to be worshipped irrespective of its consequences?

The advance of civilization *is* helping "primitive" societies to modernize themselves. There is increasing urbanization. The school system is reaching out into the remote parts of the country. But urbanization has led to a breakdown of traditional social structures without replacing them, creating a sense of disorientation or anomie. Moral and value education has not kept pace with the literacy program. Culture has become marginal and elitist. People have lost their personalities to become numbers in an ever increasing amorphous mass.

In a competitive world, becoming increasingly smaller owing to modern means of communication, people feel the need for organizing themselves. But organizations have the tendency to transform themselves from instruments of service to centers of power. There is a progressive centralization that reaches out beyond national boundaries to the formation of power-blocs. Leadership is achieved through military might, not through moral authority.

Material, economic, social and political development should be at the service of human development. But as a matter of fact, they succeed in enslaving and dehumanizing persons. Instead of the people humanizing nature, they are themselves dehumanized. The economic, social and political elite seem to benefit from this situation. But actually they also become pawns in the power game. They are more slaves of the system than its masters.

God's promise of a community of love, of sharing, of joy, of freedom seems totally absent from this process. People have succeeded in the extraordinary task of enslaving themselves. Priorities have gotten mixed up. The first need, then, is to create an awareness that development has meaning and value only in relation to humanity. The world is for people. The human person is the center of the universe. Every advancement, in whatever sphere, must contribute to the building up of the human community. For this, moral development must go hand in hand with material development. When people lose sight of this goal, progress loses its purpose and direction.

FREEDOM

The Reign of God is like a seed. The seed is buried deep in the earth and it dies. But that death is the starting point of its life and growth. The growth is the manifestation of the living force it has and it takes place in a constant dialectic with the non-living material world that surrounds it. Only a totally hostile atmosphere can stifle its growth.

Every child is born into a world. It is hemmed in on every side by a variety of factors—familial, cultural, social, economic. None of these completely controls its growth. But it is in a constant interaction with these factors as it grows into mature manhood. The only obstacle that can stifle its growth is the denial of its freedom.

People—humanity—are also a seed. The happy community promised to them by God is something that they have to grow into. But this growth is a dialectical process. Humanity is not a plant in a glass house. It is in a world consisting of the material, economic, social and political structures that it has itself evolved. But the human spirit, in freedom, can transform them. It can change what it has created. (I speak, of course, of the new humanity, redeemed by Christ and energized by the Spirit). The many reform movements and liberation struggles that ornament the history of every people are enduring witnesses to this hope. The power of people to realize their full humanity as people in spite of and in the midst of the shackles of *karma* and *maya* is axiomatic in Indian tradition. From Buddha to Gandhi through Nanak and Kabir, Indian history is a string of liberation movements from the various bonds that keep human creativity enslaved.

If the pictures of humanity marching towards its ultimate freedom and fulfillment do not look very bright today, one reason is that the social and structural dimensions of the problem have not been fully realized. People often worked for the personal freedom of themselves and of others. This led them to opt out of the structures rather than work to transform them, perceiving freedom as purely personal and interior. Today, however, there is a growing awareness of the global dimensions of the problem and the need to face it publicly as a global community.

The term global may be taken in two senses. Geographically, no isolated freedom movements would be effective today. Humanly speaking, the battle for freedom should be fought at all levels: material, economic, social, and political. One can also add religion to this list, for when it loses its Spirit of freedom the religious dimension, too, can become oppressive law.

Where there is freedom and a clear vision of the goal, everything can become a factor for growth. Scientific progress can enable people to use leisure for creation. The media of communication can promote awareness rather than diffuse propaganda. Goods can not only be produced in abundance, but be shared and distributed equitably. Human communities can be built up on the basis of love and service rather than fear and power. Communication can promote global unity rather than facilitate exploitation. Thus people's creativity and inventiveness can be put to positive ends of building a happy human community.

CREATIVITY

This leads me to my third observation. The true image of the new person is not the worker, but the creator. There may have been a period when to work and to create were the same thing. But it is not so today, except in a few cases of artistic production. Both may involve the same type of physical and/or mental effort. Yet they are different kinds of experiences. Work corresponds to a need that has to be met and produces goods. Creation is life, gratuitous: it has no purpose beyond the act itself. Work is painful and is undergone as an unavoidable drudgery. Creation is an experience of joy and harmony. Work is repetitive. Each creative act is unique. Work, while it is not necessarily dehumanizing as in many forms of industrial labor, is still alienating. Creation humanizes nature, imprints the personality of the creator on matter, imposes order and harmony on a divided world. Work isolates. Creation promotes communion through self-expression; it is a celebration. Machines can replace people at the work bench. Creation is typically a human activity. Work handles and shapes the clay of life. Creation breathes into it the Spirit.

While work produces the innumerable structures that constantly enslave humans, creation breaks out of those structures. Without the creative activity of people, the world would be a drab prison by now. Work provides human subsistence; creation gives meaning to human life, and makes it worth living. While work repeats the cycle of nature, creation provides the substance of history.

The noblest aspect of the creative spirit in people is the creation of relationships and of community. The deepest creative activity is to love. Here we have the interplay of two freedoms and converging creative movements. There is a dialogue of joy and of discovery. This is perhaps the most challenging type of creation that people are called upon to undertake, imitating, in the process, the creative interplay of the Father, Son and Spirit.

Human persons are historical beings, not only because they live in history. People do not merely subsist in space and time. The animals do it too. They make history. Their future is what they make it. Work has a finality: it produces something. Creation is play: it recreates an experience; its purpose is made of the stuff of freedom. While working one *does* something; while creating one simply *is* — oneself.

To be oneself, to live, one does not need any special knowledge, or technique, or resources. To love, to sing, to dance, to be spontaneous in self-expression, to celebrate is part of human life. Even the poor have their song and dance, their stories and humor, their celebrations and festivals. They probably have a more ready smile on their lips and find more joy in the simple things of life than their sophisticated rich neighbors who are burdened with mental and emotional problems. Creativity is not only for the elite; it is possible for all. Festivals, holy days and pilgrimages and *rites de passage* bring masses of people together in a common, joyful and creative affirmation of life and humanity, of love and fellowship. It is a bourgeois society that has made of art the obscure language of an alienated elite and has imposed on the masses, through the communications media, a mechanized "democratic" culture.

Making people human is to free them for celebrative affirmation of life; it is to minimize work and to maximize creative interaction among peoples. It is in this perspective that we must place the growing dialogue between cultures, religions and peoples. The culmination of this movement of creation cannot be foreseen: it is an object of hope (cf. Rom. 8:24).

CONCLUSION

In the past we have fought for freedom to create for the individual or for a class. Today we must promote the freedom of all peoples. The new world cannot simply be the work of an elite. The masses must be liberated. They can and will create their world of love and life, of joy and fellowship. Only they can change the world.

Christ is the new human person whose creative Spirit brings freedom. "God's Spirit joins himself to our spirits to declare that we are God's children. Since we are his children, we will possess the blessings he keeps for his people" (Rom. 8:16-17). It is our ministry to announce this good news (1 Pet. 2:9) and to give account of the hope that is in us (1 Pet. 3:15). To make people free to create is our service to the world. That is the way God has chosen to make real his promise of a new heaven and a new earth. "Now I make all things new" (Rev. 21:5).

12

Evangelization and Ecumenism

"To ask the world to unite in a common humanity centered in Jesus Christ is flabby advice," says Robert McAfee Brown, "when those making the request are not even able to unite themselves."[1] The scandal of disunity among Christians is nowhere more evident than in the missions where the Churches, all of them claiming to proclaim the Good News of salvation in Jesus Christ, speak in a multiplicity of voices and often act in a competitive spirit.

CHANGES IN UNDERSTANDING MISSION

Missionary Coordination and the Birth of Ecumenism

The missionaries, goaded on by the zealous young leaders of the Student Christian Movement, were the first to feel the need for coordination among themselves. With the aim of achieving this, a world missionary conference was called at Edinburgh in 1910. Though the gathering was not the first of its kind, historians hail the event as the birth of the modern ecumenical movement. Not only did this meeting speak about collaboration among missionaries; it also sought to give collaboration institutional voice and shape. It formed a continuation committee which, after years of effort, paved the way for the International Missionary Council (IMC). The IMC was constituted in 1921. It set itself the goals of stimulating thinking and investigation on missionary questions and making the results available to all missionary societies, of helping to coordinate the activities of the national missionary organizations and bringing about united action where necessary in missionary matters. National Christian Councils were formed.[2]

The younger Churches of Asia were particularly active in this movement towards collaboration. It concerned them directly. Besides, confessional differences often seemed to them to be impositions from abroad.[3] Their commitment was to Christ and to his Good News. They were not heirs to a history of disagreement and division. Doctrinal differences, often couched in a language and in cultural forms foreign to them, seemed much less acute. This has given rise to reunion movements at a local level. In my own country, the Church of South India was constituted in 1947 and the Church of North India in 1970.

Though the Edinburgh conference wisely decided to confine its attention to practical matters, it was an assembly of missionary societies rather than of churches. It gave rise to two complementary movements. Those who felt that cooperation need not be confined to mission lands but could also take place in the older churches, founded the "Life and Work" movement with the slogan "doctrine divides, service unites."[4] Others realized that we cannot live and work together without bringing up, sometime or other, doctrinal issues. These founded the "Faith and Order" movement.[5] As progress was made along these lines, an organization bringing together the churches was felt to be imperative and so the World Council of Churches (WCC) was founded "to do whatever we can do together."[6]

We see how the ecumenical movement owes its origin to the exigencies of evangelization. This intimate connection between ecumenism and mission was further demonstrated when the IMC merged with the WCC in 1961, at the latter's third assembly in New Delhi.

Missionary Cooperation and the Roman Catholic Church

The Roman Catholic Church did not form part of this history. Recognizing in herself the only true Church of Christ, her evangelical work was directed to other Christians as much as to members of other religions. The Octave of Prayer for Christian Unity meant, for many, praying for the return of the stray sheep into the true fold. Even when there was a slow thaw in this climate, there was no attempt at any sort of collaboration in the missions: error had no right to propagate itself. In this atmosphere of caution, the Second Vatican Council represents a definite turning point.

The Vatican II Decree on Ecumenism exhorts all Christians:

> Before the whole world, let all Christians profess their faith in God, one and three, in the incarnate Son of God, our Redeemer and Lord. United in their efforts, and with mutual respect, let them bear witness to our common home, which does not play us false.

This common witnessing, however, is restricted immediately to "cooperation in social matters" in this decree.

> Cooperation among all Christians vividly expresses that bond which already unites them, and it sets in clearer relief the features of Christ the Servant. Such cooperation, which has already begun in many countries, should be ever increasingly developed, particularly in regions where a social and technical revolution is taking place. It should con-

tribute to a just appreciation of the dignity of the human person, the promotion of the blessings of peace, the application of gospel principles to social life, and the advancement of the arts and sciences in a Christian spirit.[7]

This cooperation is not something specifically Christian since "all men, without exception, are summoned to united effort." But the call to Christians is more insistent and meaningful.

The Vatican II Decree on Missionary Activity takes us a little further on the road to ecumenical cooperation in mission. An important declaration of principle brings out the close connection that exists between ecumenism and evangelization.

... the division among Christians damages the most holy cause of preaching the gospel to every creature and blocks the way to the faith for many. Hence, by the same mandate which makes missions necessary, all the baptized are called to be gathered into one flock, and thus to be able to bear unanimous witness before the nations to Christ their Lord. And if they are not yet capable of bearing full witness to the same faith, they should at least be animated by mutual esteem and love.[8]

Taken in isolation, this text may not take us much further than the Decree on Ecumenism. The scandal of disunity in the mission is recognized. But a common witness seems to be considered a thing of the future, when unity would have been achieved. The real intention of the Council Fathers is, however, specified later. Speaking of the instruction and training to be imparted to the neophytes in the question of ecumenism, the Second Vatican Council says:

The ecumenical spirit too should be nurtured in the neophytes. They should rightly consider that the brethren who believe in Christ are Christ's disciples, reborn in baptism, sharers with the People of God in very many riches. Insofar as religious conditions allow, ecumenical activity should be furthered in such a way that without any appearance of indifference or of unwarranted intermingling on the one hand, or of unhealthy rivalry on the other, Catholics can cooperate in a brotherly spirit with their separated brethren according to the norms of the Decree on Ecumenism.

To the extent that their beliefs are common, they can make before the nations a common profession of faith in God and in Jesus Christ. They can collaborate in social and in technical projects as well as in cultural and religious ones. Let them work together especially for the sake of Christ, their common Lord. Let His Name be the bond that unites them. This cooperation should be undertaken not only among private persons, but also, according to the judgement of the local Ordinary, among Churches or ecclesial communities and their enterprises.[9]

Let us first note that ecumenism is not considered dangerous in the missions. There is no attempt to shield the neophytes from the danger of indifference. There is no desire to bolster up their self-confidence and self-identity as Christians by refusing to accept that other Christians are also Christ's disciples. The Decree on Ecumenism had only said timidly that "all proclaim themselves to be disciples of the Lord."[10] Indifference remains a danger and has to be guarded against. But this danger need not paralyze us or goad us into competitive self-assertion. On the contrary, there must be cooperation in a brotherly spirit.

This cooperation need not be restricted to social and technical projects but can include cultural and religious ones. A common profession of faith is possible and should be made. The source and motive for this cooperation is not any practical convenience; it is Christ the Common Lord who gathers together his disciples. For the first time the Roman Catholic Church in council recognizes that the partners in this collaboration are not merely the separated brethren as individuals, but churches and ecclesial communities.

In the planning of missionary activities, the Sacred Congregation for the Evangelization of Peoples is told to "search out ways and means for bringing about and directing fraternal cooperation as well as harmonious living with the missionary undertakings of other Christian communities."[11] We note the special mention of "harmonious living." Ecumenical cooperation in the mission is not merely an "operational adjustment" in view of deploying the available meager resources in the best possible way. There must be communion in life that seeks to "remove, as far as possible, the scandal of division." St. Paul tells the Galatians:

> You are, all of you, sons of God through faith in Christ Jesus. All baptized in Christ, you have all clothed yourselves in Christ, there are no more distinctions between Jew and Greek, slave and free, male and female, but all of you are one in Christ Jesus (Gal. 3: 26-28).

Witnessing to this Good News of unity and peace is bound to be less effective if the witnesses are not able to proclaim it with one voice. But this communion in life should not remain merely an interdenominational phenomenon. It must characterize the missionary undertakings. Harmonious living is more than fraternal cooperation; it implies active sharing of personnel and resources. This should be the object of a positive effort, something to be sought after, not just tolerated when it is inevitable.

The WCC Calls for Common Witness

The Third Assembly of the WCC at New Delhi in 1961 "urges the Churches to seek together in each place the help of the Holy Spirit in order that they may receive power to be together Christ's obedient witnesses to their neighbors and to the nations."[12] It also launched a movement named Joint Action for Mission (JAM). The characterization of this movement by the Fourth Assembly at Uppsala is enlightening.

It is difficult to describe just when JAM takes place for, more than a methodology, it is a way of being and acting in mission together. It goes beyond cooperation, although cooperation is essential before JAM. It moves towards unity but unity does not necessarily mean that there will be JAM. In its essence it means that the Churches in any given area look together at the state of God's mission in this area and determine together where the crucial frontiers are. Then in a spirit of self-sacrifice and self-denial, they agree to the redeployment of available resources in personnel and funds to meet the new needs.[13]

May we draw the readers' attention to the phrases "beyond cooperation" and "God's mission."

Joint Commission on Common Witness

In May 1970, a Joint Theological Commission consisting of Roman Catholic and WCC representatives prepared a study document on *Common Witness and Proselytism.*[14] After specifying that the basis and source of the common witness of the churches "is given in Christ", the document lists the different areas where cooperation is possible. The churches are called upon to "cooperate with God in deploying his gifts for the reconciliation of all men and all things in Christ" wherever men are in need of help. Some areas of such social concern are: the "development of the whole man and of all men," the defense of human rights and the promotion of religious freedom, the promotion of peace and justice, health and other social services. Cooperation is also possible in the "production, publication and distribution of joint translations of the Scriptures." The preparation of a common text which could serve as the basis for an initial catechesis on the central message of the Christian faith is possible. Common prayer and common worship for each other and for the world are on the increase. Therefore the inability to celebrate the Eucharist together as *the* sign and manifestation of unity in the one sacrifice is all the more keenly felt. Then the document speaks about common witness.

The central task of the Churches is simply to proclaim the saving deeds of God. This then should be the burden of their common witness; and what unites them is enough to enable them in large measure to speak as one. Indeed all forms of common witness are signs of the Churches' commitment to proclaim the Gospel to all men; they all find in the one Gospel their motivation, their purpose and their content.

Whether in witness or service, the Churches are together confronted by the fundamental issues of the nature and destinies of men and nations; and while they face these questions they encounter men of other religions, or men who are indifferent or unbelievers who hold to a variety of ideologies. But at this vital point of mutual engagement, the Churches become aware not only of their shared understanding of the Gospel but also of their differences.[15]

The document then goes on to list the differences. All Christians believe that Jesus Christ has founded one church, and one alone. Yet today many Christian communions present themselves as the true heritage of Jesus Christ. In the context of religious freedom, such convictions have to be respected. But they reduce the possibilities of common witness. Agreement on the major affirmations of the faith based on the scriptures and early tradition could coexist with differences in interpretation. Cooperation in social concerns can also be limited by differences in the solutions offered to moral problems: for example, those concerning family ethics: divorce, abortion, responsible parenthood. Rivalries and enmities of the past and the resentment they have caused may also present obstacles to cooperation. A spirit of mutual forgiveness and openness to correction can however surmount these obstacles.

Pope Paul VI's *Evangelii Nuntiandi* in 1975, though it devoted a paragraph to the theme (No.77) and thus underlined the need for unity for effective witnessing, did not really say anything new. *Mission and Evangelism—An Ecumenical Affirmation* marks a new step in the awareness of the churches for their common witness. After recognizing their common call to proclaim Jesus, the churches spell out their common perception of Christian mission. Mission is a call to conversion, addressed both to individuals and to groups and nations. The lordship of Christ is to be proclaimed to all realms of life. Common witness should be the consequence of the unity of the churches with Christ in his mission. This is a challenge to unity among the churches. Mission leads to the planting of the church in different cultures, which however should not be detrimental to its basic unity. Christ is the model for doing mission. This is seen particularly in the proclamation of the Good News to the poor. Today, mission is in and to six continents. Everywhere the churches are in missionary situations. Respect for the freedom of others will lead us to dialogue with them, especially with those of other living faiths, facilitating in this manner a collaboration to be communities of freedom, peace and mutual respect: "This ecumenical affirmation is a challenge which the Churches extend to each other to announce that God reigns, and that there is hope for a future when God will 'unite all things in him, things in heaven and things on earth' (Eph. 1:10).[16]

MISSIONARY COOPERATION IN INDIA

The great majority of the missionaries in India, not to speak of the ordinary Christians, might understand the need for collaboration in social and developmental projects. The need and urgency for common witness may not be obvious to them. It might seem, on the contrary, dangerous. Is it not significant that in the Declaration of the Nagpur Theological Conference on Evangelization, even the word "ecumenism" is completely absent? We do not find it either in the index of the collection of the Nagpur papers.[17] The National Consultation in Patna did better; it had a workshop on ecumenism. But what it says is still woefully inadequate, even if it reflects the general sentiment among the missionaries in the country. India has not yet caught up with the Second Vatican Council. The Patna Declaration (in numbers 83-84) realizes that Christian disunity is an obstacle to evangelization and that unity must be fostered through self-renewal and shared prayer. It has this to say on cooperation:

> Ecumenical collaboration in the fields of health services, education and social works can powerfully promote deeper fellowship. . . . Some Churches have made remarkably good use of the media of social communication, like the press, radio and cinema. More united efforts are recommended in these fields, particularly in the distribution of the Sacred Scriptures and in promoting the study of and meditation on the Word of God.

Ecumenism is spoken of under the section on "Obstacles to Evangelization." Christian disunity is perceived as an obstacle to be removed. There is no hint of any positive evaluation of the role of ecumenism in mission. Within this atmosphere, one is not surprised to read in the report of the workshop on Evangelization and Ecumenism, "It was also stated that reunion with the Catholic church on the part of Orthodox and Protestants had slackened off because of ecumenism." Almost ten years after the Decree on Ecumenism of the Second Vatican Council and in the light of the developments since then, this attitude is shocking. *Ad Gentes* spoke of "unanimous witness," "common profession of faith," "fraternal cooperation in missionary undertakings" and "harmonious living." These attitudes, obviously, are not yet shared by the Church in India.

Precept and Practice

Fortunately our practice of ecumenism is a little better than what our ideology would suggest. The presence of members of other denominations either as observers or as full members in the conferences and seminars organized by the churches is becoming more frequent. Sometimes conferences, especially in the line of dialogue with members of other religions, are even organized in collaboration.

The All-India Seminar on Ecumenism which took place in Bangalore in December 1970 declared: "In a country where the majority are non-Christians, it is urgent and imperative for all Christians to bury their differences and bear a united witness to Jesus Christ."[18]

No concrete proposals, however, were made except in the socio-economic field and for the joint diffusion of the Scriptures. In July 1973 a Coordinating Body of the Catholic Bishops' Conference of India, the National Christian Council of India and the Orthodox church was formed at a meeting of representatives of the churches in Bangalore. The statement adopted by the meeting stated that Christian unity was a precondition for truly effective witness and service.

Obstacles

Among the many obstacles that stand in the way of our commitment to common witnessing, I will speak here of three that are more fundamental than others. These are an overly ecclesial interpretation of mission, a fear of the danger of indifferentism, and a too narrow understanding of the meaning and purpose of evangelization.

No common witnessing is really possible till all Christians realize that our mission is not our own but only the manifestation and actualization of the mission of Christ. Salvation is a gift of God and Jesus Christ is the only mediator. It is Christ who announces the Good News of salvation in and through the witnessing and serving community. The churches fulfill a ministerial function in this proclamation which is addressed by Christ to the whole world. The Spirit is active in the world unto the realization of the plan of God in Jesus Christ for the liberating and re-creative unification of the world. The primary purpose of evangelization is to make disciples of Christ, not to increase the membership of the churches.

We must first of all, therefore, realize the relativity of the ministry of the Church in relation to Christ's mission. The church or the missionary is only an instrument in God's hands. As St. Paul wrote to the Corinthians:

> After all, what is Apollos and what is Paul? They are servants who brought the faith to you. Even the different ways in which they brought it were assigned to them by the Lord. I did the planting, Apollos did the watering, but God made things grow. Neither the planter nor the waterer matters: only God, who makes things grow. It is all one who does the planting and who does the watering, and each will duly be paid according to his share in the work. We are

fellow workers with God; you are God's farm, God's building (1 Cor. 3:5-9).

A missionary must always keep in mind this vertical dimension of mission. It is Christ who saves, who brings together, who renders the mission fruitful.

Jesus Christ wanted the church, which he sent on its mission, to be one. He wanted this unity to be an element, a sign in their witness:

> I pray not only for these, but for those also who through their words will believe in me. May they all be one. Father, may they be one in us, as you are in me and I am in you, so that the world may believe it was you who sent me (John 17:20-21).

But in fact the church is divided. The nature of the relationship of these churches between themselves and with regard to the one church of Christ is a complex question.[19] But the mission given by Christ to the disciples to be his witnesses in the world is one in which all the baptized share. It is a common responsibility. It is common, not because they all belong to one visible community. It is common because all confess one and the same Jesus Christ as Lord before the whole world. They base their faith on the same Scriptures and their Christian life is nourished by the same Spirit. They share the same sonship of Christ as adopted children of the Father. In the context of this common responsibility, no single church can claim the exclusive privilege of being the sole witness to Christ.

God's Word is addressed to all people. It is present to every one. "The Word was the true light that enlightens all" (John 1:9). Its unifying and liberating mission embraces the whole universe (cf. Col. 1:20; Eph. 1:3-4). The mission of the Church, however, is actually limited in space and time. The Church is for the whole world and all people. But it is effectively witnessing only in certain areas where it is actively present. Its activity does not exhaust the action of Christ and the Spirit. While the Church proclaims and makes present the saving Word of God, it has no claim to an exclusive mediation. This situation, of course, raises the question, what then is specific to the mission of the Church? The Church and the missionary have to answer this question to their satisfaction if their mission is not to appear to them meaningless. But we shall not enter into it here. We shall be satisfied with pointing out how this truth relativizes to a certain extent the mission of the Church in relation to the mission of Christ.

In the light of these few remarks, we may say that no single church can exclusivistically identify its own mission with the mission of Christ. Secondly, no one church can claim to mediate the totality of the mission given by Christ to the baptized. Within the totality of the mission, one or another church might claim a special position in accordance with what she thinks of her own nature. But most churches, the Roman Catholic Church and the churches and ecclesial communities who are members of the WCC, agree that they have a common mission in which all share. This is made clear to us by the documents I have cited in the first part.[20]

Unfortunately this consensus does not today include a number of evangelical groups, who seem to proselytize among other Christians, especially in Latin America. These groups are not open to dialogue and local churches seem uncertain about the ways of handling this problem. Independent churches in Africa and new religious movements that claim a certain Christian parentage pose a different type of challenge. While dialogue with them may be difficult, they do provoke us to examine ourselves and see why the traditional churches are not meeting adequately certain real needs of the people which these newer groups seem to meet. A study by the Pontifical Councils for Interreligious Dialogue and Ecumenism confessed:

> Very few people seem to join a sect for evil reasons. Perhaps the greatest opportunity of the sects is to attract good people and good motivation in those people. In fact, they usually succeed best when society or Church have failed to touch good motivation.[21]

The document goes on to list a number needs and aspirations that "are seemingly not being met in mainline Churches." The recognition of real needs and good motivation is certainly a call to respect and dialogue.

The idea of common sharing, however, does not say everything. The community of Christians is divided. Its basic unity in Christ is overlaid by differences in doctrine and practice. Each church, naturally, claims to transmit most faithfully the Good News of Jesus Christ, without denying that the other churches also bear witness to the same Word, though in an imperfect manner from their point of view. Each church presents itself as the true heritage of Jesus Christ. It would be insincere if it were to do otherwise. But this real difference cannot mask the fact that among themselves and especially before the world, the unity of the churches in Christ is more basic than the factors which divide them. And this fact cannot be left out of the witnessing. The basic unity as well as the diversity must be stressed in the proclamation.

Common Witness and Indifferentism

This leads us to a second point. In any program of common witness, the danger of indifferentism can be real. An unskillful presentation of the fact of unity in diversity in Christian witnessing can lead to a spirit of relativism which either overlooks or downgrades the differences. But the solution is not to simplify a complex reality and to present the faith as if disunity did not exist.[22] The Second Vatican Council does well to remind us that ecumenism must be nurtured even in neophytes. It is not a secret doctrine reserved for mature Christians who can take it and from which those still young in their faith must be shielded. What is needed is not simplification, but fuller information. Only in the context of a complete witness, can common witness avoid the danger of indifferentism.

This complexity of Christian witnessing, however, does lead to difficulties of a practical nature. Witness leads to faith and faith normally leads to Baptism (Matt. 28:19). Baptism is not only rebirth in the Spirit and sharing in the filiation of Christ. It is also incorporation into a community of believers—a church. To which church will those who are converted by common witnessing be aggregated? This question cannot be solved in the abstract, simply in terms of principles. The factors of the actual situation should be taken into consideration.

In the first place, common witness does not mean that witness is done jointly from beginning to end, including the catechesis which is part of initiation. Common witness can be given only about the basic points on which one agrees. This area of agreement and, therefore, of common witnessing might vary according to the churches who are partners in the project. The community of witness will be in function of the unity they have achieved. While cooperation is possible in the fields of overall human development, the distribution of the Bible, basic proclamation of the Good News especially through the mass media and an introductory catechesis, as the neophytes advance in their inquiry and express a desire for membership in the Christian community, the churches will have to go on their own. Spatial and personal factors as well as doctrinal factors may intervene at this stage. The liberty of the neophyte to choose under the guidance of the Holy Spirit should be respected.[23] No one can be forced, overtly or covertly, into a church. Secondly, common witnessing does not mean impersonal witnessing. The Word of God does not come to people as a system of truths to be intellectually examined and accepted. It is made present and concrete to them through historical events. This is the incarnational economy. Hence personality factors come into play. A neophyte might decide to join one church rather than another because of the person through whom he heard the Good News or to whom he is attracted. The reason may be personal; it may be accidental. The choice of a church might also depend on which church is most visible, present and active in a geographical, cultural or human area.

A spirit of openness and tolerance is only possible and, perhaps, justifiable where denominational divisions are seen as being only provisional insofar as there is an active ecumenical movement for regaining unity. In this atmosphere of mutual respect and active convergence, denominational affiliations, while important, become secondary in relation to the basic adherence to Christ which faith in Him implies.

Ecumenism, then, is part of evangelization, no longer in the old sense of "converting the heretics and schismatics" and of bringing them into the true fold. Whatever be the special role we might assign to our own church in the realization of the divine plan for the unity of the Body of Christ, this unity is still to be achieved. We do not know what form this unity is going to take. We can only move forward under the guidance of the Spirit. Such a sentiment will help us to avoid absolutizing everything associated with an individual Church's traditions and will enable us to distinguish the essential from the accidental, the central from the peripheral, the unchangeable from the changeable.

Evangelization Is Wider than Planting of the Church

A third difficulty that one might have against a common witness is a narrow understanding of evangelization. The Decree on Missionary Activity of the Second Vatican Council (in article 6) declared the specific purpose of the Church's missionary activity to be "evangelization and the planting of the Church." Many would prefer to identify both purposes. Evangelization, however, is wider than planting of the church, though the former might lead to the latter.

The Church mediates God's self-communication to humans in Jesus Christ. God's self-communication means a new being and a new life for people in a new world. It is a new creation. It is not only for individuals, but also for social groups, cultures and civilizations. It is not only for a person's soul; it is for the whole person and for all that is human, in and through which one expresses oneself. It is for the whole creation which is for the sake of the humanity. This new human person, new heaven and new earth are not merely for the next world. They are also for this world. The Church, then, is not simply a body of men and women seeking new adherents. It is a force for the transformation of the world working from within as it were, like leaven, through word and life.

The building up of the Church is not just a question of baptizing a certain number of persons. It is incarnating the Church in a new culture. Besides, making new members is only one aspect of her mission. The other aspect of making Christ present to a human group and of mediating his mission may be accomplished in a thousand different ways, individual or collective, through silent witness or vigorous protest.

If we understand evangelization in this way, we see at once what a wide field there is — as wide as the world — where the churches can act together, and bear witness to the liberating force of the Good News in word and deed in the social, political, cultural and religious spheres. No activity that can represent a value of the Gospel need be excluded. Much of the difficulties arising from the factor of disunity would be present only in the case of activities directly oriented to the planting of the church.

Evangelization Aids Ecumenism

If ecumenism is a must for evangelization to be effective, then it is also true that effective evangelization can be a sure force for ecumenism. Evangelization is a slow transformation of people and their world. Collaborating in such a work, the churches soon see how often they agree on solutions to social and cultural problems. Face to face with the world in their effort to dialogue with other religions and cultures, they would realize how united they really are. Then misgivings and wrong notions begin to disappear. Their common effort to incarnate themselves in a local culture might dispel a number of historically and culturally conditioned divisive factors. The effort to find a new expression is really an effort to differentiate the essential from the accidental, the meaning from the forms that express it, the intentions from the structures which embody them.

CONCLUSION

The goal of evangelization, as it is for ecumenism, is implementing and furthering the plan of the God who wishes to "bring everything together under Christ, as head, everything in the heavens and everything on earth" (Eph. 1:10). The work is God's. But our narrowness and selfishness place obstacles in God's way. The first requirement is one of conversion—conversion from absolutizing *my* church to serving the plan of God—and spiritual renewal. Then we must keep our heart open and be docile to the inspirations of the Spirit.[24] Reading the signs of the times, we have an opportunity "together to make a unity in the work of service, building up the body of Christ. In this way we are all to come to unity in our faith and in our knowledge of the Son of God, until we become perfect, fully mature with the fullness of Christ himself" (Eph. 4:12-13).

13

The Laity and the Church
in Mission

When mission was thought of as happening in foreign lands making present the institutional Church in places where it did not yet exist, the missionaries had to be primarily priests, helped by religious. These persons were needed to care for the churches, schools and other institutions put up in the mission. But today we are conscious that the whole Church is in mission and that mission is everywhere the Gospel has to be made present to people who need its challenge. In such a situation the lay people too can be part of God's mission. The implications of this for the lay people can be fully understood only when we have a clearer idea of the place and role of lay people in the Church. At the risk of simplification, I would like to focus on three areas.

The dignity and mission of the laity are usually based on their baptismal priesthood. The field of their apostolic action is identified as the secular world. Their specific place in the Church is articulated in terms of the charisms that differentiate roles in a hierarchical community. While we easily acknowledge the positive thrust of these affirmations, it is the implied exclusions that cause us concern. The baptismal priesthood is opposed to the sacramental priesthood from which it is different not only in degree but in kind. In a hierarchical context this seems to imply an inferior status for the laity in the Church. The secular world is opposed to the sacred which by implication is the field of activity of the clergy as opposed to the laity. An ecclesiology while being holistic may be inward looking, more preoccupied with status and roles than with collaboration in view of mission. In the following pages, I propose to take a fresh look on some of these basic principles. It would hopefully lead us to new insights, thus enriching our view of the vocation and mission of the laity in the church and in the world.

THE COMMON VOCATION AND DIGNITY OF THE PEOPLE OF GOD

The sacrament of baptism is seen as the root of the dignity and mission of the laity. In baptism, all the people of God participate in the priesthood of Jesus with its threefold prophetic, cultic and pastoral functions. One recalls the text of St. Peter: "You are a chosen race, a royal priesthood, a holy nation" (1 Peter 2:9). This dignity is common to all the baptized and prior to the diversification of charisms and ministries. But the problem is that this diversification is often seen today in hierarchical terms. The Catholic laity find themselves canonically at the lowest rung of a ladder that leads upwards through lay ministers who are "set apart" in virtue of a charism for the service of the community, the consecrated laity or religious who try to live the perfection of their baptismal vows, the priests whose priesthood is different not only in degree but in kind, the bishops who have the fullness of priesthood. Is this differentiation a functional articulation of an apostolic body in view of mission or is it an order of dignity?

According to competent exegetes, the text from the First Letter of St. Peter that we referred to above does not speak about the individual Christian but of the whole Christian community of which a person who is baptized becomes a member. Albert Vanhoye has written:

> The communication of the priesthood to the Church as a whole, as a "priestly organism," reveals a characteristic aspect of the mediation of Christ ... Christ is not, in fact, an external mediator between mankind and God, who would endeavour by his good offices to re-establish a proper understanding between the two parties. He is the one who, in his own person, has brought about the complete union between mankind and God, for the benefit of all mankind. For this reason the priesthood of Christ is fundamentally open to participation. Whoever is faithful to Christ is associated with his priesthood, for he finds in Christ an immediate relationship with God ... The priesthood of Christ was not achieved in a ceremony, but in an event, the offering of his very life. The priesthood of the Church does not consist in carrying out ceremonies, but in transforming actual existence by opening it up to the action of the Holy Spirit and to the impulse of divine love ... When the priestly people unites itself through a life of love with the action of Christ's offering, it releases a dynamic of love which spreads throughout the world and progressively transforms it.[1]

The whole community is the new people of God, the sacrament of God's Reign, the Temple that God is building up in history, of which Christ is the cornerstone (1 Peter 2:4–5). They participate in the priestly task of

Jesus, the only mediator, who is transforming the world into God's King-dom. This participation is their dignity and is common to the clergy and the laity. Within this totality, the clergy are but the servants—ministers—of this mystery. When the community gathers in worship, it is the whole community united with Christ—the Mystical Body of Christ, head and members—that worships. Within the priestly community, the ordained min-ister is a sign and is given a special gift of grace in view of ministerial function, not as a person. At ordination, one is not reborn in the same way as when one was baptized. The functional nature of the sacramental grace appears clearly if we remember the traditional phrase: "Whether it is Peter or Judas who baptizes, it is Christ who baptizes." One could add: Christ, head and members, that is, the Church. The ordained minister has author-ity. It is not given as power over others, but for service, as a leadership function that does not set one apart or above the community but is exercised in communion with the community. A hierarchy in function is not neces-sarily a hierarchy in dignity or significance. Every person is unique in the plan of God. Every person is called to play his or her role in building up the the Reign of God. Since God's Reign embraces every type of cosmic and human reality and every type of activity, every role is an integral, essential role in the Reign. Every person is to be judged for his or her faithfulness in fulfilling his or her role. An "objective" comparison is irrel-evant from this point of view. A religious is called to be a symbolic witness to some values of the Reign; an ordained minister is called to a role of leadership in the community; a lay person is called to be a politician or a worker or a scientist: each vocation is the manifestation of the charism which is God's gift to each one and he or she will be judged by his or her faithfulness to that vocation.

In the eucharist, which is the summit and center of Christian life, the ordained minister has a necessary ministerial role. But it is the action of the whole Mystical Body of Christ, head and members. The minister is a sign of Christ's headship of the community: but in such a way that Christ's headship is not replaced, nor mediated, nor sacramentalized by the min-ister. Christ is very much present and active and the Mystical Body is active with him. There are internal differentiations: but these are precisely inter-nal and integral to the totality of the celebration.

THE CLERGY AND THE LAITY

It is in this context that it may be good to avoid the term "priesthood" in talking about the laity because of the ambiguities of its meaning. The term has a cultic connotation in common usage. Because of this, the ordained minister becomes the first analogue and the laity are reduced to second-class status inevitably, though perhaps unconsciously. One should rather talk in terms of the Reign of God, the call of all Christians to be witnesses to it and to build it up among themselves and in the world, of the diversity and complementarity of charisms, and of the need for each one to be faithful to his or her call. In this totality, it is easier to understand the dignity and mission of the people of God as a whole than the precise role that the ministers play within the community and the way they relate to it. We cannot talk in vertical terms because the ordained ministers do not come in between Christ and the community. We cannot use horizontal terms because they are not the mere representatives of the people. The distinction between the people of God and the ordained ministers is not an adequate one because they are part of the people. The people do not receive their identity or mission from the ministers but from God, Father, Son and Spirit. As Vanhoye points out:

> The absence of all reference to presbyters in 1 Peter 2,4-5 shows that the priesthood of the Church is not based on their ministry; its basis is elsewhere and the text indicates this: it is Christ, in the mystery of his passion and resurrection.[2]

It is in this holistic perspective that we must look at the questions concerning the relationship of the laity to the ordained ministers with regard to their mission. In virtue of one's membership in the people of God, each one has a charism and a vocation. The recognition of this charism by the community is a natural process: by their fruits they will be known — it is a natural outcome of their witness. This recognition does not even need to be verbalized or publicly expressed. A formal recognition becomes necessary only when a person with a special charism serves the community not only in one's own name but in the name of the community, as somehow representing the community. Then the person is given a ministry by the appropriate authority acting in the name of the community. For special kinds of services, such a ministry might require the sacrament of orders. But we could also have non-ordained ministers. I think it is better to restrict the term ministry to such services that are done in the name of the community. Such a recognition also implies an authentication of the charism. Another form of recognition is seen when a group of people attempting to give expression to a particular type of charism is authenticated. Such group authentication can have many forms. In a simple way it may guarantee that a particular path pursued in common by a group corresponds to the perfection of Christian life. Another form would be when the group sets itself apart symbolically through religious vows in community as a witness of Christian life to the others. A third manner would be when such setting apart also involves a call to a particular type of service to the community. In all these cases there is a formal delegation or mission on the part of church authority only when there is a ministry or a service in the name of the community. Ministry of this type involves an official function in the community. While such ministries are inevitable in any institutionalized community, it would be a mistake to think of every service in the community as a ministry. Sometimes one speaks of the various ways in which a Christian may be called to live out his charism and mission as states of life. They do have a certain public identity which specifies their inter-relationships. But it is not helpful to think of these states as if they were ontological attributes of persons or to rank them as more or less perfect.

THE SACRED AND THE SECULAR

It is in trying to further specify the role of the laity that one often sees the use of the phrase "the secular world." This phrase supposes a twofold contrast between the Church and the world and the sacred and the secular. Sometimes one speaks of the temporal, opposing it probably to spiritual or eternal. At the institutional level, the Church and the world may be confronting each other, the one acting on the other. But Christians cannot be seen as representing the Church facing the world, unless they have offices in the Church and so belong to the institution. An ordinary Christian belongs at one and the same time to the Church and to the world. Even for the officials, the distinction is not absolute, but only relative and of the institutional order. As institutions—that is to say, public, social and structured realities—they have their autonomy. This autonomy is even strengthened today by the differentiation among institutions that seem to characterize the modern process of secularization. This is seen for instance in the varying relationships between the Church and the state according to variations both in space and in time. But an ordinary Christian, who does not hold an office either in the Church or in the state, cannot dichotomize his belongingness to these two realities in the same manner. He has to integrate them in his life where they relate to each other as religion and society: religion providing the motivation, inspiration and orientation from an ultimate perspective and society embracing the socio-economic, political and cultural levels of existence in which this ultimate perspective should find realization and fulfillment. Both the clergy and the laity live this double belongingness. It could become a problem for the clergy and even for the laity if they represent the Church as an institution in an official capacity: they cannot then also be involved as officials in the public institutions of the world, especially the state, without causing confusion and tension. Therefore what determines the extent of involvement of the Christian in the world is not whether one belongs to the clergy or the laity, but whether one has an official, representative role in the Church. Obviously this role may be more or less central in the institution and it would qualify the mode of involvement too. Today, for instance, if we think of lay ministers, we have a group of lay people who have a representative role in the church and therefore whose role in politics, for instance, will be limited. According to current understanding, an ordained minister has a representative role in the Church. Jurisdiction is normally linked to order. But we have in practice a variety of situations. There are ordained ministers who also have an institutional responsibility or office in the Church like diocesan bishops and parish pastors. Some ordained ministers do not have an office in the Church: but they are involved full-time in scientific research, in education, in developmental work or in spiritual ministry. We speak of hyphenated priests like priest-workers. The role of presidency that these exercise during a sacramental celebration need not involve the same official status and obligations as those of a parish pastor. Further articulations in this area are possible in the future. On the other hand we may have, in the future, non-ordained ministers who will have a full-time responsibility in the Church and play roles of leadership. In such a complex situation, it would be difficult to think of the clergy and laity as being somehow co-terminous with the Church and the world, respectively.

The contrast between the sacred and the secular is even more problem-atic. While current practice does not encourage ordained ministers in polit-ical office, every other area of the world is open to their activity: I have just mentioned the hyphenated priests. On the other hand, a lay person is not simply a secular figure. Not only have they integrated the sacred in their secular life and work; they are full participants in the sacred activity of the eucharist, with all that this implies. Today lay ministers seem to be taking up more representative roles within the Church-community. To speak of secularity as the special or primary characteristic of lay activity and spirituality seems to be quite inadequate. I do not mean to say that in contemporary society all distinctions between the Church and the state, religion and politics, faith and culture, economic and social structures have disappeared. On the contrary, secularization may even have radicalized some of these differences to the detriment of the totality. No one person is equally involved at the same time in every field of activity; specialization is also one of the traits of modernity. But special competence, involvement, or even leadership in one field should not isolate specialists from the others, especially because all fields mutually influence one another. All fields of activity could be open to every one in various ways according to each one's charism. There seems no need to exclude the clergy from the world. On the contrary, their prophetic presence may be very necessary calling them to witness and to proclaim not only by words, but even more by example. One cannot exclude the laity from the Church either: they also are the Church. On the other hand, sacred and secular are theological constructs, rooted in reality, indicative of an aspect or of a sphere of life and activity but not directly translatable in concrete, institutional terms. Yet, this is what we often keep doing.

The situation becomes more complex if we think of the Church in the multireligious societies of Asia. Our neat distinctions between the Church and the world would not easily apply here, because the Church is but one among the many religions. In the context of interreligious dialogue and collaboration in the promotion of common human and spiritual values, the Christian can still witness to his faith convictions, but can hardly claim to be the only or even the privileged promoter of these values. There is indeed a rightful distinction between religion and society. But it would not correspond to the distinction between the Church and the world. The non-Church is not merely the secular world, it is also the sphere of other religions. Our talk about the Church and the world often ignores this factor. It has been said, I think with truth, that the Vatican II Document on the Church in the Modern World has no theology of religions.[3] Religions did not figure in its neat contrast between the church and the world. Such neat contrasts may help clarity of thought. But we should not be surprised if they are not adequate to account for the full concrete reality of the contemporary world.

FOCUSING ON THE KINGDOM

We need then a twofold corrective to our way of talking about the laity. On the one hand, rather than look at the laity from the perspective of a worldview that we have worked out in the abstract, we can join them where they are and try to understand the complexity of their experiences as people who have to integrate in their personal lives a variety of elements, sacred and secular, ecclesial and worldly, and do that in a very pluralistic context. On the other hand, we could also revise our perspective into a more holistic one. I think that the element that could provide such a total view is the Reign of God. The reality of the Reign integrates the Church and the world, the sacred and the secular, Christianity and other religions. The vision of the Reign renews the awareness of the Church as a pilgrim, which has not yet fully incarnated the Reign in itself, but which still has a mission to witness to it and promote it, while acknowledging its presence and action in mysterious ways outside its boundaries. This twofold limitation would induce an attitude of listening, dialogue and collaboration. The vision of the Reign would also transcend, while integrating, the sacred and the secular. There is no activity in the world that does not in some way contribute to building up the Reign since the promotion of justice is now recognized to be an integral part of evangelization. From the point of view of the Reign, there is nothing merely secular any more. Sacred and secular may be easy labels to describe certain fields of life and activity. But what is important is the call to build up God's Reign whatever be the field of one's life and activity. In the light of the Reign of God even the secular becomes the sacred.

The focus on the Reign would also help us to think more about the mission of the Church than about its internal structures in talking about the laity. When we do have to talk about the internal structures, we would do so in the light of mission. For the moment, talk about the internal structures is bound to be concerned with the rights and the duties of the clergy and the laity within the Church and with participation and collaboration. This situation is not going to change unless we have rethought the identity and role in the community, not so much of the laity, but of the ordained minister. Talk about the secular world as the sphere of action of the laity may implicitly reserve the sacred sphere of the Church to the clergy. Such thinking does not correspond to the contemporary awareness of the Church as the People of God and as a communion. One of the reasons for not giving the laity their proper place in the Church is probably the exaggerated place claimed by the clergy, often for historical reasons. We may not be able to discover the identity and mission of the laity without, at the same time, discovering the true place and role of the clergy in the Church and its mission.

CONCLUSION

A reflection on the laity which remains intra-ecclesial, with the Church separated from the world, even if one searches for a total ecclesiology, would be very inadequate. The laity is then identified internally as non-ordained minister and characterized extrinsically by secularity. Speaking about the Church as a communion or as a family may help to soften the internal tensions a little without in any way solving them. Realizing the priestly character of the whole people of God, one would understand more clearly the ministerial role of the ordained ministry. Focusing on the mission of the whole Church would relativize, without ignoring, the internal differentiations and structure, inevitable in any organism. The stress on the Reign of God would make us transcend the easy dichotomies between the Church and the world, the sacred and the secular and understand better the mission of a pilgrim Church in a pluralistic situation. An appreciation of and respect for each one's vocation would enable us to avoid complexes of superiority and inferiority based on roles and status on the one hand and, on the other, consider positively and inclusively every type of life and work the People of God are engaged in, in the context of the Reign of God.

14

Collaboration in Mission

Is there a crisis of the missions? Many factors of the present situation seem to indicate there is. A more positive appreciation of other religions seems to reduce the urgency of proclamation. A broadened view of mission seems to discourage the specific task of building the Church. The crisis of secularization has brought the mission to our door steps so that the "foreign missions" seems no longer urgent. The growing responsibility of the local churches seem to have led the missionary institutes to a crisis of identity. Vocations in general and missionary vocations in particular are on the decline. One can multiply reasons that seem to indicate that there is indeed a crisis of the missions. On the other hand, the younger churches seem to be enthusiastic in evoking a "new age" in mission.[1] In such a complex situation, we can speak about the relevance of the missions only after we have explored the changes both in the way we understand mission today and the situation in which we have to evangelize.

A NEW VISION OF MISSION

Before the Second Vatican Council, missions referred to countries where the Church was not yet fully present. Establishing the Church was the aim of the missionaries who left their homeland to work in the missions. But the effort to find a theological basis for mission at the Council changed this clear view of the missions. *Ad Gentes*, 2 speaks of mission, not in territorial, but in Trinitarian and Christological terms:

> The Church on earth is by its very nature missionary since, according to the plan of the Father, it had its origin in the mission of the Son and the Holy Spirit. This plan flows from "fountain-like love," the love of God the Father.

It goes on then to say what is mission.

Its aim is to open up for all men a free and sure path to full participation in the mystery of Christ (AG, 5).

This task . . . is one and the same everywhere and in all situations,
although, because of circumstances, it may not always be exercised in
the same way. The differences which must be recognized in this activity of the Church, do not flow from the inner nature of the mission
itself, but from the circumstances in which it is exercised (AG, 6).

We see here an effort to distinguish "mission" from the "missions." After
this initial broadened view the document goes on to restrict missionary
activity to the missions as it says: "The special end of this missionary activity
is the evangelization and the implanting of the Church among people or
groups in which it has not yet taken root." Commentators such as H. Godin,
who, in the 1940s, wondered whether France itself had become a mission
country, foresaw that the broader concept of mission would eventually pre-
vail.[2] That was exactly what happened almost within a decade at the Synod
of Bishops on Evangelization. The passage from the word mission to "evangelization" is itself significant. In the post-synodal document *Evangelii
Nuntiandi,* 17, Paul VI proposes a new way of looking at things.

Evangelization has been defined as consisting in the proclamation of
Christ our Lord to those who do not know him, in preaching, catechesis, baptism and the administration of the other sacraments. But
no such defective and incomplete definition can be accepted for that
complex, rich and dynamic reality which is called evangelization without the risk of weakening or even distorting its real meaning.

Pope Paul goes on to observe: "Evangelization means the carrying forth
of the good news to every sector of the human race so that by its strength
it may enter into the hearts of men and renew the human race." It is within
this broad context that Paul VI situates what he calls "first proclamation,"
which is directed primarily to those who have never heard the Good News
of Jesus, but also to the children and to the dechristianized (cf. articles 52–
53).

This development can be traced back theologically to certain perspectives which emerged at the Second Vatican Council itself, especially in On
the Church, On the Church in the Modern World, and On the Other
Religions. One could point to three of these perspectives. The first is the
unity and universality of God's plan for the world being realized in Jesus
Christ, which reaches out in the power of the Spirit to all human beings
and leads them in various ways to the ultimate fulfillment of the Kingdom.[3]

The second is the role of the Church as the sacrament of this Kingdom
in the world, both as its symbolic first fruits and as its servant through word
and witness.[4] The Church is not to be identified with the Kingdom. The
focus of proclamation is the promotion of the Kingdom and is not narrowed

down to *plantatio ecclesiae*. The building up of a local church whose very existence and mission is to be at the service of the Kingdom, transforming the world as leaven, is an essential though not an exclusive element of building up the Kingdom. It is essential because of the incarnational economy. It is not exclusive because the action of the Spirit is not restricted to the mediation of the Church-community.[5]

The third perspective is the dialectic between Gospel and culture so that the very being of the Church is ordained to the transformation of the world.[6] All these perspectives have been further developed in the years after the Council. Rather than trace this development, we shall see the new vision of mission that they give rise to.

AN INTEGRAL VIEW

The new vision of evangelization is an integral one. It emerges out of the context of the local Church in which the good news is being announced, in an incarnational perspective. Proclamation is not made in the abstract, but is linked to a specific situation and a specific moment in history. "It is God's Good News contrasted with the bad news of that specific situation."[7] The bishops of Asia, for instance, identifying the specific characteristics of their situation as poverty, religious pluralism and a rich cultural heritage, see evangelization as a dialogue with these realities of Asia. They speak of

a Church in continuous humble and loving dialogue with the living traditions, the cultures, the religions — in brief, with all the live realities of the people in whose midst it has sunk its roots deeply and whose history and life it gladly makes its own.[8]

Evangelization as inculturation, dialogue and liberation has almost become the leitmotif of mission congresses in recent times.[9] These are not three separate activities; however, they constitute but one mutually involving action which is evangelization and proclamation of the Kingdom.

The Gospel values cannot really transform a culture in a multireligious situation without entering into dialogue with the other religions which also animate that culture and without challenging the unjust structures to which the culture gives rise, as, for example, the caste system in India. One cannot liberate the poor from all that oppresses them if one does not succeed in transforming the worldview and the value system of the whole population with the help also of the other religions, challenging them to be prophetic and not legitimizing the status quo.

Interreligious dialogue would be meaningless if it remained simply an exchange of religious experiences that did not lead to a mutual collaboration towards a transformation of culture and the liberation of the poor. Although inculturation, liberation and dialogue are different types of activities, each with its own goals and canons of adequacy, they converge on liberation of human beings in community. Otherwise, they run the risk of alienating their participants from the lived life of their communities. When they do converge, they can become three integral dimensions of the one activity—evangelization—because the Christian community is making present, through word and witness, the new perspectives and challenges of Jesus Christ according to the context it faces.

The task of evangelization is universal in its outreach. The root of this universality is of course the plan of God who wishes to reconcile all things in Christ (Eph. 1:3-14). Today this universality acquires a new significance. The Ecumenical Affirmation on Mission and Evangelism speaks of "mission in and to six continents."

> Everywhere the Churches are in missionary situations. Even in countries where the Churches have been active for centuries we see life organized today without reference to Christian values, a growth of secularism understood as the absence of any final meaning. The Churches have lost vital contact with the workers and the youth and many others ... The movement of migrants and political refugees brings the missionary frontier to the doorstep of every parish (art. 37).

To the universality of this task corresponds also a universality of responsibility, because the church is mission: "For the whole world and for every part of it, it is the Church which has the responsibility of spreading the Gospel."[10]

THE LOCAL CHURCH

The Church which is responsible for this universal mission is a communion of local Churches. The Extraordinary Synod of Bishops of 1985 clarifies this:

> The unique and universal Church is truly present in all the particular Churches, and these are formed in the image of the universal Church in such a way that the one and unique Catholic Church exists in and through the particular Churches.[11]

The universal, catholic church is therefore a reality that arises from below, so to speak, because the full reality of the church is realized in every local church and the universal Church is the mutual reception and communion of local churches.[12] The universality of the Church does not primarily refer to its geographical extension throughout the world but is the dynamism of the plan of God—the "Mystery" of St. Paul—which recapitulates all things in Christ. The Word has to become incarnate in every culture and take it through the paschal process of death and resurrection. Thus each culture contributes to the catholic richness of the self-expression of the Word. To say that evangelization is the collective responsibility of the universal Church is to say that it is the responsibility of every local church for its own mission and its concern for the mission of all other local Churches. The International Mission Congress of Manila spells this out.

> What is the newness of this "new age of mission"? First, the realization in practice that "mission" is no longer, and can no longer be, a one-way movement from the "older Churches" to the "younger Churches," from the Churches of the old Christendom to the Churches in the colonial lands. Now—as Vatican II already affirmed with all clarity and force—every local Church *is* and cannot but be missionary. Every local Church is "sent" by Christ and the Father to bring the Gospel to its surrounding milieux, and to bear it also into all the world. For every local Church this is a *primary task*. Hence we are moving beyond both the vocabulary and the idea of "sending Churches" and "receiving Churches," for as living communities of the one Church of Jesus Christ, every local Church must be a sending Church and every local Church (because it is not on earth ever a total realization of the Church) must also be a receiving Church. Every local Church must be responsible for its mission, and co-responsible for the mission of all its sister-Churches.[13]

The Church is not primarily an organization. It is a group of people, a community that, inspired by the Spirit, listens to the Word and responds in acts of faith, hope and love—that is, in affirmation, celebration and service. The Word, of course, comes to them not in an ahistorical purity, but embodied in the response of another community that is different from it either in space or in time (the previous generation). It is a challenge to the freedom of the hearers and to the socio-cultural situation which it comes to transform. The response of the community to the Word—embodied in the Church—becomes integral to history and to the world which this community constructs for itself by symbolizing and humanizing the reality in which it lives. This is how the Church becomes mission to the world. What makes this process less unique than one might imagine is precisely that this ecclesiogenesis is a permanent process—a continuing process—in every Church. That is why mission is everywhere.

From the cultural point of view, the universal Church as a communion of local churches can be seen not only as a coexistence of many local churches each one embodying the Word in its cultural milieu, but also as a convergent movement towards a community in which each local church is not only challenged by the Word but by the various embodiments of the Word in all the other cultures. A concrete way in which this mutual challenge takes place is precisely through the presence in every local church of people and communities belonging to other local churches.[14]

FOREIGN MISSION

This concern for each local church for the mission of all the other local churches may be concretized by particular persons and institutes that the Holy Spirit calls forth especially for this purpose. They symbolize but do not replace what must be a concern of the whole Church.[15] They are the "foreign missionaries." Given the importance of the local church both as the place and the agent of evangelization, foreign (*ad extra*) can only mean from outside the local church.

Mission *ad extra* must be distinguished from mission *ad gentes* understood as proclaiming the Good News to people who have not yet had a chance to hear it, either in one's own local church or in another. One could move from one local church to another to be simply at the service of another church and bring a dimension of the universality of the Church as well as to make present the challenges of the riches of the Gospel as appropriated and lived by one's own culture. This would also be evangelization *ad extra*. It is possible that within a local church, first proclamation is directed to a particular ethnic, linguistic, or subcultural group. In so far as this is happening within the same local church, one could hardly speak of it as mission *ad extra*.

The urgency and need of the mission *ad extra* as one dimension of the mission *ad gentes* would depend on one's appreciation regarding the presence of the Church everywhere. At a meeting of Divine Word Missionaries in Asia it was recently said: "Today, Christians might be a tiny minority in some places but the Church has been established everywhere."[16] If this is so, numbers and percentages that might urge a greater commitment to mission *ad gentes* need not necessarily demand the same urgency with regard to the mission *ad extra*, especially irrespective of the desires of the local church and the situation of the country.

THE SOCIO-POLITICAL CONTEXT OF FOREIGN MISSION

In the wider context of mission today, mission *ad extra* cannot be a purely religious project. When we cross national boundaries, whatever may be our intentions, we will have to take serious account of cultural, political, and national factors, not as exterior to the project, but as an integral part of it.

We are living in a postcolonial era. In the former colonies, church extension is associated in the popular mind with colonialism. They certainly coincided historically and at that time the new churches were not really built up as authentic local churches. A certain assertion of autonomy on the part of the local churches is not without connection to this past. The other believers look on the Church with suspicion as something foreign and alien. Even its efforts at inculturation are suspected as subterfuges.

A related problem is the political reaction to the project of evangelization. Seen either as liberation or option for the poor or as building up the Kingdom of freedom, fellowship, and justice, evangelization has undeniable political aspects. Sometimes the opposition to evangelization may be not to Christianity as a religion in a narrow sense but to the political implications of an oppressed group becoming better educated, more aware of their situation, rights, and responsibilities, and to their becoming more organized. In such a situation, the foreign missionary is vulnerable and because of him the local church is vulnerable too. Sometimes the local church, strong or weak as it is, may not be able to be prophetic in the manner and to the extent that it desires either because it wishes to protect the foreign missionaries or to safeguard the smooth flow of foreign funds, which is considered necessary, or because it is not free or strong enough to tell the foreigners what to do or not to do.

This may seem an extreme case, though it seems to be becoming more frequent these days. But it raises the delicate point of the relationship of the local church to the foreign missionary. The local churches in Asia at least are very clear that they are primarily responsible for evangelization in their own countries. Help from other churches is welcome, not merely to make up for deficiencies, but as a sign for the catholicity of the Church. But the local church has the responsibility in the matter. From this point of view, the number or the proportion of Catholics in a particular local church is immaterial. What is important is not power or numbers, but responsibility and dedication. The International Mission Congress in Manila said:

> The meager material—even the human—resources we have, tempt us to hesitation and fear. And yet we do not lose heart nor hope, because we have known in our own lives that when we are weakest, and must rely on the power of the Spirit, then the greatest strength is given to us.[17]

This sense of hope that animates the local churches in Asia certainly contrasts with the kind of urgency that some in Europe feel, basing themselves on numbers and percentages.

Would the insistence on the responsibility of the local churches for its mission *ad intra*, even *ad gentes*, mean that foreign missionaries are not only *sent*, but also need to be *asked for* and *accepted* by the local church?

THE CULTURAL CONTEXT OF FOREIGN MISSION

If inculturation is an integral part of evangelization and one of the values of foreign missionaries lies in their being the challenging representative of the inculturated church they come from, then it would not be proper to think of them as the bearers of a disembodied, pure, "supra-cultural" Gospel. That means that they are rooted in their own culture, not merely in the past of it, but in the ongoing present. How can we provide for this?

> The more concretely the Church becomes genuinely local Churches with immediate reference to the economic, social, political and cultural circumstances and challenges, the more difficult it may be for local Churches to understand one another, the more decisions made in one area may challenge other Churches, the more likely it may be for Churches to wonder if their communion with another is not threatened. Such Churches need to learn the skills of dialogue within their common Christian commitment, able to make distinctions which a uniform approach to the Church's self-realization does not require and not only to tolerate but to appreciate differences which the localization of the Church demands.[18]

The missionaries *ad extra* in any local church would seem to be the ideal mediators in such an ongoing dialogue, apart from more institutionalized forums like the Synod of Bishops. This requires of the missionaries first of all to be people of their own culture and at the same time identify themselves enough with the local culture, speak the language, and adopt the way of life so as to be able to communicate and dialogue effectively. They have to *acculturate* themselves to the local church in order to facilitate the local church in its task of *inculturating* the Gospel in the local context. Therefore, foreign mission today can only exist in a collaborative mode. At the same time the foreign missionary has also the responsibility of bringing back to the local church of his or her origin the riches of the local church where he or she is in mission.

If the local church is responsible for its mission and the foreign missionary comes as a helper, a missionary community that is made up entirely of foreign missionaries appears anomalous today. One would rather expect that a person coming from abroad joins a local group engaged in mission. One could also think of a foreign missionary who comes for a particular period and for a specific, often specialized task.[19]

If evangelization is seen really in a broad way as building up the Kingdom and not limited to *plantatio ecclesiae*, lay people engaged in every kind of ecclesial or secular activity could be as good bearers of the Good News *ad gentes* and *ad extra* as priests, brothers and sisters.

CONCLUSION

Mission *ad extra* is a coresponsible task of all the churches. Therefore one could talk about mutuality in mission so that one would like to think of missions not only in North-South terms, or perhaps today in South-South terms, but also in South-North terms. The seeming impracticality of this perhaps underlines the vision of mission that we are still working with on the one hand and the socio-cultural factors that are inseparable from mission which we might tend to think of as a purely religious project.

In a world that is becoming progressively unified owing to the increase and rapidity of communications, economic, and even cultural interdependance and mutual political influence, mission *ad extra* needs no great justification, since such mutual presence and aid is becoming common even in the secular sphere. What is important is a real mutuality that is based on authenticity on and respect for the freedom and identity of the other. Our concern is how we can give structural expression to the developing theology of the Church as a communion, also in the field of mission. A greater sensitivity to the cosmic outreach of the divine plan and action that includes the totality as well as all the aspects of the human world would make us open to the dynamism of history in which God is in mission to recapitulate all things in Christ and the Spirit so that God "may be everything to every one" (1 Cor. 15:28).

Conclusion

Mission: From Vatican II into the Coming Decade

The Second Vatican Council inaugurated a paradigm shift in the theology of mission. One could schematize the change as a movement from "the missions" to "the mission" and then on to "evangelization." Before the Council, one spoke of the missions as territories where the church had not yet been firmly planted. So missionaries went out to do so. Mission was seen as Church extension.

THE SECOND VATICAN COUNCIL

Searching for a theological foundation, the Council rooted mission in the Trinity. "The Church on earth is by its very nature missionary," it said, "since, according to the plan of the Father, it has its origin in the mission of the Son and the Holy Spirit" (*Ad Gentes*, 2). The whole Church is in mission everywhere, though the concrete tasks might vary according to circumstances of time, space and need. Other documents of the Council also contributed perspectives that led to a development of the theology of mission in the succeeding decade. The Document on Other Religions (*Nostra Aetate*) spoke of God as the common origin and end of all peoples. The Document on Mission (*Ad Gentes*) referred to the "seeds of the Word" in other religions. The Constitution on the Church in the Modern World (*Gaudium et Spes*) said that the salvific action of God reaches out to all peoples in ways unknown to us. *Gaudium et Spes* also pointed to the autonomy of the secular world with which the church is called to dialogue. The Decree on Religious Freedom (*Dignitatis Humanae*) upheld the primacy of conscience and the visibility and social nature of its pursuit of truth. The Constitution on the Church (*Lumen Gentium*) spoke of it as the sacrament of unity of all peoples and the beginning of the Reign of God.

New Perspectives

In the years since the Council, experience of a postcolonial world, the awareness of being a world church, and theological reflection has led to

179

the emergence of new perspectives in mission theology and praxis. The SEDOS seminar on the future of mission saw inculturation, interreligious dialogue and liberation as integral dimensions of mission. It also pointed to the growing importance of the local churches in the process of mission. Today, inculturation is seen as the task not only of the younger churches, but also of the older ones faced with secularization and modernity. One speaks of *re-evangelization of a dechristianized society*. A certain legitimacy is recognized to other religions in the plan of God, especially after the symbolic event of Assisi in October 1986, when the Pope came together with leaders of other religions to pray for peace. Interreligious dialogue focuses then not only on mutual understanding, but on a common experience of God and collaboration in the promotion and defense of common human and spiritual values. Liberation demands an option for the poor, a call to conversion of individuals and social groups and work for the change of unjust and oppressive structures. There has also been a growing awareness of mission in and to six continents. Every local church is responsible for its own mission and coresponsible for the mission of all other local churches. Mission *ad gentes*, called first proclamation by *Evangelii Nuntiandi*, is now everywhere. Mission *ad extra* or foreign mission is more and more seen as "collaboration in mission."

A Paradigm Shift

Reflecting on these new developments in the theory and praxis of mission, theologians have proposed a paradigm shift. The focus of mission is not the Church, but the Reign of God: the church is indeed to be built up, but as the servant of God's Reign. The mystery of God's action, in Christ and in the Spirit, reaches out to the whole world in ways unknown to us, and the Church is called to serve this mystery in collaboration with all people of good will. The fulfillment of the plan of God is in the future and the Church, in company with others, is on pilgrimage. While the Reign of God will be fully realized only on the last day and will be God's gratuitous gift, it is also our task and we are called to contribute to its building up in history through creative development and through struggle for liberation from oppressive structures. The interplay of the freedoms of God and of the human person in the process of salvation is a factor for pluralism in history and in the world. Therefore, the concrete task of mission in a particular situation has to be discerned carefully. Today, mission without mystery is oppressive.

A Different Point of View

Looking back again at this history of the development of theology with regard to mission, in the context of contemporary experience, I ask myself whether we do need to take another step to meet the challenges of the next decade. Before the Council, the theology of mission was done by missionaries from their point of view. It was a view from a "center" towards a "periphery." The Council and the post-Conciliar period brought a welcome deepening and broadening of perspectives. But the approach was from above, from the Trinity, conceptual and abstract. Scholastic theologians delight in dealing with universal concepts. Mission is everywhere and every one is on mission. It is true that a greater attention is paid to the reality of the world: its cultures, religions and the poor. But when mission is everything, I think that it loses in focus what it gains in breadth. This stage in the reflection has brought to us many new and rich elements. Perhaps it is now time to look at them from a different point of view.

I would like to specify this different point of view as looking from the periphery and from below. *From the periphery:* that is, as an observer from a third-world younger church, which in the eyes of many still represents an object of mission. I look at the situation as an Indian. Persons from Africa, Latin America, or elsewhere in Asia may look at it differently. I also see this perspective as one *from below:* that is, approaching mission not conceptually, but questioning it from the experience of contemporary reality. In doing this, I only highlight elements that are generally present in ongoing reflection on mission. For instance, when I consider mission as inculturation, interreligious dialogue and liberation, I want to ask a lot of questions. Sharing them with you will be one way of evoking this different point of view.

SOME QUESTIONS

Inculturation as an integral dimension of mission is described as the incarnation of the gospel in a particular culture. When a group encounters the Gospel and changes its attitudes and manner of behavior, this change finds expression in its way of life: its symbols and art, its spirituality and celebration, its social relationships. If the group is not prevented from doing so, such cultural expression of the Gospel is a natural, creative process. Conversion of this group of people is mission. But I do not see why their expression of the Gospel in their own cultural forms should be considered mission. A local church in trying to be itself is not doing mission. The many factors that prevent it from being itself are not mission problems. A missionary who comes from outside the culture may have difficulty in the necessary process of acculturation: learning the language, adapting to the living conditions. These may be problems *for the missionary.* They are not problems *for mission.*

The Gospel is on mission to a culture precisely when it is counter-cultural. When the Gospel raises its prophetic voice against what is sinful and limited in a culture, then it is doing mission. Such mission may suffer from over-inculturation. St. Paul was being a missionary when he proclaimed that in the risen Christ all were equal so that there were no longer Jew nor

Greek, slave nor free, male nor female. But when he went on to exhort slaves to obey their masters or to forbid women from speaking in the church, he was being a practical man of his time, not a missionary.

When we had a negative view of the other religions as a whole, though recognizing the presence of good and holy elements in them, then the other religions were objects of mission. They eventually had to be done away with. But the situation changes when we acknowledge a certain legitimacy to the other religions as elements in the plan of God. In a multireligious society, people can live together in harmony only if they understand each other. But an interreligious dialogue that is devoted to the mutual understanding and removal of prejudices, however necessary, does not seem to be mission. It should be the normal way of life. But religions do engage in mission when they challenge each other's limitations and lack of response to God. They are also doing mission when together they play a prophetic role in society in the promotion and defense of common human and spiritual values. Then they are acting as servants of God's own mission in the world.

To the poor the Gospel comes as the good news of liberation. The Church is called to struggle for justice in the world taking the side of the poor. But the focus of the struggle for justice with the poor is to struggle for the change of unjust socio-economic, political, cultural and even religious structures. One cannot change these sinful structures without converting the sinners who are responsible for them, because these structures are not impersonal. One can of course witness to Christian love through catering to the needs of the people and offering them development assistance. But it seems to me that the real objects of mission in such a situation are the people responsible for the structures of oppression.

What Is Mission?

I feel that by speaking of mission broadly as inculturation, interreligious dialogue, and liberation, we risk losing its precise focus. It is true that everything we do can be relevant to the building up of the Reign of God. But what have we gained by making everything mission? I suggest that we gain by envisaging mission as primarily prophecy. The Melbourne Mission Congress of the World Council of Churches said: "Proclamation is always linked to a specific situation and a specific moment in history. It is God's Good News contrasted with the bad news of that specific situation."[1] This is a good criterion for evaluation when we seek to determine what is mission in a particular situation. Mission is a call to conversion. When Jesus began his mission, he said: "The time is fulfilled, and the reign of God is at hand; repent and believe in the gospel" (Mark 1:15). His teaching and his parables challenged his hearers to a decision. Even his miracles were not just acts of compassion, but symbolic acts that provoked reflection on his person and his message. He preached the gospel to the poor; but he also challenged the rich, the wise, the powerful. That is why he went to his death. Should we not recover this prophetic dynamism of mission?

CONTEMPORARY CHALLENGES TO MISSION

What are the sinful situations in the world today that demand the prophetic proclamation of the Gospel? For reasons of convenience, let me keep to the culture-religions-justice scheme, though we shall see how intertwined they are. My aim is not to make an exhaustive list, but to point to a few highlights.

From a *cultural* point of view, I have three concerns: inequality, consumerism and violence. Paul proclaimed the equality of all human beings in the risen Christ. But we are far from having realized it even within the Church-community. In the world, there is much discrimination based on race, caste, sex, religion, nationality, color, ethnicity, etc. The inequality is all the more painful and oppressive because most human groups today proclaim the ideal of a democratic society based on the individual rights and dignity of every human person. The discrimination can take many subtle forms that are demeaning to the dignity of the person concerned.

One often hears about the secularization of modern culture. Secularization has a positive side to it insofar as it promotes a differentiation between the social institutions such as religion, politics, economics and culture. In its negative aspects, one speaks of the disappearance of religion and of the spread of unbelief. I think that many people have not become less religious. Rather they have little time and energy for the practice of religion. It is not an intellectual crisis of belief, but a moral crisis of desire. Science and technology can be used or abused. People have chosen to abuse them in the pursuit of pleasure and plenty. There is always the desire for more. Selfishness leads to individualism and to competition. Collective selfishness oppresses the poor. A materialistic attitude to life and the world leads to the erosion of human and spiritual values and eventually to alienation and meaninglessness.

Unbridled competition and alienation lead to violence. One does violence to oneself in the form of drugs in an effort to escape boredom and failure in the contest of life. Selfish pursuit of pleasure leads very easily to violence against others to meet one's own needs. Collectively, violence takes the form of war. The flourishing arms industry is an evidence of this ongoing violence in human society. A violent person has no respect for the other. Violence is an indication of the breakdown of community structures. It is also the manifestation of the loss of hope. It is the fruit of a life without love. Humanity today also violates nature. Unbridled exploitation and plunder of nature would ultimately lead to the destruction of nature itself, and with it, of humanity.

In the sphere of *religion*, we are faced with two kinds of challenges: fundamentalism and communalism. Fundamentalism is the reaction of a person whose religious security is threatened. It is one way of fighting alienation and loss of meaning. One holds on fanatically to the truths one has. One does not want to question them for fear of losing them and with them one's bearings in the moral world. Fundamentalist groups are found in all religions today and they tend to be aggressive proselytizers and intolerant even of their own co-religionists.

Communalists think that because they share the same religious belief they have the same economic and political interests. Communalism uses religious sentiment and emotion for political and economic ends. It is often inspired by a small elite in pursuit of their own power but it sways a whole multitude. In one sense, fundamentalism and communalism are not really religious problems and should be tackled at the social and political levels. But we could also attack them by the promotion of authentic religion open to the world and to history, in dialogue with other believers and aware of the Church's potential for playing a prophetic role in society, as well as by encouraging the autonomy of the secular in its own sphere.

The promotion of *justice* poses a particular type of challenge to the very identity and self-awareness of the Church. On the one hand, the Church has to be involved in the social and political life of the people. On the other, the Church should keep its distance in order to be able to prophetically challenge the world. I do not think that making the Church the preserve of the clergy and assigning the world to the laity will solve the problem. The Church as an institution, unlike Hinduism or Buddhism, for example, enjoys a public presence and voice. At the same time, its very institutional character may lead it to become self-defensive or to compromise and thus to lose its prophetic voice. A strong foreign presence in the local Church also seems to inhibit prophecy.

Our option for the poor may sometimes lead us to concentrate only on economic poverty. For many people, living poorly, unless they are in absolute misery, poverty may seem less of a problem than living without human dignity and freedom. Freedom can be denied in many different ways. What strikes our eyes, of course, is the lack of political freedom in totalitarian regimes of the right and of the left. But people can be enslaved in many ways, even in the so-called democratic societies, to money, to the machine, to bureaucracy, to prejudice, to ideology, to media-promoted disinformation. Promotion of inner and outer freedom so that people can be agents of their own transformation and growth is the real challenge today.

The Church claims to be the sacrament of the Reign of God. In the early Church there was an attempt to construct ideal communities, though there were difficulties in communities such as that of Corinth. When the church began to conform to the world, monks and later also religious took up the challenge of building model communities. They cannot be adequate models because the celibacy of community members leads them in fundamentally unique directions. Today one speaks of basic ecclesial communities. But unless the Church seeks to provide a model and a vision of an alternate community, not only at the local level but also at national and international levels, its witness will be less credible. Christians are not just called to be prophets but the sacrament and beginning of the Reign of God.

A HOLISTIC AND GLOBAL VIEW

A further step in our process of reflection is to see these and other challenges to mission holistically and globally. A holistic approach would see how much these challenges are interconnected. We cannot transform any culture unless we dialogue with other religions that also animate the culture and unless we can change the concrete socio-economic and political context that condition people's lives and attitudes. Interreligious dialogue should lead to a common prophetic voice in the growth of both culture and the world. A true liberation from oppressive socio-economic and political structures could hardly be achieved unless the people change their world-views and attitudes and draw inspiration and motivation from true religion. Therefore all these challenges have to be faced in an organic manner.

Both because of the communications revolution and increasing economic and political interdependence, the challenges of mission have taken on a global character. Religious pluralism is a reality everywhere. Intercultural contacts and influences are increasing, promoted by the pervasive and rapid media of communication. Though different cultures may react to science and technology differently, the impact and some of the problems may be common. At the economic and political level, the problems of the poor in the Third World have their roots also in the First World and the best way of helping them, besides making them independent, is to influence the decision makers in the First World.

Cross-Cultural Mission

Mission today therefore has international dimensions. This internation-ality is not merely geographic. It has deeper theological roots: the universality of the plan of God and the catholicity of the Church. Meditating on the life, death and resurrection of Jesus, both Paul and John discover the universal extent of the Mystery—the plan that God revealed in Jesus. While Paul speaks of the cosmic Christ who was at the beginning and in whom all things will be united at the end, John speaks of the Word in whom all things were made and who unites all peoples in the very life of the Trinity. The role of the Spirit in this process of unification is also stressed by both. The Church speaks of itself in the Second Vatican Council and since as the "sacrament" and "servant" of unity. Recent documents of the Church end with appeals for collaboration to all peoples of good will.

The universal dimensions of the plan of God and of the service of the Church take concrete form in the catholicity of the Church. Catholicity is not mere geographical universality. It is not merely called to become incarnate in each culture becoming authentic local churches. All the local churches are called to become a community in pluralism—a communion. As the Vatican II Constitution on the Church says:

> In virtue of this catholicity, the several parts bring their own gifts to one another and to the whole Church, so that the whole and its several parts grow by the mutual sharing of all and by a common effort towards the fullness of unity.[2]

International mission is therefore not a tactic for the better placement of resources and personnel. It is the expression and demand of the catholicity of the Church.

In the context of each local church being responsible for its own mission and coresponsible for the mission of all the churches, internationality will take the form of mutuality in mission. This gives us a new perspective on mission *ad extra*. I think that we should speak today of cross-cultural mission. In practice this will be the responsibility of some people who hear a special call for it. One could rapidly list a number of conditions which seem essential for their success. They should not only be sent, but also asked for and accepted. They would probably go for specific jobs that require specific skills. They have to acculturate themselves—that is, learn the language, adapt oneself to the way of life, and adjust to the climate—in order to be effective. They have a special role of mediation between the local churches. To the local church that receives them, they bring the riches of the cultural expression of the Gospel of their own local church. In turn they carry back to the church that sent them, the riches that they have experienced in the church where they are working. If we understand this subtle interplay of the local and the foreign, one can wonder whether a completely foreign missionary community can be really meaningful today, except in special circumstances, where it could meet particular needs for a particular time. Missionaries would go not only from the North to the South, but also from the South to the North.

Priorities

If we look at mission in a global perspective we see needs and problems everywhere. Not only primary evangelization, but the ongoing challenge of the Gospel, is needed everywhere. God may also inspire various people to different and particular tasks—work for human development, struggle for justice, cross-cultural mission, and interreligious dialogue. But if we consider the various challenges of mission today and seek to prioritize them, I think that the most urgent problem is the moral one of consumerism and its consequent exploitative and oppressive structures. Commerce becomes supreme and everything else—religion, culture, politics and social relationships—becomes subservient to it. There is a loss of the sense of transcendence. People have no time for religion. They become slaves to machines. The discoveries of science and the powers of technology are abused for selfish ends. The poor become poorer. The facility of modern communications makes control and exploitation easier and faster. The concern for the common good and the attention to moral and spiritual values break down. A rising individualism and competition undermine human relationships and community. Violence in all its forms increases. Whole peoples are at the mercy of market forces unconcerned with the plight of the marginalized.

In my view, the need of our age is for a "spiritual humanism"—*humanism*, so that people can become free and masters of their own destiny—*spiritual* so that this destiny is open to transcendence and is inserted into the plan of God for the world.

Though this need for the Gospel is everywhere, I think that it is particularly acute in the First World. As post-Christians, Northerners' sensitivity to the challenges of the Gospel is often blunted. From a global point of view, the epicenter and the key for the solution of most of the problems are in the First World because of its economic, political and, in many places, cultural dominance, thanks to the media. The elite of the First World also inspire and control, not to say corrupt, the economic and political elite of the Third. Therefore, if one can read the signs of the times and discern priorities, I wonder whether the most important and challenging locale for mission today is not the First World. Speaking to a group of Asians in April, 1947, Gandhi said:

> If you want to give a message to the West, it must be the message of love and the message of truth . . . The West today is pining for wisdom. It is despairing of a multiplication of Atom bombs . . . It is up to you to tell the world of its wickedness and sin—that is the heritage your teachers and my teachers have taught Asia.[3]

I should specify that Gandhi included Jesus among the teachers of Asia. Gandhi's proposal is not less relevant today, even though not only Asians but all people of good will are called to carry this message today.

Where there is growing indifference to religion, where there is a moral crisis of values, where one finds the roots of unjust and oppressive contemporary structures, there one sees the priorities for mission today and tomorrow. I wonder whether—in a world which is becoming increasingly a global village—a re-evangelization of the Christian world may not be a more credible witness to the rest of the world than missions in Asia or Africa. Such an effort would also lead us to re-examine the cultural and historical structures in which we carry the challenge of the Gospel in our mission *ad extra*, especially if they have not had much success at home.[4]

CONCLUSION

I have proposed that we rediscover the specificity and relevance of mission as prophecy. With this as a criterion, we can discern the contemporary challenges of mission in the realm of culture, religion and justice. I have made my own list. I have pointed to the global nature of these challenges and evoked the need for mutuality in mission. Both the plan of God for the world and the catholicity of the Church as communion demand that mission today be mutual and cross-cultural. Briefly analyzing the signs of the times, I have suggested a double but closely linked priority. From the point of view of global challenges, the consumerist and commercial culture, backed up by economic and political structures, demands our attention. From a spiritual point of view, the First World seems to be the place that needs a prophetic voice most urgently.

The Church today is called to commit itself to an international moral movement of peoples. It is in pilgrimage towards the Reign of God in the company of all peoples of good will. It has to be true to its own identity as the witness of the good news of Jesus, of his death on the cross and of his resurrection. It has also to hear the call to be the servant of unity in the world. While being a community rooted in Jesus, the Church needs to have open frontiers, ready to dialogue with every one. Opting for the poor, it must prophetically confront the unjust oppressor. In humility it has to be sensitive to the mystery of the action of God in the world. It should be open to the creative newness of the Spirit. Its horizon is God's own mission of universal reconciliation, when God will be with God's people. Then God "will wipe away every tear from their eyes, and death shall be no more, neither shall there be mourning nor crying nor pain any more, for the former things have passed away" (Rev. 21:4).

Notes

1. THE ENCOUNTER OF RELIGIONS

1. Cf. André Bétéille, *The Idea of Natural Inequality and Other Essays* (Delhi: Oxford University Press, 1983), pp. 88–89.

2. Cf. Richard K. Fenn, *Toward a Theory of Secularization* (Society for the Study of Religion, 1978); Peter Glassner, *The Sociology of Secularization* (London: Routledge and Kegan Paul, 1977); Philip E. Hammond (ed.), *The Sacred in a Secular Age* (Berkeley: University of California, 1985); David Martin, *A General Theory of Secularization* (Oxford: Blackwell, 1978).

3. M.K. Gandhi, *The Story of My Experiments with Truth* (Ahemdabad: Navjivan, 1945), p. 615.

4. See, for example, John Paul II, *Sollicitudo Rei Socialis*.

5. *The Constitution of India*, Preamble.

6. Cf. M. Amaladoss, "Theological Bases for Religious Pluralism," in S. Arulsamy (ed.), *Communalism in India* (Bangalore: Claretian, 1988) (pp. 72–82 in this volume); *Theses on Inter-religious Dialogue* (FABC Papers 48); *Living and Working Together with Sisters and Brothers of Other Faiths* (FABC Papers 49).

7. *Nostra Aetate*, 1.

8. Cf. FABC, "Evangelization in Modernday Asia," 14–15, in *For All the Peoples of Asia* (Manila: 1984).

9. Secretariatus pro Non-Christianis, *Bulletin* 64 (1987), pp. 56–57.

10. See, for example, John Paul II, Speech in Madras, in *Origins* 15, 36 (Feb. 20, 1986) 598; *Sollicitudo Rei Socialis*, 47.

11. Cf. Peter H. Merkl and Ninian Smart (eds.), *Religion and Politics in the Modern World* (New York: New York University Press, 1985).

12. Cf. Felix Wilfred, "Dialogue Gasping for Breath? Towards New Frontiers in Inter-religious Dialogue" in FABC Papers 49, pp. 32–52.

13. J. C. Murray, *We Hold These Truths* (New York: Sheed and Ward, 1960).

2. APPROACHES TO POPULAR RELIGION

1. Zev Barbu, "Popular Culture: A Sociological Approach," in C.W.E. Bigsby (ed.), *Approaches to Popular Culture* (Bowling Green: Bowling Green University Press, 1976) 39–68; Seth Siegelaub, "Preface: Working Notes on Social Relations in Communication and Culture" in Armand Mattelart and Seth Siegelaub (eds.), *Communication and Class Struggle*, Vol. 2 (New York: International General, 1983) pp. 11–16.

2. D.G. Mandelbaum, "Transcendental and Pragmatic Aspects of Religion," *American Anthropologist* 68 (1966) 1174–1191.

3. Aloysius Pieris, "Towards an Asian Theology of Liberation. Some Religio-Cultural Guidelines," *Vidyajyoti* 43 (1979) 261–284.

4. Robert Redfield, *Peasant Society and Culture* (Chicago: University of Chicago Press, 1956).

5. McKim, Marriott, "Little Communities in an Indigenous Civilization," in Charles Leslie (ed.), *Anthropology of Folk Religion* (New York: Vantage, 1960) 169–218.

6. R.L. Stirrat, "Sacred Models," *Man* 19 (1984) 199–215.

7. Gananath Obeyesekere, "Social Change and the Deities: Rise of the Kataragama Cult in Modern Sri Lanka," *Man* 12 (1977) 378.

8. Ursula Sharma, "Theodicy and the Doctrine of Karma," *Man* 8 (1973) 347–364.

9. Gabriele Dietrich, *Religion and People's Organization in East Thanjavur* (Madras: Christian Literature Society, 1976) p. 137.

10. Obeyesekere, "Social Change."

11. Francis Jeyapathy, "What is Popular Religion?" (Unpublished paper).

12. James Dow, "Universal Aspects of Symbolic Healing: A Theoretical Synthesis," *American Anthropologist* 88 (1986) 56–69.

13. John O'Donohue, *Spirits and Magic–A Critical Look* (Eldoret, Kenya: Gaba, 1981).

14. Meinrad P. Hebga, *Sorcellerie et Prière de délivrance* (Abidjan: Inades, 1982).

15. Sudhir Kakar, *Shamans, Mystics and Doctors* (London: Unwin, 1982).

16. Jaime Bulatao, "Local Cases of Possession and their Cure," *Philippine Studies* 30 (1982) 415–425.

17. Eric de Rosny, *Healers in the Night* (Maryknoll, N.Y.: Orbis Books, 1985).

18. Aylward Shorter, *Jesus and the Witch Doctor* (Maryknoll, N.Y.: Orbis Books, 1985).

19. Cf. Sharma, "Theodicy."

20. Cf. Obeyesekere, "Social Change"; Paul C. Wiebe, "Religious Change in South India: Perspectives from a Small Town," *Religion and Society* 22,4 (1975) 27–46.

21. Dietrich, *op. cit.*, p. 131.

22. Victor Turner, *The Ritual Process* (Chicago: Aldine, 1969).

23. Maurice Bloch, "From Cognition to Ideology," in R. Fardon (ed.), *Knowledge and Power* (Edinburgh: Scottish University Press, 1985).

24. Mircea Eliade, *Images and Symbols* (London: Harvill, 1961).

25. Carl G. Jung, *Man and His Symbols* (London: 1964).

26. Mary Douglas, *Natural Symbols* (Harmondsworth: Penguin, 1973).

27. K. Marx and F. Engels, *On Religion* (Moscow: Progress, 1957) p. 38.

28. Max Weber, *The Sociology of Religion* (Boston: Beacon, 1963) pp. 269–270.

29. Gunnar Myrdal, *Asian Drama* (New York: 1968), Vol. I, p. 103.

30. Dietrich, *op. cit.*, pp. 136–137.

31. A.M. Abraham Ayrookuzhiel, "Religion, Spirituality and Aspirations of the People," *Religion and Society* 25, 1 (1978) 29. See also his "A Study of the Religion of the Hindu People of Chirakkal (Kerala)," *Religion and Society* 24,1 (1977) 5–54.

32. Vieda Skultans, "The Management of Mental Illness Among Maharashtrian Families: A Case Study of a Mahanaubhav Healing Temple," *Man* 22 (1987) 661–679.

33. Obeyesekere, "Social Change."

34. Arvind Sharma, "New Hindu Religious Movements in India," in James A. Beckford (ed.), *New Religious Movements and Rapid Social Change* (London: Sage, 1986) 220–239.

35. Christian Parker, "Popular Religion and Protest against Oppression: The Chilean Example," *Concilium* 186 (1986) 28–35.

36. Cf. Akos Ostor, *Culture and Power* (New Delhi: Sage, 1984).

37. Maurice Bloch, "From Blessing to Violence: History and Ideology in the Circumcision Ritual of the Merina of Madagascar," *Current Anthropology* 27 (1986) 349–360.

38. Cf. Louis Dumont, "A Structural Definition of a Folk Deity of Tamil Nad: Aiyanar, the Lord," in William A. Lessa and Evon Z. Vogt (eds), *Reader in Comparative Religion: An Anthropological Approach* (New York: Harper and Row, 1965) 189–195; C. J. Fuller, "The Hindu Pantheon and the Legitimation of Hierarchy," *Man* 23 (1988) 19–37.

39. Jonathan Parry, "The Brahmanical Tradition and the Technology of the Intellect," in Johanna Overing (ed.), *Reason and Morality* (London: Tavistock, 1985) 200–223; R.L. Stirrat, "The Shrine of St. Sebastian at Mirisgama: An Aspect of the Cult of the Saints in Catholic Sri Lanka," *Man* 16 (1981) 185–200.

40. Victor Turner, *The Ritual Process* (Chicago: Adline, 1969).

3. OTHER SCRIPTURES AND THE CHRISTIAN

1. The Second Vatican Council, *Nostra Aetate*, 1.

2. I do not offer any elaborate theology of religions here. I shall come back to this point briefly later.

3. D.S. Amalorpavadass, *Research Seminar on Non-Biblical Scriptures* (Bangalore: 1974) referred to hereafter as RSNBS.

4. For a critical review of the Seminar, see M. Amaladoss, "Non-Biblical Scriptures in Christian Life and Worship," *Vidyajyoti* 39 (1975) 194–209.

5. This and the following numbers within brackets refer to the *Final Statement of the Seminar*. Cf. RSNBS, pp. 681–695.

6. Even this relatively low-key use of the scriptures of other religions was disallowed by church authorities.

7. Cf. J. Neuner, "Holy Scripture and Community," RSNBS, 179–189; L. Legrand, "Letter and the Spirit: The Role of the Book in the Christian Economy," RSNBS, pp. 53–77.

8. J.N.M. Wijngaards, "The Integration into Scripture of Originally Non-Jewish Religious Literature," RSNBS, pp. 78–98.

9. Report of the Bible Workshop, RSNBS, pp. 117–135.

10. J. Dupuis, "The Cosmic Economy of the Spirit and the Sacred Scriptures of Religious Traditions," RSNBS, pp. 117–135.

11. J. Puthiadam, "Reflections on Hindu Religious Texts," RSNBS, pp. 300–314.

12. Cf. G. Michael, "The Divine Origin of the Prabhandam," *Ibid.*, 48–430; X. Irudayaraj, "Self Understanding of Saiva Siddhanta Scriptures," RSNBS, pp. 445–454.

13. *Dei Verbum*, 11.

14. Cf. RSNBS, pp. 280–382. See also G. Gispert-Sauch, "Sacred Scriptures in Indian Religions," *Vidyajyoti* 39 (1975) 217–222.

15. Cf. RSNBS, pp. 489–545.

16. Cf. J. Vempeny, *Inspiration in the Non-Biblical Scriptures* (Bangalore: 1973) with the comments on the book by G. Gispert-Sauch, *Vidyajyoti* 38 (1974) 182–189. The latter gives in note 2, page 182 references to other articles on the subject.

17. On the theology of religions, see E.J. Sharpe, *Faith Meets Faith* (London: 1977). He has a good bibliography; Alan Race, *Christians and Religious Pluralism* (London: 1983), also with a good bibliography; Thomas Emprayil, *The Emerging Theology of Religions* (Rome: 1980); J. Neuner (ed.) *Christian Revelation and World Religions* (London: 1967); J. Pathrapankal, *Service and Salvation* (Bangalore: 1973); J. Hick and B.L. Hebblethwaite (eds.), *Christianity and Other Religions* (London: 1980).

18. J. Dupuis, *op. cit.*, RSNBS, p. 131.

19. G. Gispert-Sauch, "Inspiration? Some Comments on a Recent Book," *Vidyajyoti* 38 (1974) 187.

20. J. Dupuis, *op. cit.*, RSNBS, p. 134.

21. J. Neuner, *op cit.*, RSNBS, p. 185.

22. G. Soares-Prabhu, "The Inspiration of the Old Testament as seen by the New and its Implication for the Possible Inspiration of Non-Christian Scriptures," RSNBS, pp. 105–106.

23. J. Dupuis, *op. cit.*, RSNBS, p. 132.

24. A. Dulles, *Models of Revelation* (Dublin: 1983), p. 190.

25. J. Wijngaards, "Judgement of the Bible on the Other Sacred Scriptures?," *Vidyajyoti* 39 (1975), 216.

26. Cf. RSNBS, pp. 686–689.

27. Abishiktananda, *Hindu-Christian Meeting Point* (Delhi: 1976); M. Amaladoss, "An Indian Reads St. John's Gospel" in C. Duraisingh and C. Hargreaves (eds.), *India's Search for Reality and the Relevance the Gospel of John* (Delhi: 1976), 7–21; Vandana, *Waters of Fire* (Madras: 1981).

28. G. Soares-Prabhu, "Commitment and Conversion. A Biblical Hermeneutic for India Today." (Unpublished paper).

29. RSNBS, p. 693. Cf. R. Panikkar, *Mantra-Manjari*, *Vedic Experience* (Delhi, 1983).

4. DIALOGUE AND MISSION: CONFLICT OR CONVERGENCE?

1. See Mary Motte and Joseph R. Long (eds.), *Mission and Dialogue*, (Maryknoll, N.Y.: Orbis Books, 1982), pp. 633–642.

2. J. Neuner (ed.), *Christian Revelation and World Religions* (London: Burns & Oates 1967).

3. Cf. Paul Knitter, *No Other Name?* (Maryknoll, N.Y.: Orbis Books, 1985), p. 191.

4. Karl Rahner, "Basic Theological Interpretation of the Second Vatican Council," *Theological Investigation XX* (New York: Crossroad, 1981), pp. 77–89.

5. Cf. K. Rahner, *The Shape of the Church to Come* (London: SPCK, 1974).

6. *Lumen Gentium*, 16.

7. *Gaudium et Spes*, 22. Cf. also John Paul II, *Redemptor Hominis*, 14; Secretariatus pro Non-Christianis, *The Attitude of the Church towards the Followers of Other Religions* (Rome: 1984), 22.

8. *Nostra Aetate*, 2.

9. Statement of the Plenary Assembly of the Federation of Asian Bishops' Conferences, Taipei, 1974: "Evangelization in Modern Day Asia," 14–15. Text in *For All the Peoples of Asia*, Vol. 1 (Manila: IMC Publications, 1984), p. 30. See also *Redemptor Hominis*, 6 and 12: "It is the question of respecting everything that has been brought about in him by the Spirit, which "blows where it wills.""

10. K. Rahner, "Christianity and Non-Christian Religions," *Theological Investigations*, vol. 5 (London: Darton, Longman & Todd, 1966), pp. 115–134.

11. *Dignitatis Humanae*, 3.

12. Cf. M. Amaladoss, "Symbol and Mystery," *Journal of Dharma* 2 (1977) 382–396.

13. Consider the strong statement of K. Rahner: "Christian faith is aware of a universal history of salvation, common to all mankind, existing from the very outset, always effective, universally present as the most radical element of the unity of mankind, not first slowly spreading out from a particular and tangible manifestation. The universalism of the one salvific will of God in regard to all mankind, which establishes the final unity of mankind, is the sustaining ground of all particular history of salvation and religion." See "Unity of the Church—Unity of Mankind," *Theological Investigations*, vol. 20, pp. 160–161.

14. *Lumen Gentium*, 1.

15. Ibid., 8.

16. *Unitatis Redintegratio*, 3.

17. *Lumen Gentium*, 8.

18. My christology owes much to K. Rahner. For a brief but comprehensive exposition of his positions, see his *Foundations of Christian Faith* (New York: Seabury, 1978), pp. 176–320.

19. Consider, for example, the questions, How should we understand the Eucharist as sacrificial in the context of the once-for-all character of Christ's sacrifice on the cross? What is the Church's "priestly" role?

20. Consider the question of the performative formulae of the Latin tradition with the priest speaking "in persona Christi" and the declarative formulae of the Greek tradition.

21. Christology and ecclesiology are obviously related. The relation between the Church-community and Church-mystery is compared to the relation between the two natures in Christ by *Lumen Gentium*, 8.

22. See Rahner, "The One Christ and the Universality of Salvation," *Theological Investigations*, vol. 16, (London: Darton, Longman & Todd, 1970), especially pp. 212–216.

23. See K. Rahner, *Foundations*, p. 290.

24. See Wilhem Thusing in Wilhem Thusing and K. Rahner, A New Christology (London: Burns & Oates, 1980), p. 180.25.

25. K. Rahner, *Foundations*, pp. 316–318.

26. R.J. Schreiter, "The Anonymous Christian and Christology," *Missiology* 6 (1978) pp. 29–52.

27. This is my objection to the tendency represented by Paul Knitter and to his own conclusion. I am open to the idea that traditional formulae like that of Chalcedon need revision and improvement. But I feel that too narrow a focus on the Christological problem is not helpful.

28. Rahner observes: "If we face squarely and uncompromisingly the fact of the Incarnation which our faith in the fundamental dogma of Christianity testifies to,

then we have to say plainly: God can become something. He who is not subject to change in himself can himself be subject to change in something else" (K. Rahner, *Foundations*, p. 220).

29. For further clarification of this christological position, please see chapter 7, "The Pluralism of Religions and the Significance of Christ" in this volume.

30. Cf. FABC, "Evangelization in Modern Day Asia."

31. Patrick D'Souza, "Church and Mission in Relation to the Kingdom of God especially in a Third World Context," in *Towards a New Age in Mission II* (Manila: IMC Publications, 1981), pp. 42–43. The report of the theological workshop can be found in *For All the Peoples of Asia*, p. 224.

32. *Evangelii Nuntiandi*, 19.

33. John Paul II remarks, "In this ecclesial activity it is also necessary to avoid exclusivism and dichotomies. Authentic dialogue becomes witness and true evangelization is accomplished by respecting and listening to one another. Even though "there is a time for everything" (cf. Eccl. 3:1–8), prudence and discernment will teach us what is appropriate in each particular situation: collaboration, witness, listening, or exchange of values." Speech to the Plenary Assembly of the Secretariate for Non-Christians, No. 5. See *Evangelii Nuntiandi*, n. 7.

34. K. Rahner, "The One Christ, and the Universality of Salvation," *Theological Investigations*, vol. 16 (London: Darton, Longman & Todd, 1979), p. 219.

35. Cf. Secretariatus pro Non-Christianis, *op. cit.* "In dialogue also, the Christian normally nourishes in his heart the desire of sharing his experience of Christ with his brother of another religion (Acts 26:29; ES 46). On the other hand, it is natural that another believer would similarly desire to share his faith ... Dialogue thus becomes a source of hope and a factor of communion in mutual transformation" (nn. 40,43).

5. THE SYMBOLIC DIMENSION OF CHRISTIANITY

1. J. Neuner (ed.), *Christian Revelation and World Religions* (London: 1967); J. Pathrapankal (ed.), *Service and Salvation* (Bangalore: 1973); D.S. Amalorpavadass (ed.), *Research Seminar on Non-Biblical Scriptures* (Bangalore: 1974).

2. See J.R. Pierce, *Symbols, Signals and Noise: The Nature and Process of Communication* (New York: 1971); R. Barthes, *Elements of Semiology* (London: 1967); A.J. Greimas, *Du sens* (Paris: 1970); J. Kristeva, "Le geste, pratique ou communication?," *Language* 10 (1968); 48–64: G. Mounin, *Introduction à la sémiologie* (Paris: 1970); F. de Saussure, *Cours de la linguistique générale* (Paris: 1968); M. Amaladoss, "Religious Rite as Symbol," *Jeevadhara* 5 (1975) 319–328.

3. Terry Eagleton, *The Body as Language* (London: 1970): Sam Keen, *To a Dancing God* (New York: Harper and Row, 1970).

4. C. Levi-Strauss, "Introduction a l'oeuvre de Marcel Mauss," *Sociologie et anthropologie* (Paris: 1968); Mary Douglas, *Natural Symbols* (Pelican: 1973).

5. V. Turner. *The Ritual Process: Structures and Anti-Structure*, (London: 1969). See also Turner's "Pilgrimage and Communitas," *Studia Missionalia 23* (1974), 1–23.

6. THEOLOGICAL BASES OF THE PLURALISM OF RELIGIONS

1. Secretariatus pro Non-Christianis, *Bulletin* 64 (1987) 150.

2. *Gaudium et Spes*, 22.

3. *Nostra Aetate* 1.

4. *Dignitatis Humanae*, 3.

5. Federation of Asian Bishops' Conferences (FABC), "Evangelization in Modern Day Asia," 14, 15, in *For All the Peoples of Asia* (Manila: IMC Publications, 1984), p. 30. See also Reports of the Bishops' Institute for Interreligious Affairs I–III, ibid., pp. 181–205.

6. Cf. *Origins* 15 (Feb. 20, 1986), p. 598.

7. Secretariatus pro Non-Christianis, *Bulletin* 64 (1987) 56–57.

8. For Indian theologians, I hardly go into an elaborate theology of religions for my purpose here. It may suffice to recall a few landmarks, for example, J. Neuner (ed.), *Christian Revelation and Word Religions* (London: 1967); J. Pathrapankal (ed.), *Service and Salvation* (Bangalore: Theological Publications in India, 1973), pp. 165–306; D.S. Amalorpavadass (ed.), *Research Seminar on Non-Biblical Scriptures* (Bangalore: NBCLC, 1974).

9. See Eph. 1:10; Rom 8:19–22; 1 Cor. 15:26.

10. *Towards a New Age in Mission* I–III (Manila: IMC Publications, 1981).

11. See Felix Wilfred, "A Matter of Theological Education: Some Critical Reflections on the Suitability of 'Salvation History" as a Theological Model for India," *Vidyajyoti* 48 (1984) 538–556.

12. This is eminently true of Jesus himself.

13. The Four Gospels within the New Testament tradition are good examples.

14. Cf. F. Müssner, *Histoire de l'herméneutique* (Paris: Cerf, 1972); Paul Ricoeur, *Essays on Biblical Interpretation* (Philadelphia: Fortress Press, 1980).

15. Theologians would speak of ordinary and extraordinary ways.

16. See Ian Thompson, *Religion* (London: Longman, 1986); Peter Berger, *The Sacred Canopy* (New York: Doubleday, 1967); M.B. McGuire, *Religion, the Social Context* (California: Wardsworth, 1981); Anthony P. Cohen, *The Symbolic Construction of Community* (London: Tavistock, 1986); Clifford Geertz, *The Interpretation of Cultures* (New York: Basic, 1973).

17. Cf. M. Amaladoss, "Other Scriptures and the Christian," *East Asian Pastoral Review* 22 (1985) 104–115 (pp. 31–42 in this volume); Avery Dulles, *Models of Revelation* (New York: Doubleday, 1983).

18. See for instance Christian Duquoc, *Provisional Churches* (London: SCM, 1986); Walter Kasper, *Jesus the Christ* (New York: Paulist, 1976), pp. 264–265.

19. Cf. Hans Urs Van Balthasar, *Truth is Symphonic* (San Francisco: Ignatius, 1987); Bernard Lonergan, *Doctrinal Pluralism* (Milwaukee: Marquette, 1971); David Tracy, *The Analogical Imagination* (New York: Crossroad, 1981); idem, *Plurality and Ambiguity* (San Francisco: Harper and Row, 1987).

20. *Lumen Gentium* 5 calls it the seed and the beginning.

21. This is the difficulty with the "anonymous Christians" of Karl Rahner. See "Anonymous Christianity and the Missionary Task of the Church," in *Theological Investigations*, vol. 12 (New York: Seabury, 1974), pp. 161–178. For a more positive appreciation of other religions see K. Rahner, "On the Importance of the Non-Christian Religions for Salvation," *Theological Investigations*, vol. 18 (London: Darton, Longman and Todd, 1984), pp. 288–295.

22. I am aware that there are religions which do not speak of a personal God and such statements will have to be suitably broadened to take them into account. See Aloysius Pieris, "The Place of Non-Christian Religions and Cultures in the Evolution of a Third-World Theology," *East Asian Pastoral Review* 19 (1982) 26–27.

23. Cf. Philip E. Hammond (ed.), *The Sacred in a Secular Age* (Berkeley: University of California Press, 1985).

24. Cf. M. Amaladoss, *Faith, Culture and Inter-religious Dialogue* (New Delhi: Indian Social Institute, 1988).

25. Cf. Peter H. Merkl and Ninian Smart (eds.), *Religion and Politics in the Modern World* (New York: New York University Press, 1985).

26. We have very competent surveys in Alan Race, *Christians and Religious Pluralism* (London: SCM, 1983); Paul Knitter, *No Other Name?* (Maryknoll, N.Y.: Orbis Books, 1985); Arnulf Camps, *Partners in Dialogue* (Maryknoll, N.Y.: Orbis Books, 1983); Gavin D'Costa, *Theology and Religious Pluralism* (Oxford: Basil Blackwell, 1986); Peter Schineller, "Christ and the Church: A Spectrum of Views," *Theological Studies* 37 (1976) 545–566; Reginald H. Fuller and Pheme Perkins, *Who is This Christ?* (Philadelphia: Fortress, 1983), pp. 149–161.

27. See, for instance, Ignatius Puthiadem, "Diversity of Religions in the Context of Pluralism and Indian Christian Life and Reflection," in M. Amaladoss, T.K. John, and George Gispert-Sauch (eds.), *Theologizing in India Today* (Bangalore: Theological Publications in India, 1981).

28. See, for instance, George Khodr, "The Economy of the Holy Spirit," in Gerald H. Anderson and Thomas F. Stransky (eds.), *Faith Meets Faith: Mission Trends* No. 5 (Ramsey: Paulist, 1981), pp. 36–49.

29. The eminent transcendentalist would be Karl Rahner. See his summary statement in K. Rahner and W. Thusing, *A New Christology* (London: Burns and Oates, 1980), pp. 3–41. For the eschatological point of view, see John B. Cobb, *Christ in a Pluralistic Age* (Philadelphia: Westminster, 1975). For a very different eschatological perspective, George Lindbeck, *The Nature of Doctrine, Religion and Theology in a Post-liberal Age* (London: SPCK, 1984). There are hosts of others who hold varying shades of Logos Christology within not too wide a spectrum. Just a sampling: Walter Kasper, *Jesus the Christ* (New York: Paulist, 1976); Gerald O'Collins, *Interpreting Jesus* (Ramsey: Paulist, 1983); Kenneth Cragg, *The Christ and the Faiths* (London: SPCK, 1986); M.M. Thomas, *Risking Christ for Christ's Sake* (Geneva: WCC, 1987); Christian Duquoc, "Christianity and its Claim to Universality," *Concilium* 135 (1980) 59–69.

30. Cf. Swami Abhishiktananda, *Intériorité et révélation* (Paris: Présence, 1982); *La montée au fond du coeur* (Paris: O.E.I.L., 1986); Raymond Panikkar, *The Unknown Christ of Hinduism* (London: Darton, Longman and Todd, 1981); *Intra-religious Dialogue* (New York: Paulist, 1978); "The Myth of Pluralism: The Tower of Babel—A Meditation on Non-Violence," *Cross Currents* (1979) 197–230.

31. I have spelled out my own approach, along the line of Abhishiktananda and Panikkar, in chapters 4 and 7 of this volume.

32. See, for instance, G. O'Collins *Intrepreting Jesus* (Ramsey: Paulist, 1985), pp. 133–168.

33. N.A. Nikam and Richard McKeon (eds.), *The Edicts of Asoka* (Bombay: Asia Publishing House, 1959), pp. 49–50.

34. *The Bhagavad Gita* 9, 21–24.

35. S. Radhakrishnan, *The Hindu View of Life* (London: 1927), p. 43.

36. T.L. Mehta quoted in John B. Carman, "Bangalore Revisited: Balancing Understanding and Evaluation in the Comparative Study of Religion," in Frank Whaling (ed.), *The World's Religious Traditions* (Edinburgh: T&T, Clark, 1984), p. 229.

7. THE PLURALISM OF RELIGIONS AND THE SIGNIFICANCE OF CHRIST

1. See M. Amaladoss, S.J., "Theological Bases for Religious Pluralism", in S. Arulsamy (ed.), *Communalism in India* (Bangalore: Claretian Publications, 1988), pp. 115–138 (chapter 6 of this volume).

2. See Paul F. Knitter, *No Other Name?* (Maryknoll, N.Y.: Orbis Books, 1985); Alan Race, *Christians and Religious Pluralism* (Maryknoll, N.Y.: Orbis Books, 1982); Gavin D'Costa, *Theology and Religious Pluralism* (Oxford: Basil Blackwell, 1986).

3. See, for instance, the use of the term "myth" in two books that John Hick has edited: *The Myth of God Incarnate* (London: SCM, 1977); with Paul F. Knitter, *The Myth of Christian Uniqueness* (Maryknoll, N.Y.: Orbis Books, 1987). It is true that the word myth may be used to mean a symbol that affirms a deeper truth. Yet for Christians God Incarnate is not a "myth" in the same way as the creation narratives in the Book of Genesis.

4. See Leonard Swidler (ed.), *Toward a Universal Theology of Religion* (Maryknoll, N.Y.: Orbis, 1987), especially the strong critique of the idea of rationalist approaches by R. Panikkar, pp. 118–153. See also Wilfred Cantwell Smith, *Towards a World Theology* (Maryknoll, N.Y.: Orbis Books, 1990).

5. I use the word "witness" not in a passive sense as weaker than proclamation, but in the full biblical sense of "martyrion."

6. In the context of dialogue with Buddhism, it may be problematic to speak constantly about God as I am doing in this paper. Nevertheless, I speak in a Christian context to Christians and so I use a Christian language.

7. See M. Amaladoss, *Education in the Faith in a Multi-Religious Context* (New Delhi: Jesuit Educational Association, 1988), pp. 3–4.

8. See A. Pieris, "The Buddha and the Christ: Mediators of Liberation," in Hick and Knitter (eds.), *The Myth of Christian Uniqueness*, p. 162.

9. See R. Panikkar, "The Jordan, the Tiber and the Ganges", in Hick and Knitter (eds.), *The Myth of Christian Uniqueness*, p. 104.

10. This occurs through the action of the Word (Wisdom) and the Spirit. See John Paul II, *Redemptor Hominis* 6, 11; and *Dominum et Vivificantem*, 53. See also *Ad Gentes*, 4 and *Gaudium et Spes*, 22.

11. In the middle ages, St. Thomas Aquinas held that even non-Christians were justified at the time of their first moral judgment, if they chose the "Good." Cf. *Summa Theologiae* I-II, q.89, a.6.

12. Cf. R. Panikkar, "Un presente senza catture", *Rocca* (October 1, 1987) 54–59. See also Panikkar's "The Jordan, the Tiber, and the Ganges," in *The Myth of Christian Uniqueness*, pp. 89–116; Edward Schillebeeckx, *Jesus in Our Western Culture* (London: SCM, 1987), p. 2–3; Christian Duquoc, "Appartenance ecclesiale et identification chretienne", *Concilium* 216 (1988) 141–152. The words of Jacques Dupuis are also suggestive: "It is true to say that, while Jesus is the Christ, the Christ is more than Jesus. To deny this would amount to denying the real transformation, emphatically affirmed by the entire New Testament, of Jesus' manhood as he is raised by the Father. The meta-historical Christ, or cosmic Christ is universally present and active in human history." This citation is taken from Dupuis's unpublished manuscript "Theology of Religions, Christian or Universal." A similar distinction between the two poles in the personality of Jesus is made by K. Rahner in *Foundations of the Christian Faith* (New York: Seabury, 1978) p. 290; and by

Wilhem Thusing, in W. Thusing and K. Rahner, *A New Christology* (London: Burns and Oates, 1980), p. 180. C. Duquoc in A. Ngindu Mushete (ed.), *Bulletin de Théologie Africaine* (1985), p. 294, underlines the necessity "maintenir un écart, non une opposition, entre Jesus et Christ. Christ est le nom de l'ouverture universelle de Jesus, Christ donne l'Esprit au Père. Jesus est celui qui a designe dans une particularité jamais absolutise cette ouverture."

13. See Gerald O'Collins, *Interpreting Jesus* (London: Geoffrey Chapman, 1983) p. 167: "If it was Jesus' humanity that made his dying and rising possible, it was his divinity that gave that dying and rising a cosmic value."

14. See Walter Kasper, *Jesus the Christ* (London: Burns and Oates, 1976), pp. 188–189.

15. See the reflection of R. Panikkar on the difference between the "concrete" and the "particular" and the "universal" and the "general" in *The Jordan*, in Hick and Knitter (eds.), *Myth of Christian Uniqueness*, p. 107.

16. See John O'Donnell, "In Him and Over Him: The Holy Spirit in the Life of Jesus," *Gregorianum* 70 (1989) 24–45: "Pneumatology offers us the key to grasp the universality of God's saving purposes without dissolving the uniqueness of the Incarnation" (p. 45).

17. See John 16: 5–15. K. Rahner in *Theological Investigations*, vol. 17 (New York: Crossroad, 1981), p. 43, says: "Christ is present and efficacious in the non-Christian believer (and therefore in the non-Christian religions) through his Spirit." Walter Kasper in *Jesus the Christ* says something similar: "The Spirit who is operative in Christ in his fullness, is at work in varying degrees everywhere in the history of mankind" (p. 268). Cf. also C. Duquoc, "Christianity and its Claim to Universality," *Concilium* 135 (1986), 64.

18. See O'Collins, *Interpreting Jesus*, p. 167.

19. Cf. Duquoc, *Provisional Churches* (London: SCM, 1986).

20. Cf. Mt. 10: 16–25 and parallels; John 15: 18–21. K. Rahner speaks of the "Church of the Little Flock" in *The Shape of the Church to Come* (London: SPCK, 1974).

21. Cf. Matthew Lederle, *Christian Painting in India* (Bombay: Heras Institute, 1987), pp. 65–66.

8. EVANGELIZATION IN ASIA: A NEW FOCUS?

1. International Congress on Mission, *For All the Peoples of Asia* (Manila: IMC Publications, 1984).

2. Ibid., p. 215.

3. 1971 Synod of Bishops, "*Justice in the World*," Introduction.

4. *Evangelii Nuntiandi*, 20.

5. Pope John Paul II, "The Attitude of the Church towards the Followers of Other Religions" (Rome: 1984), p. 6.

6. *Evangelii Nuntiandi*, 18.

7. See *For All the Peoples of Asia*, p. 14.

8. See *Ad Gentes* 1 and Severino Dianich, *Chiesa in missione* (Milano: Paoline, 1985).

9. Mary Motte and Joseph Lang (eds.), *Mission in Dialogue* (Maryknoll, N.Y.: Orbis Books, 1982), p. 634.

10. *Origins* 15 (February 20, 1986) 598.

11. *Evangelii Nuntiandi*, 18.

12. For those philosophically inclined I may point out that here I am using only personal categories of call, response, freedom, relationship, dialogue, etc.

13. *For All the Peoples of Asia*, p. 100.

14. Ibid.

15. D. S. Amalorpavadoss (ed.), *The Indian Church in the Struggle for a New Society* (Bangalore: NBCLC, 1981), p. 62.

16. Parig Digan, *Churches in Contestation* (Maryknoll, N.Y.: Orbis Books, 1984)

17. *America* (March 22, 1986) 220.

18. See, Nikhil Chakravarty, *The Times of India*, January 2, 1986.

9. INCULTURATION: PERSPECTIVES AND CHALLENGES

1. See M. Amaladoss, *Do Sacraments Change? Variable and Invariable Elements in Sacramental Rites*. (Bangalore: TPI, 1979)

2. *Sacrosanctum Concilium*, 40.

3. Cf. Aloysius Pieris, *An Asian Theology of Liberation* (Maryknoll, N.Y.: Orbis Books, 1988).

10. MODERNITY: THE INDIAN EXPERIENCE

1. S. S. Acquaviva, *The Decline of the Sacred in Industrial Society* (Oxford; Blackwell, 1979), pp. 201–202.

2. See Philip E. Hammond (ed.), *The Sacred in a Secular Age* (Berkeley: University of California Press, 1985); Thomas Luckmann, *Life-World and Social Realities* (London: Heinmann, 1983); Roland Robertson, *The Sociological Interpretation of Religion* (New York: Schocken, 1970); David Lyon, "Rethinking Secularization: Retrospect and Prospect," *Review of Religious Research* 26 (1985) 228–243; Richard K. Fenn, *Toward a Theory of Secularization* (Society for the Study of Religion, 1978); Peter Glasner, *The Sociology of Secularization* (London: Routledge and Kegan Paul, 1977).

3. Allan R. Brockway and J. Paul Rajashekar (eds.), *New Religious Movements and the Churches* (Geneva: World Council of Churches, 1987).

4. Langdon Gilkey, *Society and the Sacred* (New York: Crossroad, 1981); Andrew M. Greeley, *The Unsecular Man* (New York: Schocken, 1972).

5. Gene Outka, "Equality and the Fate of Theism in Modern Culture," *The Journal of Religion* 68 (1987) 275–288.

6. Peter L. Berger, *Facing Up to Modernity* (Harmondsworth: Penguin, 1979) p. 110.

7. Michael Hout and Andrew M. Greeley, "The Center Doesn't Hold: Church Attendance in the United States, 1940–1984," *American Sociological Review* 52 (1987) 341. See also Meredith B. McGuire, *Religion: The Social Context* (Belmont: Wadsworth, 1981), pp. 216–224.

8. David Martin, *A General Theory of Secularization* (Oxford: Blackwell, 1978).

9. Cf. Antonio Perez-Exclarin, *Atheism and Liberation* (London: SCM, 1980).

10. David Hay and Ann Morisey, "Secular Society, Religious Meanings: A Contemporary Paradox," *Review of Religious Research* 26 (1985) 213–227.

11. See Michael J. Buckley, *At the Origins of Modern Atheism* (New Haven: Yale University Press, 1987).

12. Robert E. Webber, *The Church in the World* (Grand Rapids: Zondervan, 1986).

13. Robert N. Bellah, *Beyond Belief* (New York: Harper and Row, 1970).

14. For varied relationships between the state and religion see Peter H. Merkl and Ninian Smart (eds.), *Religion and Politics in the Modern World* (New York: New York University Press, 1985).

15. David L. Gosling, *Science and Religion in India* (Madras: Christian Literature Society, 1976).

16. Gabriele Dietrich, *Religion and People's Organization in East Thanjavur* (Madras: Christian Literature Society, 1977), pp. 136, 131, 137.

17. A. M. Abraham Ayrookuzhiel, "A Study of the Religion of the Hindu People of Chirakkal (Kerala)." *Religion and Society* 24 (1977) 5–54.

18. A. M. Abraham Ayrookuzhiel, "The Living Hindu Popular Religious Consciousness and Some Reflections on It in the Context of Hindu-Christian Dialogue," *Religion and Society* 26 (1979) 23.

19. A. M. Abraham Ayrookuzhiel, "Religion, Spirituality and Aspirations of the People," *Religion and Society* 25 (1978) 29. See also A.M.A. Ayrookuzhiel, "An Enquiry into the Idea of God and Pattern of Worship in a South Indian Village," *Religion and Society* 26 (1979) 77–90; Paul C. Wiebe, "Religious Change in South India: Perspectives from a Small Town," *Religion and Society* 22 (1975) 27–46.

20. M. M. Thomas, *The Secular Ideologies of India and the Secular Meaning of Christ* (Madras: Christian Literature Society, 1976) p. v.

21. Yogendra Singh, *Modernization of Indian Tradition* (Delhi: Thomson, 1973), p. 214.

22. David Mandelbaum, "Transcendental and Pragmatic Aspects of Religion," *American Anthropologist* 68 (1966) 1174–93.

23. Peter L. Berger, *A Rumour of Angels* (Garden City: Doubleday, 1969).

24. For a confirmation of my thesis with reference to Sri Lanka see Gananath Obeyesekere, "Social Change and the Deities: Rise of the Kataragama Cult in Modern Sri Lanka," *Man*, N.S.12 (1977) 377–396. "Whatever its significance for Western society, the secularisation thesis is clearly inapplicable to contemporary southern Asia, where intellectuals not only continue to believe in their higher religions, like Buddhism and Hinduism, with increased conviction, but, more surprisingly, continue to adhere to those spirit cults which are decried and sometimes condemned by these higher doctrinal traditions" (p. 378).

25. See T. N. Madan, *Non-Renunciation* (Delhi: Oxford University Press, 1987).

26. Louis Dumont, *Homo Hierarchicus*, 2nd ed., (Chicago: University of Chicago Press, 1980).

27. Hans-J. Klimkeit, "Indigenous Elements in Modern Tamil Secularism," *Religion and Society* 23, 3 (1976) 80.

28. M. Amaladoss, "Tolerance and Religious Faith: Some Models and Problems," *Indian Theological Studies* 20 (1983) 199–215.

29. Milton Singer, "The Great Tradition of Hinduism in the City of Madras," in Charles Leslie (ed.), *Anthropology of Folk Religion* (New York: Vantage, 1960) pp. 158, 164. As a matter of fact, the diversity within Hinduism may not be greater than the diversity within Christianity, if we take together all the groups in the world that identify themselves as Christian.

30. Bipan Chandra, *Communalism in Modern India* (New Delhi: Vani, 1984); T.

N. Madan, "Secularization and the Sikh Religious Tradition," *Social Compass* 33 (1986) 257–273.

31. See Robert D. Baird (ed.), *Religion in Modern India* (Delhi: Manohar, 1981); "Secularism and Secularization," *Religion and Society* 18 (1971).

32. M. Amaladoss, "Befreiung: ein interreligioses Projekt," in Felix Wilfred (ed.), *Verlass den Tempel* (Herder: Freiburg, 1988), pp. 146–178.

33. Ashis Nandy, *Traditions, Tyranny and Utopias* (Delhi: Oxford, 1987); Sudhir Kakar (ed.), *Identity and Adulthood* (Delhi: Oxford, 1979).

34. Philip Mathew and Ajit Muricken (eds.), *Religion, Ideology and Counter Culture* (Bangalore: Horizon, 1987).

35. Paul Valadier, *L'Église en proces* (Paris: Calmann-Levyu, 1987).

12. EVANGELIZATION AND ECUMENISM

1. Robert McAfee Brown "Whence and Whither," in *The Challenge to Reunion* (New York, 1963), p. 9. Cited in Pedro S. Achutegui, S.J., "Missions and the Ecumenical Dimensions," in *Ecumenism and Vatican II* (Manila: 1972), p. 118.

2. For details and documentation see *A History of the Ecumenical Movement, 1517–1948*, ed. by Ruth Rouse and Stephen Charles Neill (London, 1954), especially chapters 8, 9, and 11; Hans-Ruedi Weber, *Asia and the Ecumenical Movement* (London: 1966): K.M. Brown, *The Ecumenical Revolution* (London).

3. Rouse and Neill, *Ecumenical History*, p. 473.

4. At Stockholm in 1925.

5. At Lausanne in 1927.

6. At Amsterdam in 1948.

7. *Unitatis Redintegratio*, 12.

8. *Ad Gentes*, 6.

9. *Ad Gentes*, 15. See A. Gilles de Pelichy, "L'Oecumenisme dans le décrét sur l'activité missionnaire de l'église," *Irênikon* 39 (1966), 355–361; *International Review of Missions* 56 (1967).

10. *Unitatis Redintegratio*, 1.

11. *Ad Gentes*, 29.

12. *The New Delhi Report* (London: 1962), p. 257.

13. *The Upsala Report 1968* (Geneva: 1968), p. 233.

14. The full text can be found in *The Ecumenical Review* 23 (1971) 9–20.

15. Joint Theological Commission, *Common Witness and Proselytism*, 17–18.

16. *The Ecumenical Affirmation*, preface.

17. *Service and Salvation*, ed. by J. Pathrapankal (Bangalore: 1973).

18. *The Clergy Monthly* 35 (1971), 86.

19. On this point see Avery Dulles, "The Church, the Churches and the Catholic Church," *The Dublin Papers on Ecumenism* (Manila: 1972), 118–158.

20. Here we are not considering those churches who do not believe in ecumenism. See J. Bruls, "Possibilités de coopération oecumenique avec les chretiens qui n'appartiennent pas au C.O.E.," *Oecumenisme en mission*, 115–123.

21. Pontifical Councils for Interreligious Dialogue and Ecumenism, *Sects or New Religious Movements: Pastoral Challenge*. See text in Allan R. Brockway and J. Paul Rajashekar (eds.), *New Religious Movements and the Churches* (Geneva: WCC, 1987), p. 182.

22. Cf. Hans-Werner Gensichen, "Joint Action for Mission in Relation to Con-

fession," *International Review of Missions 54* (1967) 87–98; Piet Fransen, "Unity and Confessional Statements," *The Dublin Papers,* 35–78.

23. Cf. Joint Theological Commission, *Common Witness and Proselytism,* 25–37.

24. A. S. de Achutegui, *Missions and Ecumenism,* pp. 133–146.

13. THE LAITY AND THE CHURCH IN MISSION

1. Albert Vanhoye, *Old Testament Priests and the New Priest according to the New Testament* (Petersham: 1986), pp. 313, 315, 317.

2. Ibid., p. 266.

3. Cf. Joseph Phan Tan Thanh, "Religion and Religions in the Second Vatican Council," *Christ to the World* 31 (1986) 381–388.

14. COLLABORATION IN MISSION

1. Cf. Albert, *Towards a New Age in Mission,* Book I (Manila, 1981), p. 24; *Your Kingdom Come: Report on the World Congress on Mission and Evangelism* (Geneva: WCC, 1980), pp. 220–221.

2. Cf. A. M. Henry, "Mission d'hier, mission de demain," in *L'Activité missionnaire de l'église* (Paris: Cerf, 1967), pp. 434–440.

3. *Gaudium et Spes,* 22. John Paul II has strongly supported this again recently. See his speech to the Cardinals on December 22, 1986, explaining the significance of the event of Assisi where in October 1986 he came together with leaders of other religions to pray for peace.

4. See *Lumen Gentium,* 1.

5. Cf. M. Amaladoss, "Evangelization in Asia Today: A New Focus?," *Vidyajyoti* 51 (1987) 7–28 (chapter 8 in this volume); Jerry Persha, "Towards Developing an Adequate and Comprehensive Understanding of Evangelization," *Missiology* 14 (1986) 273–285; James Fergusson, "A Paradigm Shift in the Theology of Mission: Two Roman Catholic Perspectives," *International Bulletin of Missionary Research* 8 (1984) 117–119.

6. *Gaudium et Spes,* 58.

7. *Your Kingdom Come,* p. 195.

8. Federation of Asian Bishops' Conferences, *Evangelization in Modern Day Asia,* Taipei, April, 1974, No. 12.

9. Cf. Mary Motte and Joseph R. Lang (eds.), *Mission in Dialogue* (Maryknoll, N.Y.: Orbis Books, 1982) p. 634.

10. *Evangelii Nuntiandi,* 60. Cf. also *Ad Gentes,* 35, 36, 38; *Lumen Gentium,* 23; *Your Kingdom Come,* p. 220.

11. See the Synod document, section C, 2. The text refers to *Christus Dominus,* 11 and *Lumen Gentium,* 23. One could also refer to *Lumen Gentium,* 26.

12. Cf. Joseph A. Komonchak, "Towards a Theology of the Local Church," *FABC Papers* 42 (1986) p. 17; See also Komonchak, "La réalisation de l'église en un lieu" in G. Alberigo and J.-P. Jossua (eds.), *La réception de Vatican II* (Paris, 1985), pp. 107–126; Herve Legrand, "La realisation de l'eglise en un lieu," in B. Lauret and F. Réfoulé (eds.), *Initiation a la pratique de la théologie, Tome III, dogmatique 2* (Paris, 1983), pp. 143–345; Jan Kerkhofs, "Some Introductory Notes for the Theology of the Particular Church," *Verbum SVD* 27 (1986) 313–322.

13. *Towards a New Age in Mission,* Book I, p. 24.

14. Cf. The documents of Puebla of the Latin American Conference of Bishops, No. 368.

15. Cf. *Ad Gentes*, 23; *Ecumenical Affirmation*, 40.

16. Ennio Mantovanni, "Missionary Societies of the 80's and 90's," FABC Papers 43 (1986), p. 16.

17. *Towards a New Age in Mission*, p. 27.

18. Komonchok, Theology of Local Church *op. cit.*, p. 41.

19. See Ennio Mantovani, "Missionary Societies of the 80's and 90's," *FABC Papers* 43 (1986).

CONCLUSION

1. Report on the World Congress on Mission and Evangelism, *Your Kingdom Come* (Geneva: WCC, 1980), p. 195.

2. *Lumen Gentium*, 13.

3. M. K. Gandhi, *Communal Unity*, pp. 579–580, quoted in Wm. Theodore de Bary (ed.), *Sources of Indian Tradition*, vol. 2 (New York: Columbia University Press, 1958), pp. 273–274.

4. See T. K. John, "The Pope's 'Pastoral Visit' to India: A Further Reflection," *Vidyajyoti* 51 (1987) 58–66, especially p. 59.

Also of Interest

Walbert Bühlmann
WITH EYES TO SEE
Church and World in the Third Millennium
With Franciscan zest for the inner life of the ecclesia and a willingness to challenge the powerful, the author of *The Church of the Future* offers "New Commandments for the World Church": to accompany spiritual nomads in the affluent West in their search for faith ... to stand in solidarity with the poor seeking liberation ... to wonder at the riches of cultural plurality ... to experience the mystery of God's presence in the wisdom of Asia ... to see integral Christian mission as empowerment to preserve that nature of which humans are part ... to bring politics and spirituality into a coherent vision for the service of peace and justice.

"A challenging strategy for reshaping the church's mission agenda in the next century." —*James A. Scherer*
ISBN 0-88344-683-9 Paper

Lucien Legrand
UNITY AND PLURALITY
Mission in the Bible
Provides unique insights into the variety of understandings of mission displayed in two millennia of biblical tradition, while showing us how that variety is at the service of the Mysterious One who comes to us—empowering, reconciling, challenging, renewing.

"Simply excellent. ... Legrand's interpretations of scripture are carefully nuanced and, without reducing the scriptural message to one or another narrow facet, he manages to show the kaleidoscopic nature of both Jewish and Christian scriptures as they bear on mission and evangelization." —*Richard Albertine*
ISBN 0-88344-692-8 Paper

David Bosch
TRANSFORMING MISSION
Paradigm Shifts in Theology of Evangelization
This truly magisterial book examines the entire sweep of Christian mission, attending to the interplay of the *theological* and the *historical* as paradigms for the understanding and praxis of Christian mission.

"A kind of *Summa Missiologica* ... a masterly overview of all the great issues in missiology, scrupulously fair in rendering different views and wise in their assess-

ment. It will surely be the indispensable foundation for the teaching of missiology for many years to come."
— *Lesslie Newbigin*

ISBN 0-88344-719-3 Paper
ISBN 0-88344-744-4 Cloth

Jonathan Bonk
MISSIONS AND MONEY
Affluence as a Western Missionary Problem

Drawing on his own Mennonite missionary heritage and the dynamics of the Gospel's profound ambivalence toward wealth, Bonk asks us to think on some hard questions. Do contemporary Western missioners, because of their relative affluence, inadvertently subvert the gospel and hinder its inculturation among the poor? Does a missioner's wealth eventually lead indigenous people to feel hostility, conscious or unconscious, against the missioner?

"Professor Bonk makes a cogent argument. . . . I commend his book to all interested in the spread of the whole gospel to the whole world." — *Walbert Bühlmann*
ISBN 0-88344-718-5 Paper